9.50

EX LIBRIS

John R. Lambert

EYNSHAM ABBEY
1005~1228

A Small Window into a Large Room

Virgin and Child, from a 12th-century manuscript which is believed to have been in Eynsham Abbey library. *Bodl. MS. 269, f.iiiR*. St. Mary of Eynsham, St. Mary of Stow, St. Mary of Lincoln — St. Mary dominates the Eynsham story. This drawing had much to say to Eynsham monks.

EYNSHAM ABBEY
1005~1228

A Small Window into a Large Room

Eric Gordon
sometime Bishop of Sodor and Man

Phillimore

1990

Published by
PHILLIMORE & CO. LTD.
Shopwyke Hall, Chichester, Sussex

ISBN 0 85033 747 X

Printed and bound in Great Britain by
STAPLES PRINTERS, ROCHESTER

Amicus Amicis
Gratias et Lacrimas et hoc Opusculum
Tandem Natum

Contents

Part Five: A Niggling Question

Epilogue

Appendices

List of Illustrations

Frontispiece: Virgin and Child, 12th century

Illustration Acknowledgements

My illustrations owe much to the following, and I would like to express my deep gratitude to them all, not only for their permission, but for their courtesy and helpfulness: William Bainbridge (nos. 1 and 27); B.T. Batsford Ltd. (no. 8); the Bodleian Library, Oxford (Frontispiece, nos. 13, 16, 25, 26, 28-34, 43 and 44); the British Library (nos. 4 and 5); Cambridge University Press (no. 11); Courtauld Institute of Art, Conway Library (A85/962), Granada Television Ltd., and the Tate Gallery, Liverpool (no. 38); Royal Commission on the Historical Monuments of England (no. 21); Gwynneth Holt (nos. 6, 9, 36, 39, 40 and the chapter numbers); Lincolnshire Collection, Lincoln Central Library, by kind permission of Lincolnshire County Council, Recreational Services (nos. 18 and 19); the Manx Museum and National Trust (no. 40); the Isle of Man Post Office (no. 3); National Trust Photographic Library (Front Cover); the Governors of St. Olave's and St. Saviour's Grammar School, Orpington, Kent (no. 15); Oxford University Department for External Studies (no. 41); Oxford University Press (nos. 17 and 42); Oxfordshire Archives (no. 35); Oxfordshire County Council (no. 24); Phaidon Press (no. 14).

Preface

It is my hope that this little book will do six things:

   i. tell the Eynsham abbey story;

   ii. suggest corrections of currently-accepted views;

   iii. explain simple things that are often only half-understood;

   iv. encourage the further exploration which is needed;

   v. help modern readers to see how medieval men and women thought and spoke;

   vi. show how close study of one small place sheds light on a whole period, and indeed on the doings of all of us at all times.

I was tempted to focus the book on a series of colourful individuals: Aethelred, for example, wearing his uneasy crown, pondering upon the year 1000, and anticipating the end of the world; or Aelfric, learned and compassionate, a letter-writer for bishops, and rebuking an Oxfordshire bigwig for pressing him to drink too much; or Remigius, monastic executive from Normandy, risking his life to sail with the Conqueror, and duly rewarded with the bishopric of Lincoln; or Lady Godiva, the Anglo-Saxon heroine that everyone knows, named in Norman-French prayers, day by day, in Eynsham abbey; or William Rufus, remembered as the Conqueror's wayward son, and impatient as ever with clerics, sending a threatening letter to Bishop Bloet, telling him to get on with what he had promised; or Henry II, tearing himself away from hunting at Woodstock, carrying the murder of Thomas a Becket on his conscience, cantering over to Eynsham abbey, every day for a week, intent upon choosing a saintly bishop of Lincoln; or Godfrey, a worldly abbot, and capable, doubtless a great builder, but encountered in purgatory, wriggling, and writhing, and very glum indeed; or Hugh of Avalon, Carthusian of Carthusians, larger than life-size, winkled out of a meagre cell in Somerset, elevated to be bishop of Lincoln, and fearless against kings. All of these, and many more, are part of the Eynsham tale. In the end, however, it seemed right not to glamorize them, but to let them appear in the unfolding story and speak for themselves.

I am full of gratitude to all sorts of people, in many different places.

First, I must thank those responsible for the Greening Lamborn and the W.A. Pantin Trusts. Without their ready and generous financial support it would have been well-nigh impossible to produce the book at all.

Next, I must make special mention of two individuals. They are Mr. James Campbell, F.B.A., Fellow of Worcester College, Oxford, and to Dr. Brian Atkins, Fellow of St. Cross College, Oxford. Each has read my script, and encouraged me to continue, and given invaluable advice and help. Needless to say, neither of them is responsible for any mis-statements or misjudgements in my text. All are mine.

Thirdly, I must thank Dr. Nicholas Mann, of Pembroke College, Oxford, Dr. Bruce Mitchell, of St. Edmund Hall, Oxford, and Mr. Edward Wilson, of Worcester College, Oxford. Some years ago they gave me generous guidance upon Middle French, Old English and Middle English elements in the Eynsham records. They have not seen what I have since written, and, if there are errors, they are mine.

Then, the many translations from Latin: here as well I must take full responsibility — as is probably all too obvious! — for all but a few; in those cases I have noted the source. I have worked from standard printed texts, except in two instances where the printed text seemed wrong, and led me back to the manuscript.

Some years ago, four others, Mrs. Elizabeth Corner, the late Revd. Stanley Fisher, Mrs. Julie Hyde, and Miss Mary Oakeley, read an earlier version of my book. Each of them urged me on, and took trouble, and gave me great assistance. Many others have stood by me, and spared time and thought, and been patient with my slowness, through the years. I thank them all, and may perhaps single out Canon John Parker, once Rector of Stow, and therefore in charge of its great Anglo-Saxon minster, which is so closely linked with Eynsham abbey. And of course, here in Eynsham, there have been all the officers and members of the History Group, each of them eager, and supportive, and tolerant.

Nothing could have been done without the Bodleian Library or Christ Church Library, each of which has greeted this mere Cantabrigian with a warm welcome and with unfailing courtesy and service. Duke Humfrey's library, indeed, within the Bodleian, almost became a second home!

Last, but very far from least, there is my own wife. Without her constant stimulus, and sacrifice, and concern, nothing would have been completed. Her own lifelong calling and much-loved work, as the sculptor Gwynneth Holt, has suffered, and I am all the more grateful to her for her profound and sensitive contributions to this book of mine.

ERIC GORDON
Cobden, Eynsham, Oxon.
January, 1990

Part One

Before the Conquest

Records of a vanished abbey

Eynsham is a small town in Oxfordshire, five or six miles to the west of Oxford itself, half-way to Witney, and at the edge of the Cotswolds. Virtually on the Thames, and still surrounded by lovely countryside, it has a character which is all its own.

Between 1005 and 1538, except for a short period after the Norman conquest, Eynsham housed a Benedictine monastery. The abbot, in fact, and his monks owned the place and dominated its life. Their market-cross, crumbling away, well-scarred by time, stood until recently in the Square.[1] The church which they built for the parishioners still opens on the Square, but their great abbey and its wide spread of buildings, once towering behind the church, have all vanished (see illustration 1). Fragments are here and there, built into houses.

1. **Eynsham Church and Cross: engraving by Wise.** Until 1538 the great Romanesque abbey church would have dominated the background.

1

A single drawing survives, but even the ground-plan is unknown. And large parts of the abbey's story are obscure and tangled. This essay takes a new look at places, people, and purposes, especially during earlier centuries.

The primary source of information is in medieval manuscripts, and particularly in the older of two cartularies, still preserved in Christ Church library, Oxford. The Eynsham monks began this book in around 1196. Important documents were copied into it, and in the end about 600 were entered. They covered both sides of some 150 leaves of parchment, and then went on to fill up the fly-leaves. The first hand, the unknown scribe of c.1196, wrote almost one-third of the main text.[2]

Their purpose was entirely practical. This book was for abbey business; it was a handy tool of reference, at a time when abbey properties were multiplying rapidly and abbey officials frequently found themselves in litigation about their lands and rights. Medieval records tended to be cumbrous things, folded inwards, with dangling seals. Stored in chests and cupboards, they were hard to file and awkward to consult. The new cartulary would preserve the text, and make it easy of access.

And if the book had its origin in practical considerations, so also did its preservation in 1538. The abbey was dissolved, its buildings and its lands disposed of, and its few remaining monks dispersed. But shrewd minds realized that this old book might still shed light on current legal squabbles.

We look therefore for something plain and utilitarian. This is no sumptuous offering to God, full of painstaking pictures, colourful borders, and elaborate initials. It has an antique charm, of course, and its well-thumbed pages bring us into direct touch with the monks of nearly 800 years ago. But it is a book for use, not for ornament. Colour and design are used, but only to make reference easier. The documents are numbered in the margin; each one begins with a distinctive initial; each one has its own title. Numbers, initials, and titles are normally coloured red or green. The book, it seems, had simple covers of parchment at first. Later on, but still in the Middle Ages, it was bound in oak boards, and covered with two layers of sheepskin, now peeling away, and anchored by a brass stud.

Naturally enough, the first document to be entered was the abbey's foundation-charter, already nearly 200 years old. The original deed has vanished, but this copy of c.1196 survives here. It is a fascinating record from Anglo-Saxon times, and it is the subject of the first chapters of this essay.

Eynsham abbey, as would be expected, had other cartularies. A second has survived, and is also in Christ Church library, Oxford. Its main concern is with the manors which the abbey farmed during the 14th century. A third is known to have existed, and to have dealt with the abbey's properties within the city of Oxford; it seems now to be lost.[3]

Notes
1. By 1988 the cross was in such a parlous state that it had to be taken away for restoration. Its steps and its railings were left in place. Unfortunately the cross proved to be irreparable. The future of the whole structure is now under review.

2. The chapter-numbers in this book have been drawn by Gwynneth Holt. She has based them on the charter-numbers, drawn by the first scribe, in the older Eynsham cartulary, now in Christ Church library, Oxford. I am grateful for her success in capturing their original informality and spontaneity.

3. H.E. Salter's edition of both surviving cartularies, with supplementary materials and authoritative introductions, is fundamental (hereafter *E.C.*). In *V.C.H.*, *Oxon.*, vol.2, pp.65-7, he provided a summary account. All later work has been based upon his, including two major contributions, E.K. Chambers, *Eynsham under the Monks* (hereafter *E.M.*) and the Latin text of the *Eynsham Customary*, ed. A. Gransden (hereafter *E.Cust.*). For Salter and Chambers, see Appendix 13.

II

Foundation-charter

Eynsham abbey's foundation-charter is dated 1005. At first sight it is ponderous and involved, moralizing, self-congratulatory, quite irrelevant to life nearly 1,000 years later. In fact it is deeply moving and strangely contemporary. Behind its well-turned phrases there are men like ourselves, groping in the dark, very frightened, and clutching at straws.

King Aethelred II (Ethelred the Unready), 'by the grace and mercy of God, king and ruler of the realm of the English' (see illustration 2), gives authority

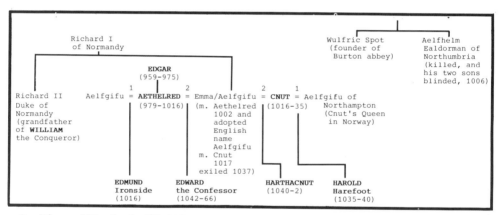

2. **Kings of England, 979-1066.** For Queen Emma/Aelfgifu, see *Campbell 1949, Barlow 1* pp.40-5, and illustrations 4-5 below. For family of Wulfric Spot, see *Charters of Burton Abbey*, ed. P.H. Sawyer (*Anglo-Saxon Charters*, vol.2), Brit. Acad., 1979.

to Aethelmaer, one of his elder statesmen, 'a man of outstanding loyalty to myself and very dear to me', to establish a Benedictine monastery, and to endow it at 'an important place, hard by the river Thames, and called Eynsham by those who live in that part of the country' (*in loco celebri juxta fluvium qui vocatur Tamis constituto, quod ab incolis regionis illius Egnesham nuncupatur vocabulo*).

Further down he calls himself 'the said king of the Anglo-Saxons, as also governor and ruler of the other adjacent nations, far and wide, and all around' (*Angul-Saxonum antedictus rex, ceterarumque gentium longe lateque per circuitum adjacentium gubernator & rector*). What was his real power? What, if any, substance lay behind such sweeping claims? What were his relationships with the rest of the royal family, and with all the notabilities (his wise men, his *witan*), whose names, more than 80 of them, crowd the end of the charter? What motives stirred within him, as also within Aethelmaer, the principal benefactor? And who indeed was Aethelmaer, and what was his background? Why was Eynsham selected, so near to Oxford, and yet (in those times) so far? What sort of place was it, and in what sense 'important'? How would English Benedictines of 1005 spend their days? How would they support themselves? What sort of men would they be, whether in social status, or in godliness of spirit, or in education? And how would they fit into the rustic community all around?

And curiosity can only deepen, when we discover that the first abbot of Eynsham was (almost certainly) Aelfric, a name to conjure with, the outstanding Christian teacher in the England of that day, a man whose sermons were printed during the reign of Elizabeth I and afterwards, a man whose full stature and image are still being rediscovered and clarified in the 20th century, a man whose bones may still lie undisturbed in Eynsham.[1]

Notes

1. Foundation charter: for text (Latin and O.E.), see *E.C.*, vol.1, pp.19-28; for general comment, see lists in *Sawyer 1968* and *Gelling 1979*; for place-names, see *Ekwall 1960*; for charters of this period, see *Stenton 1955, Brooks 1974*, and *Keynes 1980*; for authenticity, see *Id.*, p.114, n.103.

Aethelred II

Aethelred (979-1016) was a Christian king in a Christian land. The upheavals of the centuries had, of course, left their mark. Conduct was often crude and savage; dark superstitions persisted; few men and women thought deeply about their faith. Nevertheless, at the root of things, king and clergy, nobles and ordinary folk, scholars and simpletons, one and all, thought of God in the same way, looked to the same Redeemer, hoped for the same rewards hereafter, and dreaded the same punishments. The Christian revelation, embedded in the Old and the New Testaments, and in the ongoing life of the Church, was continuous with the events of the day; something of Roman culture had been taken on board, and (with it) some of its hazy Greek background. But the story was all of one piece: the relationships of God and men were still the same. There were substrata of animism and witchcraft, but this was not the day for free-thinkers, sceptics, rationalists, alternative faiths.

Against such a background it was only natural for Aethelred to make his pledges, and be anointed and crowned, in the course of the Christian Mass. The memory of kings like Saul, David, and Solomon would be relevant and contemporary: they had been chosen, and anointed, and accepted, under the guidance of men of God (1 Sam. 10, 1; 16, 13; 1 Kings 1, 39). The theology might be imprecise, and the king's actual performance might be inadequate, but the intent was clear. Kingship was a ministry: the coronation service was, in a sense, an ordination, a consecration. The king would be given grace, and could rightly look for more. As St. Paul had said, 'The powers that be are ordained of God' (Romans 13, 1).

So it was no empty formality that lay behind the opening words of Eynsham abbey's foundation-charter:

CHRIST is Lord: through endless ages he is Lord of all: Christ is our Saviour: by him were all things made.

AETHELRED: by the grace and mercy of God, king and ruler of the realm of the English, faithful defender and humble sustainer of holy Church: to all who hold office or bear authority, whether in Church or State (*omnibus ecclesiastice pietatis ordinibus seu secularis potentie dignitatibus*): may you be granted peace and blessedness in Christ our Lord . . .

(from the Latin of *E.C.*, vol.1, pp.19-28).

Nor could there be any doubt that the dynasty of Wessex, an Anglo-Saxon line, and Aethelred with it, were kings of the whole of England. The other Anglo-Saxon groupings all acknowledged Aethelred; so did the settled Norsemen in the Danelaw, across Watling Street. And there was even substance in the more grandiose title, used further down in the charter, 'King of the Anglo-Saxons, as also governor and ruler of the other adjacent nations, far and wide, and all around'. The kings of England did in fact enjoy a vague hegemony over neighbouring kings in Britain. The seniority was ill-defined, but it had been won by King Aethelstan (924-40) and sustained by his successors, each according to his strength.

The Worcester chronicler, generally described as Florence (died 1118), tells a delightful story about King Edgar. In 973, soon after being crowned, he went to Chester. There eight lesser kings, all from our islands, paid him homage, and then rowed him on the river Dee, whilst he held the tiller (see illustration 3). Even the most illiterate could read a symbol like that. And the concept of kings and sub-kings, co-existing in mutual support, was well understood.

By 1005, however, political reality was tarnishing those high phrases. Scandinavian marauders were here again. No one knew where Danish ships would strike next. They were here to plunder, and if possible to conquer. Aelfric (writing in about 996, and not yet come to Eynsham) looked back to that voyage on the Dee with wistful nostalgia:

> We have now spoken thus briefly of Swithun, and we say of a truth that the time was blessed and winsome in England, when King Edgar furthered Christianity, and built many monasteries, and his kingdom still continued in peace, so that no

3. **King Edgar on the Dee at Chester: painting by J.H. Nicholson, 1974.**
A Manx impression of this spectacular event. It is suggested that King Magnus of the Isles, being third in seniority, was pulling the third oar.

fleet was heard of, save that of the people themselves who held this land; and all the kings of the Cymry and Scots that were in this island, came to Edgar once upon a day, being eight kings, and they all bowed themselves to Edgar's rule.

(from the O.E. of *Aelfric, Saints*, as translated in 1966 edn., vol.1, pp.468-9: see also *Stenton 1971*, pp.369-70, and W.H. Stevenson, in *E.H.R.*, vol. 13 (1898), pp.505-7).

Aethelred and his *witan* met the Danish onslaught with more skill and determination than is sometimes credited. Army and navy, fortifications and garrisons, were used with vigour and courage. But England was a rich prize, and the hungry Danes were not inclined to draw back. Somehow the peril grew and grew, and in the end, though not until after Aethelred's death, and then not at once, Cnut, a Danish king, took his place (see *Hill 1981*, maps 106-29, 164-6).

Aethelred had not always been wise in his response to national danger, though not perhaps as unwise as his cruel nickname might suggest — 'Aethelraed Unraed' (Noble counsel, No counsel). He had tried to bribe the raiders off; they came back, of course, for more. He had tried foolish and treacherous massacre; it served only to increase bitterness. The events of St. Brice's day, 13 November 1002, must have made Eynsham people shudder. Here is a nearly contemporary account of what happened at St. Frideswide's church, Oxford:

Everyone in the land must have heard what happened at this church. I (sc. Aethelred) had taken counsel with my ealdormen and thegns: my decree had gone forth: the Danes, who had sprung up and sprouted in this island, like tares among wheat (*Dani qui in hac insula velut lollium inter triticum pululando emerserant*), were all to meet their just reward, and be destroyed: my decree was to be carried through to the point of death. Then those Danes who were resident in the city of Oxford made efforts to escape their fate. They broke open the doors and the bolts of this Christian shrine, and forced their way inside: there they set about making it a refuge and a stronghold against the people of the city and those who lived just by it. But, when all the populace had to follow them inside, and tried to throw them out, but could not prevail, they set fire to the timbers, and (as is plain) they burned this church down, together with its ornaments and its books.

(from the Latin of *St. Frideswide's Cartulary*, ed. S.R. Wigram, 1894-6, vol.1, pp.2f.; see also *E.H.D.*, vol.1, pp.590-3).

Things went from bad to worse. In 1009 there was a call for nationwide fasting, almsgiving, and prayer. If all joined in, for three whole days before Michaelmas, maybe archangels and angels would give aid where man was helpless. In 1010 the Danes reached Oxford, and burned it down; doubtless they recollected St. Frideswide's. In 1013 Aethelred fled the country, only to return and struggle on till his death in 1016. After a while Cnut, by now almost certainly a Christian, became king of England, married Emma/Aelfgifu (Aethelred's Norman widow), and ruled well (see illustrations 4 & 5).

It was against that backcloth of accelerating misery and defeat that Eynsham abbey had been established in 1005. God (they thought) must be very angry with English people. When the Hebrews of old had fallen away from him, he had handed them over to the powerful, but pagan, Canaanites (Judges 4, 1); perhaps things were so with England now. Perhaps the costly establishment of

4. (*left*) **Queen Emma/Aelfgifu, 11th century.** High-crowned and awesome, Queen to two Kings of England, mother of two others (see illustration 2), she receives *Encomium Emmae* (In Praise of Emma) from its monastic writer. *Brit. Libr. MS. Add. 33241, f.4.*

5. (*right*) **King Cnut and Queen Emma/Aelfgifu, 11th century.** Presentation of an altar cross to New Minster, Winchester. Christ, in majesty, flanked by the Virgin Mother and St. Peter, looks down and blesses; monks below conjoin in praise; angels point to the true source of all greatness and holiness. *Brit. Libr. MS. Stowe 944, f.6.*

an abbey, and its total offering to God, and the sequel of constant praise and prayer rising from it, would turn that wrath away. Perhaps the whole situation was even more critical. Could it be that all this sorrow, disappointment and trouble were signs of the end of the world? Was it indeed that great and awful time of special tribulation which was to precede the Last Judgment (Matthew 24, 21ff.)? What more likely than that at roughly 1,000 years after the first coming of the Lord he would come again? St. Peter himself had said, 'One day

is with the Lord as a thousand years, and a thousand years as one day' (2 Peter
3, 8). So the foundation-charter continues:

> ... The anger of God is turned upon us, unwonted in its fury, and I have a deep
> concern. My heart is prayerful, my will is sound, my every desire is for peace. I
> have sat with the priests of God and with our men of counsel. I have determined
> to appease God with a never-ending display of good works and a ceaseless offering
> of praise. In these very times we are suffering the flames of battle: our goods are
> pillaged: savage enemies devastate the land: they rob us cruelly: heathen tribes
> put us to all kinds of 'tribulation':[1] they afflict us grievously: they bring us to the
> very brink of extinction. We can see that the 'perilous times', which were foretold,
> are upon us. We are those 'upon whom the ends of the world are come'.
>
> It is therefore fitting that we should look most carefully to the good of our souls.
> By what kind of life shall we earn a place with Christ, the author of all things,
> in that new age, now coming? 'For here', as the apostle says, 'have we no abiding
> place, but we seek one to come'. And if we are possessed of earthly riches, the
> question is more urgent still. We must seek that coming city with all the strength
> that we have. If those riches of ours are not shared with others, they cannot possibly
> profit ourselves at all. For, however settled and steady a man's prosperity may
> be, the day will come when, whether he wills it or not, he will lose all that he
> has. Thus it is that the sweetness of human bliss is so deeply tinged with bitterness.
> What may seem so pleasant to a man, at the moment of its enjoyment, will always
> lead to sourness at the end.
>
> Now there are two essentials, if any human activity is to be brought to effect.
> One is the will, the other the power. Lack the one or the other, and a man can
> achieve nothing. Take the will away, and no man will approach what he has no
> wish to do. Take the power away, and his will is utterly useless. Good men,
> however, possessed of a just will and honourable power, attain that ultimate good
> which is their real desire: for through the temporal affairs of this fleeting life they
> earn eternal rewards, rewards of that endless age now dawning, rewards which
> will never cease.
>
> Wherefore I, AETHELRED, by God's manifold mercy and permission the said
> king of the Anglo-Saxons, as also governor and ruler of the other adjacent nations,
> far and wide, and all around, do see that in a certain matter I stand possessed
> both of the will and of the power to act.[2] Accordingly, to aid the memories of men,
> both now and in days to come, I have caused my purpose to be set down in this
> precise and written form (*veracibus litterarum apicibus insinuare*) ...

Notes

1. Biblical references: 2 Tim. 3, 1; 1 Cor. 10, 11; Hebr. 13, 14.
2. *Keynes 1980, loc. cit.*, links the theme of 'two essentials' to Boethius, *De Consolatione Philosophiae*,
   4, 2, a work which had been translated into English by King Alfred the Great. Boethius, a
   Roman statesman and philosopher, renowned for his integrity, wrote it in prison, prior to his
   execution under Theodoric in *c.*524. For the wide range of classical education enjoyed in
   England before and after the Conquest, see *Barlow 2*, pp.217-67.

Benedictines at Eynsham

The core of the foundation-charter comes next. God is to be given a monastery. It is to be at Eynsham. Aethelmaer, a prominent layman, is prime mover in the affair.

The essence of such a gift lay in the monks themselves: not in the lands of the endowment, not in the abbey-church and its ancillary buildings, not in the protracted business that went beforehand, but in the end-product, the men who would live there for God. There was sacrifice, of course, in all the rest; but it was the surrendered lives of the monks that counted. Jesus, who had said, 'I am the light of the world', had also said, 'Ye are the light of the world' (John 9, 5; Matthew 5, 14). The monks of Eynsham would set out to be that light in their own part of a darkling world.

For centuries past the way of the monk and the nun, a way that took them right out of ordinary society, a way that entailed exemplary living founded in constant prayer, had to many Christians seemed the better way. There had been endless variations on the one theme. Climate, national temperament, influential teachers, politics, all played their part. Some were solitaries (the eremitical ideal); others lived in groups (coenobites). Some toiled away at grim austerities, feats of physical endurance; others stressed contemplation. Some were in frequent touch with normal society; others hardly at all. Some shared parish-work, pastoral ministry, with those outside; others eschewed it. Many were of the laity, more and more were priests. Most were men, some were women. Some wrote books, some worked in kitchens, some copied manuscripts, others tilled the fields. Some were level-headed, others fanatical. There were all sorts of combinations of the varying emphases. And at all times and places, as would be expected, whatever the system, some proved to be square pegs in round holes.

All of them, however, believed that their calling was God's special demand of them, and that it was a call to something intrinsically higher, essentially better, than any aim or achievement in Christian discipleship outside in the world. They remembered the rich young ruler of the gospel story, and how Jesus challenged him to go one step further, 'If thou wilt be perfect, go and sell that thou hast, and give to the poor, and thou shalt have treasure in heaven: and come and follow me' (Matthew 19, 21). This counsel, given on one occasion to one man, was (they insisted) a general assertion of Christian principle for all men and all women at all times. They looked also to the first church, living its life in Jerusalem, and they noted that, at least for a while, its members had shared their goods as well as their prayers (Acts 2, 42ff.). Here also perhaps

6. **Christus: ivory by Gwynneth Holt, 1963.** 'If any man will come after me, let him deny himself, and take up his cross daily, and follow me.' *Luke ix, 23.* 'If ye then be risen with Christ, seek those things which are above, where Christ sitteth on the right hand of God.' *Col. iii, 1.* (It is necessary to say that this profound work, exhibited in the Royal Academy in 1963, was made from old ivory, brought here long before the present shameful trade had begun.)

was a pointer to perfection. And they looked to St. Paul's somewhat hesitant pronouncements on celibacy and marriage, and to his clear preference for celibacy. Here too, they felt, was a higher standard, for those who could take it (1 Cor. 7, 1,7,29ff.).

Whatever the virtue of the biblical arguments for a dual standard in Christian ethic, there can be no doubt that, through the seemingly endless generations of chaos and uncertainty, whilst the Roman Empire crumbled and fell apart, monasticism was paramount, not only in keeping the lamp of faith alight, but in preserving what was good in ancient culture. It had proliferated first in the deserts of Egypt (Anthony, *c.*305, and Pachomius, *c.*315). It had spread through Syria into Asia Minor (Basil, *c.*360). It had travelled westwards into Gaul (Cassian, *c.*415), and on to the British islands. And, when Christianity had been stamped down by the Anglo-Saxons, the men who had brought it back here were monks, some Celtic, some Roman. Monks had been a natural task-force for the Church, ready to hand, travelling light, especially dedicated people, subject to vows of obedience, with no domestic ties to hold them back, and no personal possessions to pin them down.

In the west of Europe, by gradual degrees, the Rule of Saint Benedict, springing from Benedict of Nursia (480-543) and his famous monastery on Monte Cassino in central Italy, had come to be known generally as '*the* Rule (*regula*)', and its observers as 'regulars'. Clergy who were not monks were 'seculars' (in the world, *seculum*). Whatever the merits of other rules, Benedict's had outpaced them all. It had proved to be moderate, sane, humane, unfussy. By no means easy to keep, it did not crush the normal man or woman down. And so it prevailed for centuries, and it still plays a major role today. Emphases may change — less or more corporate prayer, for example, or degrees of silence, or varieties of diet, or complexity of liturgy, or exercise of authority within a house, or balance between this and that kind of work — but the spirit of the founder has gone on (see *RB 1980, Butler 1924* and *Rees 1978*).

During the first centuries of Christian England monasticism had flourished. The Viking invasions, however, had made peaceful living impossible, and by 940 full observance of the Rule had virtually ceased. True, there were buildings called abbeys, minsters, monasteries, and there were men called abbots. There were even groups of men, sharing life and ministry, at major churches, and seemingly monks. But, except possibly at St. Augustine's, Canterbury, no house, no community, lived out the regular life in full. Maybe a few individuals did so in private, maybe some isolated groups, but that was all.

Since 940, however, the English scene had changed completely. New houses had been founded, and were keeping the Rule. Others, grown slack, had been regularized. By King Aethelred's time there were some 30 houses for men, and about six for women, all of them genuine Benedictine monasteries. Three men, each of great spiritual calibre, each (in their degree) influenced by recent continental reform, had led the way. Dunstan had been abbot of Glastonbury, subsequently archbishop of Canterbury. Aethelwold had been abbot of Abingdon, later bishop of Winchester. Oswald had been bishop of Worcester, later (in plurality) archbishop of York. Dunstan had died in 988, Aethelwold in 984,

Oswald in 992; but their influence lived on, and the whole Church (not only the monastic houses) had benefited (see *Knowles 1963, Stenton 1971, Barlow 1* (1979), pp.311-38, *Regularis Concordia*, and *Bateson 1894*).

The establishment of Eynsham abbey in 1005 was a late flowering of that great revival. Its main figures were Aethelmaer and (as is generally understood) Aelfric, the one a prominent statesman, the other a gifted teacher and scholar. They had already worked together, regularizing the abbey of Cerne in Dorset. Now they would turn their attention to Eynsham, Aethelmaer as founder, benefactor, adviser, friend, Aelfric as abbot.

Aethelmaer came of noble stock. He was descended from King Aethelred I, elder brother of King Alfred. His family had long moved easily in the court circles of Wessex. Of late it had begun to show a marked concern for religion and culture, part perhaps of a growing protest against centuries of violence.

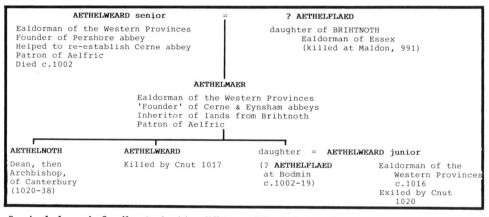

7. **Aethelmaer's family.** Authorities differ: see *Whitelock 1930, Exeter Book 1933*, F.E. Harmer, *Anglo-Saxon Writs* (1952), *Robertson 1956, Chronicle of Aethelweard* (ed. A. Campbell, 1962), and *Barlow 1.*

Aethelweard senior, his father, only recently dead (see illustration 7), had translated the English of the Anglo-Saxon Chronicle into Latin, and sent a copy to Germany, to a famous relative of his, Matilda, abbess of Essen. It is possible that he had commissioned the remarkable *Exeter Book of Old English Poetry*. As Ealdorman of the Western Provinces he was a senior figure in English life. He may well have been behind the Eynsham scheme of 1005, and planned it before his death.

Aelfric was a notable product of Aethelwold's stern traditions at Winchester. He had caught his enthusiasm. He had read widely. He had thought deeply. He had both the gifts and the desires of a teacher. His special opportunity had come in 987. At Aethelmaer's request he had been sent to Cerne abbey, charged with building up an instructed community. There, as 'monk and mass-priest' (his own words), working outside the cloister as well as within, his talent for teaching and writing had blossomed, and his fame had spread. In particular, his sermons, preached and written down in English, were soon being copied out and circulated, for use by others. All kinds of people, high and low, clerical and lay, turned to him.

By 1005 Cerne could be left to others. Aethelmaer and Aelfric could collaborate in a new venture at Eynsham. Aethelmaer, it seems, would make his home there, though not as a monk. The economics of the affair would, we may presume, be his special care; worship, teaching, the norms of the regular life, would be Aelfric's. Both men were getting older. They would (it was hoped) spend their later years in congenial company and worthwhile work. Perhaps they would contribute to England's peace and safety.

And so it was that, amidst the continuing national crisis, King Aethelred, with the ample support of his council, founded an abbey. God (it had been thought in very primitive days) could quite literally smell a succulent burnt sacrifice and be very delighted (Gen. 8, 20f.). Taking that picture St. Paul had spoken of good Christian living as 'an odour of a sweet smell, a sacrifice acceptable, well-pleasing to God' (Phil. 4, 18). Aethelred (as he said at the beginning of the charter) had 'determined to appease God with a never-ending display of good works and a ceaseless offering of praise', and to do so at Eynsham. The red line of sacrifice, integral to Jewish/Christian thinking, runs through the story. The charter continues thus:

> . . . The matter concerns Aethelmaer, a man of outstanding loyalty to myself, and very dear to me. At his earnest request, I here and now confer the privilege of liberty, in its most unconditional form, upon his monastery, now duly dedicated, in honour of St. Saviour and all his Saints, and established at an important place, hard by the river Thames, called Eynsham (*Egnesham*) by those who live in that part of the country.
>
> Aethelmaer has received this monastery in an exchange of lands with his son-in-law,[1] Aethelweard. For the 30 holdings (*mansiunculae*), which constitute Eynsham, he has given 36 holdings (*mansiones*), situate in three different places, three at Up Ottery, 10 at Little Compton, 10 at Lawling, and 13 at Shelford.
>
> Therein he is establishing monks who will order their lives by the Rule. He will himself be like a father to them, sharing his goods, and living amongst them. For the duration of his own life, he has appointed the abbot who will lead the sacred community of monks. In due course, after the abbot of his appointment, the election of abbots will follow the directions of the Rule. According to traditional practice, the choice will be made from out of the community itself. The man to be ordained abbot shall be chosen from that same community, and from nowhere else whatever, unless perhaps, through faults of character, or lack of experience, no man worthy of such a responsibility can be found there.
>
> And the choice shall be made in consultation with the king. Let the king, however, maintain his lordship over the shepherd and the flock of Christ with watchful diligence and with compassion, not tyrannizing over it, but defending the place, and giving it increase, as good custom dictates.
>
> And, except for the authority of the king, let no secular person whatsoever at any time be chosen to exercise lordship over the place: for this might lead to great damage, not to say disaster . . .[2]

Notes

1. *Genero suo*: this may have its less precise meaning, 'kinsman'.
2. Abbeys were so rich in land that kings simply had to have a voice in choosing abbots, but, at

the same time, kings afforded protection to abbeys against grasping local magnates, whether ecclesiastical or lay. They were rewarded with special prayers in the daily monastic round (see *Knowles 1963*, pp.714-5). The charter here reflects the language and the aims of the *Regularis Concordia* (see its Proem, 9-10).

Economic base

The economics of an abbey were much the same as those of a landed family, and at this time perhaps all or most of its monks would be drawn from that stock and accustomed to its standards. When life in general was rough and uncomfortable, short and hazardous, the clothing and footwear, food and drink of monks would be relatively better; they would enjoy more quiet and shelter; they would command more domestic service; and the labour of other men would deal with their heavy farming and building.

But that by no means implied that they were 'clothed in purple and fine linen, and fared sumptuously every day' (Luke 16, 19). They had surrendered all privacy; every detail of life was decided for them. Even the smallest thing could not be called their own. The joys of wife and children were not for them, and at all times, winter and summer, they spent hours in disciplined and exacting prayer in church, as well as in tedious toils in draughty cloisters. There was a degree of asceticism built into their lives, which few laymen would have cared to tolerate. Often they failed, but their whole order was a standing protest against selfishness and arrogance, as also against worshipping wealth, sexuality, and violence.

At the centre of their premises there would be the four essentials for shared Christian living — a church for prayers, a refectory for meals, a cloister for work, and a dormitory for rest and sleep. Other desirables would grow around that nucleus — a chapter-house for business, an infirmary for sick and elderly brethren, a guest-house etc., and, encircling all (for they were an enclosed order) a wall or ditch, with gate and porter (see illustration 8).

The specifically monastic quarters would stand in place of the large house, elsewhere occupied by a lay magnate, his wife and family; but the sustaining economic structure, all around, and inevitably penetrating within, would be much the same. The whole unit would be more or less self-supporting, the inner parts containing the kitchens, storehouses, workshops, bakery, brewery, stables, home-farm etc., and, by almost imperceptible links, passing into the world outside — the fields, the woods, the meadows, the pastures, the livestock, the fish ponds, the rivers, the mill, and above all the cottages and their inhabitants. Here would be produce, labour, skills, payments large and small, contributions in kind; here also smiths, potters, stonemasons, leather-workers, carpenters etc., who would support the abbey and its village and the whole interconnected estate.

And beyond Eynsham there were more distant estates, each producing its

gardens

gardens

THE WORLD OUTSIDE

THE WORLD OUTSIDE

N

1 slype (passage-way)
2 vestibule
3 chapter-house
4 parlour
5 warming-room
6 service-area
7 stores & cellars
8 little cloister
9 infirmary
  a. hall
  b. chapel
  c. kitchen
  d. misericord (for those allowed meat)

← scriptorium (writing-rooms)

b

9 a

c

d

← dormitory (over)

8

3

latrines

2

1

4

7

(for study)

5

cloister, around garth

6 refectory

church

(for novices)

cemetery

abbot's lodging

kitchen

outer parlour →

greater guesthouse

outer court

for brewing, etc.

stables & granaries

for baking, offices,

almonry

lesser guesthouse

feet

0   50   100   150   200

main gatehouse

8. **Plan of a typical 12th-century Benedictine monastery.** Based upon M. and C.H.B. Quennell, *A History of Everyday Things in England, 1066-1499*, Batsford, 1918.

quota of revenue. A few things, salt, for example, would of necessity come from outside. Some domestic staff would be resident; others would come and go. And with them a constant flow of visitors — royal and ecclesiastical officials, relatives, potential monks, messengers, pilgrims, traders, abbey-bailiffs, itinerant craftsmen, vagrants, and so on.

When not busy at their prayers (the quintessential work of God, *opus Dei*), monks would be expected to read and study. They would also have miscellaneous responsibilities of management, as well as the detailed and complex ordering of the church and its services, the copying of manuscripts, the distribution of charity, the care of those in the infirmary, the teaching of novices and boy-oblates (see illustration 9),[1] the ironing out of personal problems. Sometimes they would venture out into the world beyond, but only with the abbot's permission, and not without great circumspection.

In this Anglo-Saxon period it would be wrong to picture the vast and elaborate architectural triumphs of the Normans, but it would be equally wrong to underestimate the daring, the skill, the majesty, the imagination, the sheer craftsmanship, which Anglo-Saxons brought to their churches and their contents (see *Taylor 1965* and *Fernie 1983*). Abbey buildings might well begin with wood and thatch, and much might continue so. But only the best would do for God and his Church: churches and abbeys were built to last. Stone walls, their roofs covered with lead or tiles, would gradually replace less durable

9. **Mother and Boy: bronze by Gwynneth Holt, 1986.** Hannah gave Samuel to Shiloh; there was a time when medieval mothers gave sons to monasteries. (Photography by Sue Chapman.)

structures. First the church, and then the rest, would be improved and enriched.
Rivalry with other houses might well spur the effort. So would royal or noble
favour, burials of the famous, acquisitions of relics, varying flows of trade or
travel, and a peaceful political scene, not to mention the enterprise and vision
of an individual abbot and his chief assistants (his *obedientiaries*). By and large,
abbeys lived up to their means, sometimes beyond them, and built accordingly.

The Eynsham estate was just right for Aethelmaer's purpose. It was compact
and long-established; it was on one or two main roads; it was in the heart of
southern England, comparatively secure, tucked away between the windings of
the Thames and the confines of the Wychwood forest. The foundation-charter,
which details the landmarks, the tracks, the watercourses etc. of its boundary,
leaves the feeling that the whole estate was more or less coterminous with the
parish of many centuries later. It comprised '30 holdings', probably tenant-

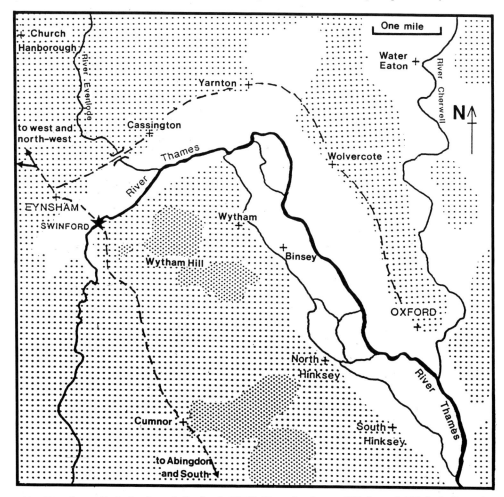

10. **Eynsham, Swinford, and Oxford, 1005.** Note: land over 200 ft. and 400 ft. indicated
by coarse and fine stippling respectively.

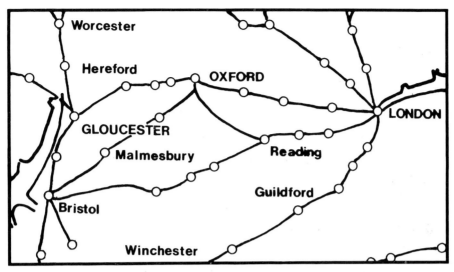

11. **London to Gloucester, *c.*1360** (via Uxbridge, High Wycombe, Tetsworth, Oxford, Witney, Burford, Northleach). Based on the Gough map, as represented in *Darby 1973*, p.175. It is impossible to provide an accurate scale.

holdings of various sizes, each with its accommodation for man and beast, as well as its own 'cabbage-patch', and a recognized share in the common fields, meadows, and so on.

The village was on a low terrace of gravel, above the flood-waters of the Thames, and commanding the important Swinford crossing of the river (see illustration 10). Much north/south traffic must have flowed this way, avoiding Oxford. The Midlands lay to the north, Abingdon, Winchester, Southampton, and the Continent to the south. There is ample evidence that human settlement was very ancient in Eynsham, even when Britons and Saxons fought for its control in the year 571:

> 571. In this year Cuthwulf fought against the Britons at *Biedcanford*, and captured four towns, Limbury, Aylesbury, Bensington, and Eynsham (*Egonesham*): and in the same year he died

> (from the O.E. of the *Anglo-Saxon Chronicle*, as translated in *E.H.D.*, vol.1; see also K.R. Davis, *Britons and Saxons. The Chiltern Region 400-700*, Chichester, 1982.)

It is not impossible that Eynsham took west/east traffic as well. The soundest route from the village to Oxford went north-eastwards at first, crossing the little river Evenlode, and then in a great curve, avoiding the Thames, and down into the city from the north. If (as seems possible) that track was a section of a major west/east route, perhaps even from Wales and Gloucester to London (see illustration 11), then Eynsham was at a very significant crossroads, and many travellers would pause, refresh body and soul, have a gossip, exchange news, visit the local shrine, leave an offering, and light a candle (see Appendix 1).

And Eynsham may also have benefited from water-borne traffic. Even in Anglo-Saxon times the Thames was already navigable as far as Oxford, and perhaps even up to Cricklade. More and more water-mills had entailed more and more weirs, and with the weirs had come flash-locks and navigation (see *Davis 1973* and *Hill 1981*, map 15).

So Eynsham was in a strategic position, and (perhaps best of all) Aethelweard junior, its current holder, was ready to part with it. We cannot tell what family-pressures he faced. The charter suggests that he drove a hard bargain, taking '36 holdings', surrendering '30 lesser holdings'. Anglo-Saxon notaries, however, often changed a word for changing's sake and, in any case, his 36 new possessions were widely scattered, hard to manage, and in some cases (for example, Up Ottery in Devon, and Lawling in Essex) uncomfortably close to the sea and its Danish raiders.

Whatever the circumstances, Aethelmaer acquired a good site, and (whether intentionally or not) gained also a monastic toehold in a curiously unmonastic part of England. Monasteries stretched across the south, reached up the west, and clustered in the eastern fenlands, but a huge swathe of the Midlands was almost destitute of them. Eynsham just crept into it.

The charter moves on to give details of sundry other lands, gathered up, and now given to the new house. In a manner characteristic of Aethelred's charters, it goes out of its way (except in the case of Shipton-on-Cherwell: see Postscript to ch.7, below) to tell how they were Aethelmaer's to give (see *Stenton 1955*, pp.74ff. and *Keynes 1980*, pp.95-8). In some cases they were bequests, seemingly entrusted to him, against such a need. The text offers a curious sense of the landed aristocracy, probably much interrelated, banding together, earnestly and generously, to help Aethelmaer get his great project off the ground.

Precise identification of each endowment-land is not yet possible. The following summary seems probable: Shipton-on-Cherwell, Shifford, and Yarnton, Oxford-shire; Mickleton, Gloucestershire; an unidentified Burton; Marlcliff, in Bidford-on-Avon, Warwickshire; Bentley, in Holt, Worcestershire; Esher and Thames Ditton, Surrey; Rameslie (roughly Rye), Sussex (see illustration 12).

They appear to be a random selection, odd bits and pieces, come somehow into Aethelmaer's hands, and now shovelled, almost indiscriminately into one box. At least in one case, however, a very sound and practical purpose is obvious: Mickleton had a firm stake in Droitwich salt and its ancient salt-ways (see illustration 12). Could it be that all the other lands had a vague or specific business value, over and above what its tenants might provide? Quantities of smaller, and often costly, material — spices, perfumes, textiles, precious metals, pigments, gems etc. — passed by well-known, well-used, tracks, on four-footed transport, across the length and breadth of England, and indeed of Europe and the Mediterranean world. And bulkier goods travelled far as well, by cart and waggon, barge and ship. Aethelred's legislation for the port of London mentions Normandy, France, Flanders, Lorraine, and the German Empire, and specifies planks, cloth, fish, wine, wool, melted fat, pepper, gloves, vinegar and blubber-fish (i.e. whales, porpoises etc.); see *IV Aethelred* in *Robertson 1925*.

Was Aethelmaer planning for less troubled times, when the Danes might have gone? Did he think of a peaceful future which never came? That network of lands might then have been valuable indeed. Shifford, upstream from Eynsham,

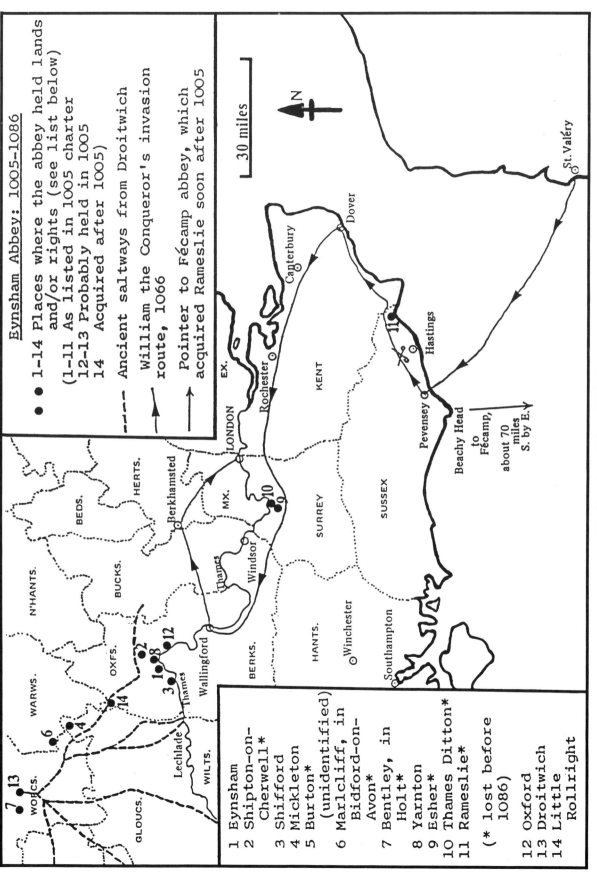

Eynsham Abbey: 1005-1086

• 1-14 Places where the abbey held lands and/or rights (see list below)

(1-11 As listed in 1005 charter
12-13 Probably held in 1005
14 Acquired after 1005)

--- Ancient saltways from Droitwich

→ William the Conqueror's invasion route, 1066

→ Pointer to Fécamp abbey, which acquired Rameslie soon after 1005

1 Eynsham
2 Shipton-on-Cherwell*
3 Shifford
4 Mickleton
5 Burton* (unidentified)
6 Marlcliff, in Bidford-on-Avon*
7 Bentley, in Holt*
8 Yarnton
9 Esher*
10 Thames Ditton*
11 Rameslie*

(* lost before 1086)

12 Oxford
13 Droitwich
14 Little Rollright

30 miles

N

to Fécamp, about 70 miles S. by E.

12. Eynsham Abbey, 1005-1086.

would give a second crossing of the Thames. Shipton would permit the crossing of the Cherwell without going through Oxford. Bentley, as well as Mickleton, had an interest in Droitwich salt, and Marlcliff was on the way to it. Marlcliff was also by the ancient Ryknield Street, where it crossed the Avon. Esher and Ditton were en route to London, long the hub of England's road-system and gateway to Europe. Rameslie had its own salt-pans, as well as its manifold cross-Channel connections (see Appendix 2). Here is how the foundation-charter sets it out:

> . . . Now these are the lands, which the said Aethelmaer has acquired for St. Saviour and all his Saints, and for the offering of service to God: they are given in great humility: they are not only from the king, but from sundry other men: some are by purchase, some by exchange; all are for the benefit of the monks who live therein: and they are granted by gift perpetual.
>
> First, five holdings in a place which the inhabitants call Shipton.
>
> Next, an estate called Shifford: this also the said man has given to the said monastery: his kinsman, Leofwine, at the point of death, had bestowed it upon him: previously it had been held by the famous Ealdorman Brihtnoth, who had been delighted to receive it from my father, Edgar, as a reward for worthy service.
>
> Likewise, he has given Mickleton to the monastery: this had been bequeathed to him by the same Ealdorman Brihtnoth: this also had been given to Brihtnoth by Edgar, and confirmed by charter.
>
> Furthermore, he has given an estate of five holdings, called Burton: he had merited such a gift from me, but had been given it by his kinsman, Aethelweard, as if from me: in effect, it was a voluntary tribute from Aethelweard to me: Aethelmaer has now given it to the monastery for the healing of the soul of his wife.
>
> The said Aethelmaer has also bought 12 holdings from me for £30: they are from the estates which a certain lady, named Leoftaet, mismanaged and forfeited: thus he has given three and a half holdings at Marlcliff to the monastery, as also two holdings of common woodland at Bentley.
>
> He has also given to the said monastery 10 holdings of common land at Yarnton: he had obtained them from his relative, Godwin, in exchange for five holdings at Studley and 10 at Chesterton.[2]
>
> There are also 20 holdings[3] at a place which local people call Esher: Bishop Byrhthelm once gave them to his kinsman, Aethelweard, Aethelmaer's father: a while before his death Aethelweard gave them to his son, Aethelmaer: Aethelmaer has now given them to the monastery.
>
> Likewise, there is land called Ditton: I had rewarded Aethelmaer with this, and confirmed it by charter: this also he has given to the said monastery.
>
> Finally, there is an estate called Rameslie, with the harbour pertaining to it: his kinswoman, Wulfwyn, committed these to Aethelmaer at her death: he has granted them to the said monastery.
>
> Let then this monastery, together with all the lands described above, and lawfully appertaining to it, be free from all service to men, excepting only military duty, or the building of a bridge, or of a fortification.[4]
>
> Now, if any man strive to confirm this our grant of liberty, and determine to establish and enlarge it, then let God Almighty increase and enlarge him with all prosperity in this present world and with blissful exultation (*felicitatis tripudium*) in the world to come. But if any man is minded to divert and to destroy the protection which our liberty affords, then let him be cut off from the fellowship of the holy church of God, as also from any share in the most holy body and blood

of Christ: and, at the day of the great judgment, may he stand condemned, together with Judas, betrayer of Christ, upon the left side of the throne, unless, humbly penitent for his disobedience to our decrees, he has rendered adequate and worthy satisfaction.

[5]These are the boundaries of the land at Eynsham. First from the 'rough lake' to Bugga's brook; along the brook to Tilgar's ditch; from the ditch to ward sty (i.e. path); from the sty to Winburh's 'stock';[6] from the stock to three oaks; along the way to the boundary tree; thence along the way to the port street; from the street to the 'swains' croft; thence to heath-field to the old ditch; thence right to the boundary-brook; along the brook into (the) Bladen; along (the) Bladen into (the) Thames . . .

(from the O.E. as translated by W.H. Stevenson in *E.C.* See also *Grundy 1933*, *E.M.*, *Gelling 1953-4*, *Cooper 1961/70*, *Steed 1961/2*, and *Bailey 1989*.)

Notes

1. For centuries past, parents or guardians had offered boys, often quite young ones, for the monastic life. The custom may well have provided a majority of the monks. It was to be forbidden by the Lateran Council of 1215, but would be slow to die. The oblation was irrevocable, and was often associated with an extra endowment of the house. It was dictated by family circumstances, as well as by any personal fitness or aspiration in the boy himself. Doubtless the boy Samuel was often called to mind (see 1 Sam. 1, 1-2, 11).

2. *Sawyer 1968*, p.278, wrongly includes Studley, Warwickshire, and Chesterton, Oxfordshire, in Aethelmaer's gift to Eynsham.

3. In this translation the nondescript word 'holding' is used for four different Latin words, *manentes, mansiones, mansae, mansiunculae*: they frequently occur in multiples of five, and probably mean *hides*, the traditional English land measurement, by this time more of a rounded assessment for tax than a precise area. The O.E. version of the Shipton land actually reads '*v. hida land*'. The other four Latin words, used in this connection, *rus, villa, villula, terra*, seem to be more general in meaning.

4. These three civic duties fell upon local land-holders, as occasion demanded. The term *trimoda necessitas* is sometimes associated with them.

5. At this point the foundation-charter moves from Latin to English, and gives nine boundaries, starting with Eynsham, the only one here translated. Each peasant would recognize the landmarks. (For Shipton-on-Cherwell, see J.Cooper, *Four Oxfordshire Anglo-Saxon Charter Boundaries*, Oxoniensia, vol.50 (1985), pp.15-23.)

6. 'Sty' means 'footpath, narrow way'; 'stock' means 'log, mark', as sign-post.

The king's wise men

Power lay with the king and the council, his *witan*, literally his wise men. They were not chosen for their wisdom; still less were they chosen by the people. But they had collective power, and sometimes collective wisdom. They were the aristocracy of their day — bearers of the blood royal, bishops and abbots from the clergy, ealdormen and thegns[1] from the laity — there by family or office, wealth or intrigue, character or ability. Decisions were made as the king moved around the land; at some meetings many were present, at others just a few. At the centre was a steady nucleus, embracing the royal family and the chief officials (see *Liebermann 1913, Robertson 1925*, and *Oleson 1955*).

The foundation-charter moves on to a brief personal statement by Aethelmaer, written in English, simple and moving, read out perhaps in the assembly. He is himself to live in his new abbey. Laymen often did so. Benefactors might well rely on their abbey for security and care in sickness, old age and death. They would have their own quarters and staff within the precinct. They would go in and out at will. As godly laymen, they would be happy in that atmosphere, and would join in such devotions as they wished. Aethelmaer, it seems, had lost his wife. His family had grown up and moved away. At Eynsham he would find companionship, and in particular his old friend Aelfric.

It is just possible that another consideration moved him. Court circles, thrown into disarray by the Danes, could pose their own dangers. Was it only coincidence that in that same year another great layman, Ordulf, the king's uncle, retired into Tavistock abbey, in Devon? Wild things were to happen in 1006, events associated with Eadric, ealdorman of Mercia. Eadric 'Streona' (the term implies grasping ambition) was to leave an unsavoury name. The year 1006 was to see him burst into treachery and violence. Had it been wisdom which prompted Aethelmaer and Ordulf to vanish from the public scene in 1005? We cannot be sure (see *Keynes 1980*, pp.211ff.)

Whatever the case, Aethelmaer had massive support in 1005. His Eynsham charter concludes with a huge list of witnesses, members of the *witan*, who agreed with and supported his plan, and put their names to its details: the king and the queen, seven royal princes, both archbishops, 12 other bishops (nearly the whole bench), 16 abbots (more than half their total), three ealdormen, and 44 thegns. The abbey could not have been launched with more prayer and concern.

Motives, no doubt, were very mixed: Aethelmaer, insuring against old age, and perhaps in fear of Eadric; the *witan*, anxious to retain lands and power, and fearful of the Danes; but (say what we will) all of them wanting more men to be better men. Together, therefore, they made this offering to God.

Liber aurelii augustini De vera et falsa
Quantum sit appetenda gra penitentia.

penitentie omnis autoritas clamat. ois
beatorum uita conat ostendere. Langores enim
sanat. leprof curat. mortuof sufcitat. fanitatem
auget: qua conseruat. Claudif gressum. aridis
copia. cecis restituit uisum. Vicia fugat. uirtu
tef exornat. mente munit et roborat. Omnia
sanat. omnia redintegrat. oia letificat. Tempe
rat successuf. cöstringit impetuf: moderatur
excessus. Ignoranf se: p hanc recognoscit. Orens
se: p hanc se inuenit. Hec e que hominef ad
anglof ducit: et creatura reddit creatori. Ista
ouem pditam mösstrut querenti: et decima drag
mam optulit anxianti. Hec dissipatore filiü
ad prem reduxit: et uulneratü a latronibus cuf
todi cändum reseruauit. In hanc omne boniü
inuenit: p hanc omne bonü cöseruatur. fugat
tenebraf. inducit luce. excocte oia ipsa ignif con
sumenf. Hec oia prudida uirago sensisti: q hoc tantü
bonü vere dilexisti. Vix eni diligitur: quod
omnino ignorat. Sup hoc bonü innixa: fortis
ee potif ad omnia bona. Itaqz uolumtate tua

13. **Eynsham Abbey library book: B IX, 12th century.** The shelf-number is in red, and written very neatly; the reference to the abbey library is in black, and added somewhat hastily. This is the opening page of Augustine's *De vera et falsa penitentia*. Bodl. MS. Laud Lat. 31, f.6R.

One extra factor must be noted. Eynsham abbey is dedicated 'in honour of St. Saviour and all his Saints'. In the English statement St. Mary and St. Benedict are added. In due course Eynsham abbey was to be 'St. Mary's, Eynsham'. Its only certain surviving library book is inscribed with Eynsham abbey's name, and also the place on the library shelves, *lib sce marie de Egnesh B IX* (This book belongs to Saint Mary of Eynsham: B9) (see illustration 13 & Appendix 3).

St. Mary (and St. Peter also) were to play a substantial part in the unfolding Eynsham story. 'The wrath of St. Mary' may seem a strange phrase, when we recall the simple and godly mother in the Gospels, but it was a near and real peril in the Middle Ages. Disease and death were close at hand, stalking every man. The Last Judgment, the wrath of the Lamb, the surrounding multitude of Saints, the adjoining throne of the Holy Mother, were dread realities, made even more vivid by the artists who served the Church. The relics, the shrines, the lights, of the Saints were tended with care. Men went on laborious pilgrimage, to secure their support. Eynsham abbey's full dedication linked the new venture with all the host of heaven. Here is how the charter continues:

> ... I, Aethelmaer, make known to my beloved lord, King Aethelred, and to all his *witan*, that I give this possession to God, and to Saint Mary, and to all his Saints, and to Saint Benedict, into Eynsham, for those who rightly observe the Rule of Benedict to enjoy after my life for ever. And I will that he who is there now shall be chief over them during his life, and that afterwards, if it shall so fall out, they choose them a chief from their convent, as their Rule enjoins upon them. And that he who shall augment this, may God Almighty grant to him the kingdom of heaven, and he who shall diminish it, may God Almighty render to him such meed as he did to him who betrayed him. And I myself will live in common with the convent, and enjoy the possessions with them during my life.

> [2]Here then is this present charter, set down in writing, in the year of our Lord's incarnation, 1005, in the third year of the current indiction,[3] in consultation with those whose names are to be seen, written out below, and witnessed by them.

> I, Aethelred, by God's grace lifted up on high and honoured with kingship, do here set my name to this charter, with the sign of the holy cross, and do confirm this our privilege of liberty. I, Aethelstan, son of that same king, here add my witness ...

> I, Aelfgifu, queen, being fully cognisant of this matter, do hereby add my witness ...[4]

Notes

1. Ealdormen (in the Danelaw called earls) were the senior lay magnates and land-holders, after the royal family. They were responsible for shires or groups of shires. Thegns (thanes) came next.
2. At this point the charter reverts to the use of Latin.
3. Indictions were 15-year periods, instituted by the Emperor Constantine for fiscal purposes, and later adopted for dating in general. The first was in 312-3.
4. Here, as elsewhere in the charter, Anglo-Saxon Latin (Anglo-Latin) reveals its tendency to be florid and affected. The assertion, 'So-and-so bears witness and agrees', is expressed in some 19 different ways: *testimonium adhibeo, testis assisto, testificans affui, non abnui, consensi, scivi* etc.; see Appendix 4.

Before 1005

What was on the Eynsham abbey site before 1005? We have to wait for the archaeologist, but something pertinent can be said meanwhile. Maybe the chief house of the village, the headman's house, stood there, perhaps with its own little church to hand. Or perhaps there was a larger parish church, one meriting the title 'minster',[1] possibly served by some sort of community. There may even be traces of a pagan shrine below that, for 'holiness' tends to inhere in places.[2] The settlement nearest to Swinford must always have had special importance.

A Midlands document, dated 864 (for text, see *C.S.*, no.509), may give a clue. It suggests that at that time Eynsham had a church with significance outside the village as well as within. Burgred, king of Mercia (see illustration 14), and his queen, Aethelswyth, grant land at Water Eaton, a village on the river Cherwell, north of Oxford, to Ealhun, bishop of Worcester. The price is heavy, and there is a stipulation that at the end of a year the bishop must pay 30s. 'to the church at *Egenes homme*'. If, as seems likely, *Egenes homme* is our Eynsham, then clearly it had an important church, able to expect and receive offerings from places at a little distance. Perhaps it housed a religious community. (For the identification, see *V.C.H., Oxon.*, vol.1, p.379 and *Gelling 1979*, pp.126f.)

Another Mercian document, dated 825 (for text, see *C.S.*, no.384), may point in a similar direction. Archbishop Wulfred of Canterbury is under severe pressure from Beornwulf, king of Mercia. He is compelled to give up a very large estate, no less than 300 hides in extent and value, at a place called *Iognes homme*. If, as is possible, *Iognes homme* also meant Eynsham, the likelihood that so huge a property, held by the archbishop himself, at such a critical point on the Mercia/Wessex boundary, contained a minster and a community is all the greater. (For the identification, see *Ekwall 1960*, p.172 and *Wormald*, in *Campbell 1982*, p.127; for hesitations, see *Gelling 1979*, pp.102-4 and *Brooks 1984*, p.181.)[3]

Those were days when Mercia had had roughly a century of dominance in England. Under kings Aethelbald (716-57), Offa (757-96) and Cenwulf (796-821) they had even counted for something in Europe, and Charlemagne had corresponded with Offa as an equal. Offa had built his great Dyke against the Welsh. Doubtless he was wary enough to watch his border-crossings with Wessex. Swinford was one of them: Eynsham must have been vital to his interests. It is perhaps significant that the four battles in which Wessex finally toppled Mercia from its predominance took place in a virtual circle around Eynsham — Burford 752, Bensington 779, Kempsford 802 and Wroughton 825.

If then (though we cannot be certain) Eynsham had had a minster and a

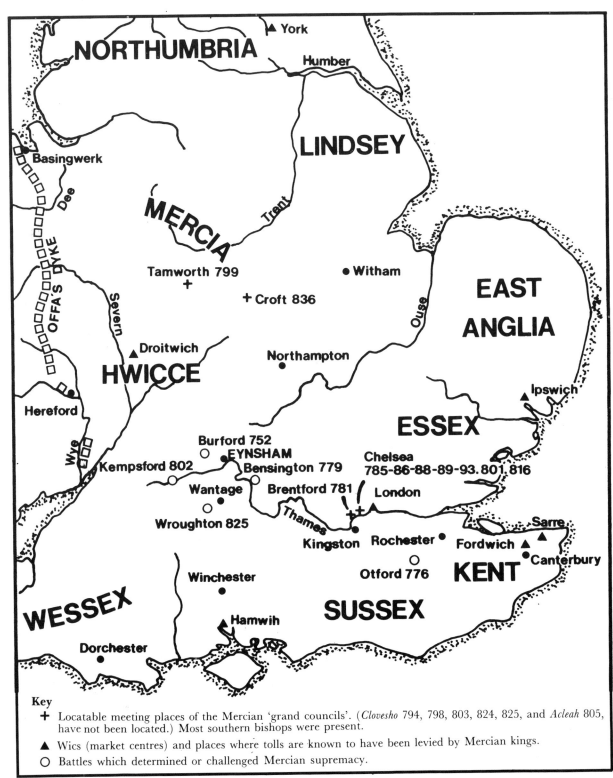

Key

+ Locatable meeting places of the Mercian 'grand councils'. (*Clovesho* 794, 798, 803, 824, 825, and *Acleah* 805, have not been located.) Most southern bishops were present.

▲ Wics (market centres) and places where tolls are known to have been levied by Mercian kings.

O Battles which determined or challenged Mercian supremacy.

14. **Mercian supremacy, 8th/9th centuries.** Based on *Campbell 1982*, p.126.

community in the ninth century, the institution may well have stumbled on until 1005, a group of soi-disant monks, avoiding regularization, tenants of Aethelweard junior, effectively a component of his estates, part of his 'property', religious in vague intent and guise, but untouched by recent reformation. In pre-Conquest England many a religious house suffered a bewildering series of changes and chances (see *M.R.H. 1971*, esp. Appendix 1). If Eynsham had become such a place, then Aethelmaer and Aelfric would have been 'cleansing' an old house, rather than founding a new one. And perhaps Aelfric's so-called *Letter to the Monks of Eynsham* was written in the way it was, because some only of the Eynsham household were really new monks, whilst others were remnants of an older group, men who had elected to stay on and toe the line, rather than to go out into the hazards of a Dane-ridden countryside.

Two phrases in the 1005 foundation-charter may well point in the same direction. One speaks of the buildings as 'duly dedicated and established (*Jure dedicato . . . constituto*)'. That may, of course, refer to recent building work, now ready for a completely new community; but it may perhaps imply hallowed structures, long in existence, now made ready for the new regime. Perhaps even more significant is the reference to Eynsham as 'an important place (*in loco celebri*)'. In the English, as well as the Latin, of that time the word 'place' often meant much more than a mere point on a map; it carried with it the meaning 'holy place'. St. Felix' place, Felixstowe, was his 'holy place'; and so with Bridestowe (St. Bridget's), Edwinstowe (St. Edwin's), St. Mary's Stow, Lincolnshire (soon to come into the Eynsham story). Thus, when a notary of 1005, in ecclesiastical employ, spoke of Eynsham as 'an important place', it is not unlikely that the place was well-known for its holiness, familiar as a resort for pilgrims, a site where somehow God's presence had long seemed to break through the mysterious clouds of human life and shed some light. Perhaps then we may await the archaeologist with extra hopefulness.[4]

Postscript to chapter 7

A recent re-examination of the St. Frideswide legend has led to important suggestions about Eynsham and its Anglo-Saxon past. See J.Blair, *Saint Frideswide Reconsidered*, in *Oxoniensia*, vol.52 (1987; publ. 1988), pp.71-127, and *Eynsham as a central place in Anglo-Saxon Oxfordshire*, in *E.R.*, no.5 (1988), pp.4-6; (for Bampton, see J. Blair, *Saint Beornwald of Bampton*, *Oxoniensia*, vol.49 (1984), pp.47-55). It is suggested:

i. that, in the seventh and eighth centuries, there may have been an Anglo-Saxon sub-kingdom, with its centre at Eynsham, but embracing Bampton to the west and Oxford to the east, and linked together by the 'highway' of the Thames. It would have been subject to the overlordship of Mercia;

ii. that each of those three places had a 'parochial area' around it, and that the three parochial areas were contiguous, and in each case centred upon a 'minster';

iii. that each minster accommodated a loosely-organized group of 'monks', 'nuns', and priests, who co-ordinated church interests throughout their own parochial area, and were supported by it;

iv. that, not infrequently, such minsters were headed by those of royal or noble blood, and that in the case of Oxford, at the beginning of the eighth century, the head was an 'abbess', Princess Frideswide,[5] later canonized (her O.E. name, *Frithuswith*, means 'Peace-Strong');

v. that Frideswide's father, with some such name as Dida, may have been head of the Eynsham-centred sub-kingdom;

vi. that the huge 300-hide estate at *Iognes homme* (see *C.S.*, no.384: date 825), tentatively identified, in the chapter above, with Eynsham, was in fact at Eynsham, and was indeed the heartland of the Eynsham-centred sub-kingdom;

vii. that the land at Water-Eaton, Oxon., whose holder paid dues to the church at Eynsham (*Egenes homme*; see ch. above, & *C.S.*, no.509: date 864), was a lingering fragment of Eynsham's formerly extensive parochial area, and on the edge of Oxford's similarly extensive parochial area;

viii. that the land at Shipton-on-Cherwell, Oxon., which seems to have belonged to Eynsham church already, when, in 1005, it became Eynsham abbey (see E1, in ch.5, above), was a similar fragment on the former Eynsham/Oxford parochial boundary;

ix. that land at Cogges, Oxon. (in this instance see *Blair & Steane 1982*, p.44, n.16, & EI: date, 1239), whose holder had to make a traditional payment (*ab antiquo*) to Eynsham abbey, was a similar lingering fragment of Eynsham's old parochial area, but in this case at its western end, where it abutted on Witney.

These possibilities spring from close study of written sources. At this point the story has to be handed over to the archaeologist. The current excavation becomes all the more exciting.

Notes

1. Anglo-Saxon legal thinking awarded certain penalties for offences against churches in proportion with the importance of the church concerned. VIII Aethelred, 5, 1 (1014), lists four grades in the proportion 8:4:2:1 — a principal church (*heafodmynstres*), a church of medium rank (*medemran mynstres*), one still smaller, though with a graveyard (*thonne git laessan*), and a country chapel (*feldcircan*); see *Robertson 1925*.

2. Ordinary folk hedge their bets. Leaders signalize conquest. Thus the Jewish temple in Jerusalem was displaced by a Roman temple on the same site, later by a Moslem shrine, later still by a Christian church, finally by the Moslem shrine again. And St. Benedict, arrived on Monte Cassino, caused a surviving temple of Apollo to be turned into a chapel of St. Martin.

3. To modern eyes *Egnesham* (1005), *Egonesham* (571), *Egenes homme* (864) and *Iognes homme* (825) seem very different; but standard spelling is a recent phenomenon, and in Eynsham's case there have been many spellings through the centuries (see *E.M.*, pp.107f.). Scribes did their best with what they heard, and broad country-speech could be very variously interpreted in writing. Other contenders are *Igeneshamme* (in a will of 971-83; see *Whitelock 1930*, pp.125ff., and *Gelling 1979*, pp.133f.) and *aet Eanham* (in some of Aethelred's legislation; see *Robertson 1925*). The former might be our Eynsham, but perhaps Inglesham, Wilts.; the latter is now usually identified with King's Enham, near Andover, Hants.

4. There was a limited excavation in 1971 (see *Gray & Clayton 1978-9*). The present writer was invited to contribute a historical note, with which a reproduction of Anthony Wood's famous 1657 drawing of Eynsham abbey ruins might be associated (see *Gordon 1978-9*). Unfortunately Willis' distorted representation of the drawing was printed (see *ib.*, 1978, Plate IV), and (worse still) the text of the main report was slightly adjusted to fit. For reproductions of Wood's drawing, see my ch.20, n.3, below.

The Oxfordshire Archaeological Unit, supported by English Heritage, began further excavation in 1989. Preliminary results are exciting, and appear to substantiate the arguments of this chapter.

5. At Eynsham we may recollect Abbess Matilda of Essen, a redoubtable person, of royal blood, enjoying learned correspondence in the 10th century with her relative, Ealdorman Aethelweard, father of Aethelmaer.

Aelfric

Aelfric's life fell into three parts: more than 30 years of preparation, in and around Winchester; nearly 20 years of hard teaching, at Cerne, in Dorset; and at the end just a few years at Eynsham. Some extracts from his writing will show the special blend of gentleness, severity, and artistry, which was his characteristic.

When quite young he had become wary of putting the complete biblical text into ill-instructed hands. Here is an extract from the Preface to his paraphrase of Genesis:

> The task is very dangerous for me or any one else to undertake, for I am afraid that if some unthinking person reads the book or hears it read, he will imagine that he may live now under the new dispensation just as the patriarchs lived before the old law was given, or as they lived under the law of Moses. I once knew that a certain priest, who was my master at the time, had a copy of the Book of Genesis and a smattering of Latin. He remarked with regard to the patriarch Jacob that he had four wives — two sisters and their respective maid-servants. His statement was correct, but he did not know, nor did I at the time, what a difference there is between the old dispensation and the new. In the beginning of things in this world, the brother married his sister, and sometimes a father had children by his own daughter, and polygamy was practised that people might increase in numbers, and one could not marry unless he wedded his own relations . . .

> (from O.E., as translated in *Benham 1916*, pp.135f.).

It seems likely that he came from a parish not far from Winchester, and that he was attracted to its cathedral-monastery by the reformed Benedictinism, which Aethelwold had introduced there. The change, however salutary, seems to have been both violent and revolutionary; and one detects a degree of relish in Aelfric's story of it, written some 40 years later. Judgment here might fend off Judgment hereafter; both belong to Aelfric's scenario (see *Gatch 1977*, pp.60ff. and *John 1983*).

> The throne of the bishops of Winchester was in the Old Minster there: but the clergy of that place were an evil-living lot, notorious for pride, and arrogance, and high living. Some of them even disdained to celebrate Mass, when their turn came. They had brought in wives, all irregularly: and now they were repudiating them, and taking others. And they were utterly given over to gluttony and drunkenness. This was something that that holy man, Aethelwold, could in no wise bear: and so, with permission from King Edgar, and as quickly as possible, he drove those wicked blasphemers of God out of the monastery, and brought over monks from Abingdon, and put them there instead, with himself both as abbot

and bishop. It so happened that, when the monks had arrived from Abingdon, and were standing at the entrance to the church, the clergy within were finishing Mass, and singing the Communion anthem, 'Serve the Lord with fear, and lift up your hearts to him with trembling: take hold of his teaching, lest ye perish from the right way.' It was as if they were saying, 'We are not willing to serve God, nor yet to sustain his teaching: it is for you to do so, lest ye also perish, like us.' So when the monks heard them sing thus, they said one to another, 'Why do we tarry without? Lo, we are bidden to go in.' The king dispatched one of his thegns also, a very distinguished man, Wulfstan by name, to accompany the bishop: and, with royal authority, he bade the clergy give place with all speed to the monks, or else submit to the monastic habit. But there and then they cursed the monastic life, and went forth from the church: three of them, however, were later converted to the regular way, namely, Eadsin, Wulfsin, and Wilstan . . .

(from the Latin of *Stevenson 1858*, pp.260f.)

Perhaps they were as bad as he says, certainly they were as irregular; but it is hard not to feel some sympathy, at least for the wives and the children!

Whatever the case, this was the place where Aelfric became a monk, thought and prayed, studied and matured, for many years, before being called to Cerne abbey. In about 987, now over 30 years of age, he became novice-master at Cerne. He was to be part of a team, regularizing this house also. Aethelweard senior and Aethelmaer had come to know and admire him, and it was under their pressure that he went.

His first concern was that his pupils, all drawn from English-speaking homes, should know their Latin, and know it well. Their basic education would be in the Latin classics. Their fundamental Christian reading would be the Latin Fathers of the western church. Their life was to be patterned and moulded by regular worship in Latin. They could not know the language too well. So he wrote a Latin *Grammar*; it followed traditional models, but its main text was in English. Then he compiled a Latin/English *Word-List* — not a dictionary, but groups of related Latin words, with their English equivalents. Finally, he produced his own *Colloquy*, that is, an imaginary conversation in Latin, introducing Latin grammar, syntax, and vocabulary, on the way; it would be learned by heart. Its first sentences stress the traditional symbol of the pedagogue (see illustration 15):

15. **The Crest of St. Olave's Grammar School.** The school is now at Orpington, Kent, but was formerly by the Tower Bridge, in London. Founded in 1571, its traditional crest still retains the birch, Aelfric's symbol of centuries earlier. It should be added that corporal punishment was already on the wane when the present writer was at the school.

Master, we boys ask you to teach us to speak Latin correctly: for we are very backward, and speak badly. What do you want to talk about? What matter what we talk about, so only as the speech is correct and useful, not empty or unseemly? Are you willing to be birched whilst learning? We would rather be birched and learn than be ignorant. But we know that you are a kindly man, reluctant to inflict blows on us, unless we force you to . . .

(for translations of *Colloquy*, see *Gem 1912* or *Swanton 1975*; for text, see *Garmonsway 1978*; for *Grammar* and *Word-List*, see *Zupitza 1880*.)

Colloquies were standard tools of education, but Aelfric's was brilliantly original and interesting.

Meanwhile, he taught and preached vigorously in English. Much of it must have been to older monks in the abbey itself, as well as to the novices. A good monastery set out to be a continuing school of Christian learning. Much also seems to have gone to lay congregations, who crowded the abbey nave, coming to Masses, and hungry to learn. Aelfric's sermons were written down, worked over, copied, and distributed, far and wide. Parish clergy used them, up and down the land. One surviving manuscript is thought to show Aelfric's own revising hand (see *Aelfric: Homilies 1* (fac.), folio 64). Two sets, known as *Catholic Homilies*, 40 in each, went out; they were tied systematically to the Christian Year and its ordered display of the main elements of the faith, but they were lucid, imaginative, sympathetic, strong in challenge (see *Thorpe 1844-6* and *Godden 1979*). Besides those 80 homilies others have survived (see *Pope 1967-8*), and also *Lives of Saints* (see *Aelfric, Saints*). Even in the 12th century, years after the Norman conquest, that great corpus of Aelfric's teaching was being copied out. It was probably his greatest legacy.

Here is part of his account of the Creation and the Fall. It is from a homily *On the False Gods*:

. . . This Trinity created the bright angels, and then Adam and Eve as human beings, giving them dominion over earthly creatures. And they might have lived forever, without death, if they had never broken that one commandment of God. Adam then dwelt in happiness, free from care, and no creature could harm him so long as he kept the heavenly behest. No fire hurt him, though he stepped into it, nor could water drown the man, even if he suddenly ran into the waves.[1] Neither could any wild beast injure him. No more could hunger, nor thirst, grievous cold, nor extreme heat, nor sickness afflict Adam in the world, so long as he kept that little commandment with faith.

But when he had sinned and broken God's behest, he lost happiness, and lived in toil, so that lice and fleas boldly bit him whom formerly not even the serpent had dared to touch. Then he had to beware of water and of fire, and to be on the watch lest harm befall him, and to provide food for himself by his own toil. Moreover, the natural gifts with which God had endowed him he had to guard with great care in order to keep them. Even so the good do still, they who with toil keep themselves from sins . . .

(from O.E., as translated in *Benham 1916*, pp.92f.)

And here is how he tried to explain the mystery of Christ's words, 'This is my body', 'This is my blood'. The lovely translation is Elizabethan, because Archbishop Matthew Parker and his fellow Anglicans thought (mistakenly) that they had found a western catholicism, more like their own, in Aelfric's pre-Norman presentation of the matter:[2]

The Apostles dyd as Christ commaunded, that is, they blessed bread & wine to housell agayne afterward in hys remembraunce. Even so also since their departure all priestes by Christes commaundement doe blesse bread & wine to housell in hys name with the Apostolike blessing.

Now men have often searched & do yet often search, howe bread that is gathered of corne, and through fyers heate baked, may bee turned to Christes body, or how wyne that is pressed out of many grapes is turned through one blessing to the Lordes bloude.

Now saye we to suche men that some thinges be spoken of Christ by signification, some thyng by thyng certaine. True thyng is and certaine that Christ was borne of a maide, & suffred death of his own accorde, & was buried, & on thys daye rose from death. He is sayd bread by signification, & a lambe, & a lyon, & a mountayne. He is called bread, because he is our life & angells life. He is sayd to be a lambe for his innocencie. A lyon for strength wherwith he overcame the strong devill. But Christ is not so notwithstanding after true nature neither bread, nor a lambe, nor a Lyon.

Why is then that holy housel called Christs body, or his bloud if it be not truely that it is called. Truely the bread and the wine which by the masse of the priest is halowed, shewe one thyng without to humayne understanding & an other thing they call within to beleving mindes. Without they bee sene bread & wine both in figure & in tast: and they be truely after their halowing, Christes body & hys bloude through ghostly mistery . . .

(from O.E., as translated in *Aelfric* c.*1567*; see illustration 16).

Coming to Eynsham in *c.*1005 Aelfric wrote his *Letter to the Monks of Eynsham*. It is in fact a *Customary*, an ordered set of details, filling out the basic Benedictine Rule, and applying it to the manifold daily practicalities of communal religious life in 10th-/11th-century England. It begins with the general sentiment that monastic life is not nearly as tough for monks of 1005 as it was for him when he was a novice in Aethelwold's time!

Abbot Aelfric: to the Eynsham brethren: greetings in Christ.

Living amongst you, I can see that you need instruction in monastic ways: you need it by word of mouth or in written form: after all it was only recently that you accepted Aethelmaer's invitation and were set apart for the monastic life. Here then are some few written extracts from the book of customs, which St. Aethelwold, bishop of Winchester, with his fellow-bishops and abbots, gathered up from all sides, and directed monks to observe, in the time of the most blessed Edgar, king of England. Until now even this little book has been completely unknown to your brotherhood. I confess that I only undertake the task in fear and trembling. I have no courage even to tell you of everything that I learned of monastic ways and customs, during the many years that I spent in his school. You might find the strictness of such great observance so utterly distasteful that you would refuse even to hear the story. Lest, however, you should remain in total ignorance of such wholesome teaching, I am setting down in this document some of the matters which are not covered by our Rule, but ought to be read by you: and I am also adding some items from a book by the priest, Amalarius. Health and happiness be yours in Christ . . .

Here are some dramatic and colourful moments for the end of Holy Week:

. . . On the three nights before Easter, we kindle 24 candles each night, and extinguish them one by one, at each antiphon and each responsory. And thus we mark the departure of Christ, our true sun. For one day is made up of 24 hours, and we continue this extinction of just so many candles for three nights: forasmuch as Christ our sun was hid three days within the sepulchre.

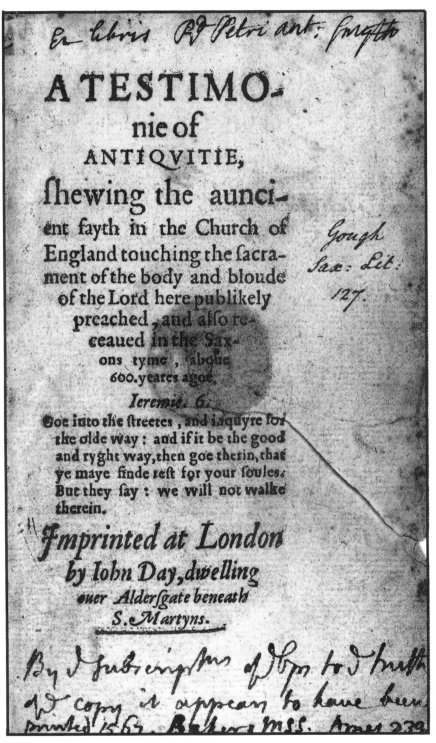

16. **Title page of *A Testimonie of Antiquitie, c.1567.*** Aelfric's Easter Sermon, as published by Anglican Reformers, in parallel Old English and Elizabethan English. 'Goe into the streetes, and inquyre for the olde way.' *Bodl. Gough Sax. Lit., 127.*

Custom teaches us that, at the Lord's Supper on Maundy Thursday, the last
antiphon at the Gospel being finished, two boys should stand in the south aisle
(*porticus*),[3] and sing in a loud voice, Lord, have mercy (*Kyrie eleison*): and two boys
in the north aisle should respond, Christ, have mercy (*Christe eleison*): and two
brethren in the western part should cry back, Lord, have mercy upon us (*Domine
miserere nobis*): and all the company should reply together, Christ the Lord is
become obedient even unto death (*Christus Dominus factus est obediens usque ad mortem*).
And thus let all do thrice: and let all offer silent prayers, on bended knees, as is
the wont: and let this manner of singing be observed, in the same form, on three
successive nights: and, if Mattins be ended before dawn, let those brethren who
wish return to their rest . . .

At None, on that same day, and on the two following days, let new fire be struck
from stone, at the entrance of the church, and let it be carried within the church
. . . And, if it pleases, when None has been sung, let there be the image of a
serpent, made ready before, and fixed to a pole,[4] and having a candle in its mouth:
and let this candle be kindled from the aforesaid fire: and let it be carried, upon
its pole, within the church, and let the lights be kindled from it: and so let it be
done on those three days . . . (see Appendix 5)

And here is provision for a hard winter:

. . . If it is absolutely essential, in winter weather, let the brethren be allowed
access to a fire. But let this not take place in the refectory. And if there befall a
spell of extreme cold, let all say and sing their prayers together in the house: but,
if the weather improve a little, let all sit together[5] in the cloister . . .

(from the Latin of *Bateson 1892*, pp.174f., 184ff., and 178.)

Over the years many great men turned to Aelfric for counsel. One of them
was Sigweard, thegn of Asthall, some 12 miles to the west of Eynsham. It was
to him that, after some hesitation, he sent his paraphrase of the Old Testament,
carrying the story on to the sack of Jerusalem by Rome in A.D. 70. The account
is vivid and horrifying, especially in the 17th-century translation used below;
but the tragic roots of anti-Semitism are very plain. The Lord had died for all
men, but the Jews are blamed:

I would have said somewhat before concerning that unhappy nation, the Jewes I
mean, who crucified our Lord: but this I thought meet first to speake, that I have
done. Many of them beleeved on Christ, but the most would not; and therefore
perished. Much misery befell them, and of all sorts, after the passion of Christ
. . . nor would they lament nor with any repentance entreat his mercy: then sent
he them horrible signes & tokens, & utter destruction afterward by the people of
Rome . . . Of the young children, all that remained after the famine throughout
all the land, they led them away to be put to worke fine purple cloth wheresoever
they were captives: & of these came the Jewes in most places yet living: this was
the reward of their wickednes; & the paine of hell thereto, which is more heavy
for them to beare . . .

(from O.E. of *Letter to Sigweard*, as translated by William L'isle, in 1623; commended in *Crawford 1922*.)

And the letter concludes with a sharp, but domestic, turn, the equivalent of
the modern slogan, 'Don't ask a man to drink and drive':

When I was with thee, thou wentst about to perswade me to drink liberally, as
'twere for delight, and beyond my custome; but know thou, deare friend, that

whoso forces another man to drinke more than he is able, shall answer for both if any harme come thereof. Our Saviour Christ in his Gospell hath forbidden drunkennesse unto all the faithfull: suffer all men that will to keep his ordinance. The holy and learned fathers also have since our Saviour put downe that enormitie by their doctrine: and taught that man should so drinke as it doe not hurt him: for over drinking surely detroyes a mans soule & safety: and much sicknesse of body comes thereon . . .

(from *Id.*).

With the same strong gentleness Aelfric spoke to all, combining an awareness of ultimate (even imminent) Judgment with persuasive and kindly tact. Wulfsige, bishop of Sherborne, and even Wulfstan, archbishop of York, himself a powerful writer, engaged Aelfric to write Pastoral Letters for them — letters which they would send to their clergy, letters of guidance and admonition, letters to carry the impetus of monastic reform into the parishes. Here is part of the Preface to one such letter, written for Wulfsige, Aelfric's bishop from 992 to 1002:

Brother Aelfric, in all humility, to the venerable Bishop Wulfsige: greetings in Christ. We have gladly done what you bade: but we have not dared to write about a bishop's responsibility: for it is yours to know . . . Nevertheless, I say that you bishops ought to speak to your clergy more often, and censure them for their negligence: for the directions of canon law, and the faith and teaching of holy church, are almost obliterated by their frowardness: wherefore deliver your own soul, and tell them how priests and servants of Christ ought to behave, lest you perish likewise, if you be judged a dumb dog (*ne tu pereas pariter, si mutus habearis canis*) . . .

(from the Latin of *Thorpe 1840*, vol.2, pp.342f; see also *Fehr 1914*, pp.1-34).

That last sentence sees all mankind, gathered and trembling, before the throne of God, with the gates of heaven and hell open to either side. And Brother Aelfric says to Bishop Wulfsige, 'Lest, at the Day of Judgment, the cry goes up, This watch-dog failed to bark: let him go down to hell with the rest!' Off would go Wulfsige, mitre and all, to the eternal flames. Both men would be familiar with Ezek. 33, esp. v.9, and Matt. 24, 45-51.

But we must not end thus. Aelfric seems, in fact, to have tried to teach every side of the Christian Church, and to cover every aspect of the Christian faith, and even to have had a master-plan to that end (see *Clemoes 1959*, pp.245f.). And as he tried to unveil wide mysteries and plumb great depths, he often turned (like all great teachers) to poetry and symbol. And here the picture of Cuthbert is relevant to him, and to us all:

Cuthbert, standing in the sea at night singing his prayers, is not merely a particular individual, cold and wet: he is a universal figure: he typifies the life of the spirit.[6] Just so, the rhythmical style is the language of the spirit. It is transcendental. The unity of its interrelated, regular sound is the artistic counterpoint of the unity of an interrelated, regular universe

(from *Clemoes 1966*, p.206).

Such was the great man, Aelfric the artist, Aelfric the visionary, second only to Bede in the Anglo-Saxon centuries, who came to live and die in Eynsham in 1005.[7]

Notes

1. Ordeals by fire or water were accepted ingredients of medieval 'justice'; see *Barlow 1*, pp.274f. and *2*, pp.159ff.

2. Aelfric would probably not have recognized himself as a precursor of the Reformation! It was simply that he lived before the doctrine of transubstantiation was precisely formulated. In making use of him, the Reformers were at great pains to distance themselves from the general stance of his day: 'But what was the condition and state of the church, when Aelfrick himself lived? In deede to confesse the truth, it was in divers pointes a Religion full of blindnes and ignoraunce: full of childysh servitude to ceremonies, as it was longe before and after: and to much geven to the love of monketye (*sic*), which now at thys tyme unmeasurablye tooke roote, and grew excessively' (from Preface to *Aelfric c.1567*).

3. Anglo-Saxon writers made strange use of the word *porticus*. It could refer to any space or room, whatever its size or purpose, attached to the main body of a church. An aisle could be so described, or a chapel, or a transept, or even a sanctuary.

4. See Numb.21, 7-9, and John 3, 14f.

5. *Simul . . . pariter . . .* Huddled together?

6. Clemoes lifts the story of Cuthbert's chilly asceticism into a lovely picture of us all — striving at prayer, but set in a universe which often seems hostile and meaningless. Bede tells the story; Clemoes reflects the strength and beauty of his Latin:

   Ingressusque altidudinem maris, donec ad collum usque et brachia unda tumens assurgeret, pervigiles undisonis in laudibus tenebras noctis exegit

   (from *Bede's Life of St. Cuthbert*, ch.10).

7. See also pioneer study in *Dietrich 1855-6*, followed closely by *White 1898*. *Westlake 1907* is an outstanding account of Aelfric's place in English literature, but ignore his statement that a synod took place at Eynsham in 1014; the event in question was probably at King's Enham, Hants. (see ch.7, n.3).

Troubled waters

Eynsham is at about the centre of southern England. By 1005 Danes were infiltrating, by estuaries and rivers, from every side. This was no time for quiet monastic life. Doubtless Aelfric and Aethelmaer did their best, but the tide of English history was against them.

In 1003 the marauders reached Wilton and Salisbury, coming through Exeter and Devon. In 1006-7 they arrived at Reading and Wallingford, through Hampshire and Berkshire. A few years later they took their revenge on Oxford, burning it down. In 1010, based now in Cambridgeshire, they swept again and again across the south, even into Wiltshire. In 1011-12, some of them captured and butchered Aelfheah, archbishop of Canterbury. In 1013, from Gainsborough, in Lincolnshire, first taking hostages from their distant kinsmen in the Danelaw, they poured across Watling Street, and drove Aethelred right out of his kingdom, and into exile in Normandy; Oxford and Winchester both surrendered. Three years later they finally conquered, and soon afterwards Cnut, king of Denmark, became king of England also (see *Stenton 1971*, pp.374-93).

It used to be thought that Aelfric lived on, throughout that chaos, and witnessed the English collapse, and did not die until *c*.1020-5. It is now thought that he died soon after 1010, aged about 53. That was when his continuous flow of writing came to an end (see *Whitelock 1943*). To lose so great an abbot so very soon, and against such a national background, must have been disastrous for the infant community at Eynsham, and deeply distressing for Aethelmaer. Perhaps he had managed to settle himself at the abbey? But how, in any case, could such a man be spared for long from affairs of state? This emergency, and that, would force him out, and, with Aelfric dead, there would be little incentive to return. We find him witnessing Sherborne charters in 1012 and 1014, and joining the western thegns at Bath, in surrender to Swein of Denmark, in 1013. Soon afterwards he vanishes from the scene.

Eynsham abbey must have felt like a motherless child. What kings had granted, kings could take away; and only a few, very great, men had strength to resist. King Aethelred had agreed with Aethelmaer that the promising little port of Rameslie, in Sussex, with its cross-Channel connections, and its lands, and its 100 salt-pans, should go to Eynsham abbey (see *D.B., Sussex*, folio 17b and note 5,1: also L.A. Vidler, *A New History of Rye*, Hove, 1934). A deed of *c*.1017 claims that, even before his death, he had changed his mind, and pledged Rameslie to Fécamp abbey, over the water, in Normandy (see illustration 12):

I, CNUT, by the grace of God, king of England: desirous of reward in heavenly places: do now make a grant perpetual to the monks of the abbey of the Holy Trinity at Fécamp:

It is the estate called Rameslie, together with its harbour, and all that pertains to it: it is precisely what King Aethelred promised to give, but forestalled by death failed to fulfil:

Thus may I have the prayers of those to whom I now give relief and solace:

I, Queen Aelfgifu, have agreed to this gift: I, Bishop Aelfsige, have subscribed: I, Bishop Leofsige,[1] have set my seal:

May joy, peace, and charity be upon those who consent to this liberty. Amen.

(from the Latin (c.1017) of a Fécamp cartulary (12th-century), as transcribed by Lenoir (18th century): see *Haskins 1918.*)

Both kings had had the formidable Emma/Aelfgifu to wife. Emma was Norman, a daughter of Richard I, count of Normandy, and sister to Richard II. Fécamp was a well-established and very powerful Benedictine house, much favoured by the lords of Normandy. Do we see signs of Emma's contriving hand? Or was it that Rameslie was useless now to Eynsham, because trade and transport were so disrupted? Or perhaps Eynsham received something in exchange, possibly Little Rollright, Oxon., added to it at some point between 1005 and 1066? Or maybe the kings of England were almost obliged to forge stronger links with Normandy? Whatever the case, Rameslie was lost, and was still in the hands of Fécamp in 1066.

By that time Eynsham had suffered other losses also — Marlcliff in Bidford, Warwks.; Bentley in Holt, Worcs.; Esher and Ditton, Surrey; the unidentified Burton; Shipton-on-Cherwell, Oxon.[2] What was left was a fairly compact group of estates, all of them in the south Midlands — Eynsham itself, Shifford and Yarnton, Oxon., and Mickleton, Glos., together with Little Rollright, Oxon.

A fascinating little document demonstrates Eynsham abbey's continued existence in c.1050-2. It is an admirable illustration of petty business of that day. The occasion is a shire-moot for Oxfordshire. The gathering is in Oxford itself. The presidents are the bishop and the earl responsible for this shire. One is Ulf, bishop of Dorchester, soon to be driven out of England; the other is Leofric, earl of Mercia, husband of the Lady Godiva, and soon to come into Eynsham records. Most of those present are Oxfordshire thegns. Two abbeys are represented, one of them the great and strong Abingdon, from over the river, the other, little Eynsham.

This document sets out the terms of an agreement, made between a certain widow, named Tova, relict of Wihtric, and the Lord Abbot, Leofstan, and all the community, of the church of St. Alban: and it concerns land called Cyrictiwa:[3]

The said woman has given three gold marks to the officials of the said community, on condition that she may hold the said land throughout her life, and her son Godwin throughout his: and, when both are dead, St. Alban shall without any gainsaying have his land back, in as good heart, and as well-provided, as it was when she received it from the officials and the church, or somewhat better:

And, in recognition of this agreement, she shall, in each and every year, at the feast of St. Peter-in-Chains, give to the monks of the church of St. Alban one measure of honey, 32 ounces in weight, by way of rent:

Whosoever shall study to preserve this arrangement without deceit, let him have the blessing of God and of the holy martyr, Alban: and whosoever shall break it, let him be excommunicate, cut off from the company of the holy church of God, and let him have the curse of God, and of St. Alban, and of all the saints. Amen:

This agreement is witnessed by Bishop Ulf: and Earl Leofric: and the abbot and all the community of Abingdon: and the abbot and all the community of Eynsham:[4] and Wagan and all the barons of Earl Leofric: and Aethelric of Glympton: and Eadric, son of Aefic: and Brihtwine of Deddington: and Leofwine of Barton: and Aethelric Smyrl and Aelfwine and Alwin of Ingham: and Leofric, son of Osmund: and Leofnoth, his brother: and Burgred and Siward and Aethelweard of Orton: and Asser, son of Tolry: and Godwine, reeve of the city of Oxford: and Wulfwine, the earl's reeve: and all the citizens of Oxford

(from the Latin of *Matthew Paris*, vol.6, pp.29f.).

Cyrictiwa seems to be Great Tew, in north Oxfordshire. St. Albans abbey did not wish to manage this land itself. It receives a useful capital sum at once, as well as the promise of a small yearly rental of honey. The widow and her son get the life security which they need. The whole transaction takes place in the presence of St. Alban himself, living, very concerned, and hard by the throne of God. This is the last surviving glimpse of Eynsham abbey before the Conquest.

Notes

1. Aelfsige II was bishop of Winchester, 1012/14-32, and Leofsige was bishop of Worcester, 1017-33; see *Barlow 1*.
2. Great Wessex families which had supported Aethelred might expect to suffer under Cnut (see illustration 7). Institutions which they had sponsored would suffer with them. Eynsham abbey lost Rameslie in *c.*1017. It is just possible that it lost Bentley in Holt at the same time (see *Kemble*, vol.6, no.1313). For a suggestion about the loss of Ditton, Surrey, see *Blair & Steane 1982*, pp.43ff. Ottery, Devon, given up by Aethelmaer in 1005, was given to Rouen cathedral by Edward the Confessor in 1061; see *Matthew 1962*, pp.25f.
3. *Cyrictiwa*. Probably not Tewin, Herts. (as Luard, ed. *Matthew Paris*); nor *Cyrictuna* (as read by *Kemble*, vol.4, no.950, followed by *Sawyer 1968*, no.1425, perhaps influenced by *Cryctina*, in *G.A.S. Alb.*, vol.1, p.39); but Church Tew (for later Great Tew), Oxon., as Salter, *E.C.*, vol.1, p.ix, *Gelling 1953-4*, vol.2, p.289, *Gelling 1979*, p.189, and *V.C.H., Oxon.*, vol.11 (1983), pp.223-47. Archbishop Aelfric of Canterbury (995-1005) had bequeathed land there to St. Albans abbey (*Whitelock 1930*, no.18).
4. The manuscript reads *et abbas et omnis congregatio Egnes Abbonduniensis et abbas et omnis congregatio Egneshamiensis*. *Egnes* is a scribal slip. Kemble makes matters worse by reading *aeccles* (= *ecclesiae*, 'of the church') each time. That left him *hamiensis*, which he read as *Hauuensis*.

Part Two

The Wilderness Years

Destruction

It is no accident that the word 'Norman' is associated with massive churches. And it was no empty display that prompted their building. The Normans (as their name indicates) were a branch of the great Norse invasions. They had settled about the mouth of the Seine, and then pressed the Bretons (cousins of our own Celtic stocks) back. At least nominally they owed homage to the kings of France. They were a vigorous people, forceful, alert, ambitious, imaginative, quick to embrace Christianity, and, having embraced it, to move with the times. In the 11th century they were welcoming the reforms which the popes, especially Leo IX (1048-54) and Alexander II (1061-73), were initiating in the Church life of western Europe. At the same time they were receiving a succession of scholars and thinkers from Italy. And when England's monastic reforms had lost impetus, an energetic monastic revival took place in Normandy.

Of course, Duke William (our future Conqueror) was superstitious. Who wasn't? His armada was held up by contrary winds, latterly at Saint-Valéry, near Dieppe, and only a parade of St. Valéry's relics, and considerable offerings at his shrine, changed the wind. As he set foot on the English shore, he slipped and bit the dust — an evil omen? 'No', said his ready aides, fearful for his confidence, 'You have hold of England, Duke: soon you will be King' (from the Latin of *Wm. Malm. G.R.*, vol.2, p.300). The stuff of chroniclers![1]

The real man could be harsh and cruel, supporting himself, no doubt, by St. Paul's appraisal of rulers, 'He beareth not the sword in vain' (Rmns. 13, 4), and harking back perhaps to David's handling of Philistines and Amalekites. But, at heart, he was a man of God, and he certainly believed himself to be the rightful heir to England's throne.

Ambition, territorial aggrandisement, and economic expansion, nerved his arm, and his warriors' arms, as they plucked up their courage, and played for heavy stakes, and risked an all-out invasion. But the Norman Church, which cheered him on and gave support, was stronger for what he and his family had done. The papal reform movement had brought discipline and stiffened morale, alike in monks and in secular clergy and in laity. Fécamp, and later Bec, had stood for lively, diligent, and intelligent monasticism. William of Volpiano (St. William of Dijon) had been followed by John (of Ravenna) at Fécamp, and the simple Norman knight, Herluin, by Lanfranc of Pavia, and then Anselm of Aosta, at Bec. These were men of great stature. State, as well as Church, had benefited by their coming. Evils such as simony (see Simon Magus in Acts 8, 18ff.) and pluralism had been attacked; celibacy had been pressed upon the parochial clergy; slackness and indolence had been rebuked.

Small wonder that the popes approved of Duke William. They pressed for more, and especially for a greater say in the appointment of church dignitaries — archbishops, bishops, abbots. But such men held much land; how could William let so much secular influence pass to Rome? So there he stayed their hand, and in fact they were well content with the loyalty he gave. His gift of the abbey of Caen was symbolic: it was a reassuring act of penance for marrying within the prohibited degrees. So he fought at Hastings under a papal banner, and there were dedicated relics around his neck. And later on he gave yet another religious house, Battle abbey, in penance for such evil as the Conquest had entailed.[2]

News of his victory would reach the Eynsham monks very quickly, and they would tremble — perhaps as members of a Church with slack leadership, but certainly as Englishmen with English lands. Probably they were members of noble families, cognisant of William's love of Church, but aware also that his distinguished followers would look for distinguished rewards, and that of all rewards land was par excellence the greatest.

We know nothing of their abbot in 1066; it is likely that so small and weak a charge had indifferent leadership. Around them was their diocese, huge and rambling, its southern boundary on the Thames, and its bishops there, at Dorchester, and its northern boundary on the Humber (see illustration 17). Its bishop was Wulfwig, an Anglo-Saxon who had come in (with somewhat dubious authority) when Bishop Ulf had been expelled. By 1066 Wulfwig was old and weak, and in 1067 he would die. Further away, high and lofty in the hierarchy, and much involved in affairs of State, was their archbishop, Stigand, holding two of the greatest English sees, Canterbury and Winchester, in plurality, and probably Anglo-Scandinavian in blood (see *Barlow 1*, pp.76-81). He was worldly and inadequate, but it would take the Conqueror four years to unhorse him.

After Hastings William gave his men a brief respite. Then, first making sure of Kent, its Channel ports and Canterbury, he marched them westwards below the Thames, avoiding London, going on into Berkshire, and finally crossing to the northern bank of the river at Wallingford. At this point Oxford was only about 14 miles ahead, and Eynsham abbey just beyond it. The monks there, at ease in Zion, hitherto untroubled by Norman reformers, must have stirred uncomfortably. But William now turned eastwards again, reached Berkhamsted, some 25 miles from London, received the city's formal submission, continued on his way (still harrying as he went), and was crowned in Edward the Confessor's newly rebuilt Westminster abbey on Christmas Day, 1066 (see illustration 12).

There followed years of insurrection and unease, whilst the subdual of England was carried through. Throne had to be turned into kingdom, and neither Norman nor English knew any other way than harrying and slaughter. The Eynsham monks must have kept an anxious eye on Oxford. It had been very important, and might well suffer accordingly. National assemblies had been held there in 1018, 1036 and 1065. No less than seven moneyers (always an index to civic status) had been at work there in the Confessor's reign. Eynsham abbey had a church there, and a few town houses. Oxford, however, was not destroyed at the Conquest: it fell into serious decay. By 1086 about 480 of its

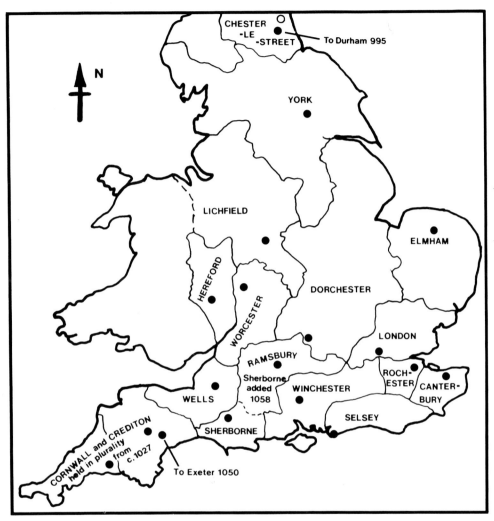

17. **English dioceses, 1035** (from *Hill 1981*, p.148).

approximately 720 dwellings were either uninhabitable or dilapidated (see *Salter 1936*, pp.20-39). It had to endure one of the Conqueror's numerous castle-mounds (still there today); there he had his garrison, to keep the natives down; but it was not sacked.

Eynsham abbey was less fortunate than the city. For some or other reason it was destroyed at the Conquest. The chronicler is quite explicit, and there is no reason to doubt his blunt assertion:

> Eynsham abbey had been laid waste at the Conquest, and its brethren had fled away, frightened of the enemy

(from the Latin of *Vita Hugonis 1864*, p.189).

The writer had been an Eynsham monk. He had had special access to the records there. Perhaps the brethren, walled close together in their secluded premises, had hatched a conspiracy? Perhaps sudden fright had overtaken the Norman soldiery, penetrating, as they were, nervously, ever more deeply, into the unknown Midlands? Perhaps they were worried for the security of the Swinford crossing? No one knows.

Whatever the case, Eynsham abbey now passed into more than 40 wilderness years, years which left a permanent mark. The ups and downs of those years are the subject of discussion; but all are agreed that the house did not stand firmly and securely again until 1109. Then it was to continue for more than 400 years, seemingly eternal.

Notes

1. Other chroniclers, for example, Florence of Worcester and Henry Knighton, enlarge upon this story.
2. For William the Conqueror's life, see *Douglas 1964*; for his ecclesiastical policies, see also *Barlow 2*.

Norman bishop

The charred remains of Eynsham abbey were entrusted to the bishop. So were its lands and tenants. What more natural? It was God's property, and to God's man it went. A quick rebuilding might well have been expected, but it was not to be.

The bishop, it should be said, was very busy. His lands were numerous (17 or so items in Oxfordshire alone), and widely scattered. Their number was a royal reward, their dispersion a royal policy. Layers of stewards and under-stewards would manage them. Revenues would filter slowly to the bishop's treasury. Eynsham abbey can only have been a very small fish in a very large net.

By 1067 Remigius was bishop. He was a Norman monk, and had been almoner at Fécamp. He had brought his abbey's quota to William's holy war; he had been with the duke at Hastings. Not surprisingly he was William's first appointment to an English bishopric. The apparent element of simony was to dog his steps for years (see Appendix 6).

Although Gerald of Wales was to try to get him made a saint, spirituality had never been Remigius' strong suit. That said, however, he was probably a shrewd and a wise choice for a tough assignment. John of Ravenna had left his mark on Fécamp, and it was a breeding ground for good monks. That Remigius was almoner suggests business capacity. That he was fit for the rigours of William's expeditionary force suggests a body and a spirit still able to cope with travel and strain. He was to hold his taxing see for 25 years, outliving the Conqueror, and entering on the cloudy days of William Rufus.

His diocese was enormous, a great wedge of the east Midlands, no less than eight shires — Oxford, Buckingham, Northampton, Bedford, Cambridge, Huntingdon, Leicester, Lincoln. They also embraced Rutland, which had not yet attained shire status. Once there had been bishops of Lindsey (that is, north Lincolnshire); the Danes had driven them out. There had been bishops of Leicester also; they had met the same fate. The whole territory had fallen (ecclesiastically speaking) under bishops of Dorchester, right down on the Thames.[1]

It was a far cry from the Humber. Otherwise Dorchester had advantages. It was convenient for Winchester and London, and bishops had often to share in the king's great councils there. It was one of the bishop's most ancient estates; tradition was with him. More than that, Dorchester had especially sacred memories: St. Birinus had been there, Birinus the seventh-century apostle from

Rome to the West Saxons, Birinus the first bishop of Wessex. He had had his cathedral at Dorchester, and as, in another age, Remigius said his prayers with his secular canons in his own cathedral there, he would feel well content to be near Birinus in the blest communion of the saints.

For five years he worked on from Dorchester, presumably doing what most great men had to do. He would go on safari around his territory, taking attendant clergy, office staff, and a considerable domestic cavalcade with him, and meeting his people where they were. There were ministrations which only a bishop could offer; men would seize their chance when a bishop came near. It would be a restless and a wearisome life, though bishops, even more than abbots, lived as nobles did, and were cushioned from many of the pains and discomforts of ordinary men. Herein perhaps was recompense, and herein also a certain peace for wise decision making.

In 1070 Lanfranc came from Caen to Canterbury, and with the new archbishop the pace of reform quickened. One result (ultimately of great significance for Eynsham abbey) was that in 1072 Remigius moved his see from Dorchester to Lincoln. He was no more central to his diocese than he had been before, but the move was in keeping with church policy of the day. Popes, kings, archbishops were all agreed. The Anglo-Saxons had often been well content with country sees on remote estates; the Normans wanted them in cities and towns, built-up places, commercial vortices, strategic military centres. The movement had begun before the Conquest. In 995 the body of St. Cuthbert had been moved from Chester-le-Street to Durham. In 1050 the see for Devon and Cornwall had gone from Crediton to Exeter, in 1058 that for Dorset, Wilts., and Berks., from Ramsbury to Sherborne. Now the see of Elmham, for East Anglia, went to Thetford, and later to Norwich. The see of Sherborne moved again, this time to Salisbury. The see of Selsey, serving the south Saxons from Selsey Bill, moved to Chichester. Lichfield, for the west Midlands, went to Chester, and Dorchester to Lincoln. It was a mighty upheaval, somehow natural to modern eyes, but doubtless very disturbing to Anglo-Saxons of the day. Most of the bishoprics were at the same period filling up with Normans; so also the secular baronies. A glance at the map shows that the removal of sees created a strong ring of 'ecclesiastical strong-points', 15 in all, encompassing the land — Durham, York, Lincoln, Thetford/Norwich, London, Rochester, Canterbury, Chichester, Winchester, Salisbury, Exeter, Wells, Hereford, Worcester, Chester. Their prayers and their presence might combine to serve some of the same ends as the 200 or so castle mounds (see illustration 17).[2]

In Lincoln's case there was another, and more subtle, nuance. The archbishops of York had long coveted Lindsey (just south of the Humber) for their province and diocese; but Lincoln was in Lindsey. So, when Lanfranc helped Remigius to remove his see from Dorchester to Lincoln, he was in effect saying to Thomas I, the very redoubtable archbishop of York (1070-1100), 'No, the diocese of Lincoln, and with it my province of Canterbury, and with that a degree of extra nearness to the throne, go right up to the Humber.' The archbishops of York would rumble on for years, but at the moment when Remigius went to Lincoln they had virtually lost.

Much of Remigius' future effort now lay in building his new cathedral on Lincoln hill, much also in a sound ordering of the lives and activities of its 21 secular canons. And much went into establishing archdeaconries in every shire, splendid tools of episcopal delegation, comparatively little employed in England until that time. And all the while there was a share in the work of State as well: bishops and king must work close together. Remigius was even one of the Commissioners for the Domesday Survey, and deeply involved in its astonishing, but very tedious, amassing of landed detail. He shared with Earl Walter Giffard, Henry de Ferrers, and Adam, brother of Eudo, the king's steward, in dealing with the circuit comprising Gloucester, Worcester, Hereford, Stafford, Shropshire, and Cheshire (see *Galbraith 1974*, pp.38f.).

The bishop's move from Dorchester to Lincoln had such a profound effect upon the fortunes of Eynsham abbey that it is especially worthwhile to look at the royal decree which formalized the matter. Lincoln cathedral still has what appears to be an original copy from the Conqueror's time. Its spare diction and its precise planning unfold the clear dissecting judgments of Archbishop Lanfranc and his senior staff:

> WILLIAM, king of England: to Sheriff T., and to all the sheriffs in the bishopric of Bishop Remigius: greeting.
>
> You are to know that I have transferred the seat of the bishopric of Dorchester to the city of Lincoln.
>
> I have done so with the approval of Pope Alexander and his legates, as also of Archbishop Lanfranc and other bishops of my realm, and in consultation with them.
>
> There also I have given sufficient land, free and quit of all customary dues, for the raising up of the Mother Church of the whole bishopric, as also of its other necessary buildings.
>
> Now, to this same Mother Church, for the salvation of my own soul, it is my wish to give certain benefaction:
>
> first, I grant it the two manors, Welton and Sleaford, and what goes with them:
>
> next, the churches of three of my manors, Kirton, Caistor, and Wellingore, together with their lands and tithes: to these I add the whole tithe of the total render of those same manors:[3]
>
> also, two churches in Lincoln, to wit, St. Lawrence's and St. Martin's.
>
> Furthermore, at the urgent plea of Bishop Remigius, I grant to the same Church:
> a manor called Leighton,[4] which at a recent date and with my authority Earl Waltheof[5] gave to the said bishop:
>
> and another manor called Wooburn, which some while ago I myself gave him together with his pastoral staff (*quod sibi olim cum episcopali baculo concesseram*).[6]
>
> There are also four churches, namely, Bedford and Leighton, Buckingham and Aylesbury: they were held by the bishop's predecessors, and I gave them to him for his lifetime: now, with his consent, and by his grant, I confer them upon the same Church, together with all that pertains to them: the benefaction is for all time, and I confirm it with my royal authority.
>
> Witnesses: Lanfranc, archbishop, and E., sheriff

(from the Latin of L2/2: see also facsimile, plate 4, there).

Notes

1. For early bishops of Lindsey, Leicester, and Dorchester, see *H.B.C.*
2. Two more dioceses (Ely and Carlisle) were created in the 12th century, and then no more until the 16th century.

3. At this period churches were treated as items of property, to be given away, bequeathed, subdivided, forfeited etc.
4. Leighton Bromswold, Hunts.; next, Wooburn, Bucks.; below, Leighton Buzzard, Beds.
5. In 1076 Waltheof, earl of Huntingdon, was beheaded for his part in the abortive 'earls' rebellion' of 1075.
6. This assertion demonstrates the authenticity of the whole document. The Church would not have forged it. See F.M. Stenton, with L 2/2.

Domesday

Men might fight, men might pray, men might toil and hew — so went the traditional division of manly function. Sometimes the lines between were smudged. The Conqueror found manly fulfilment in his English mission, and hardly ever enjoyed unmanly ease again.

He was known as William the Bastard, for men are cruel.[1] Medieval French jingles, about him and his knights, could begin, '*Bastard, Baignard, Brassard . . .*' (see *Hardy 1862-5*, vol. 2, pp.2ff.) Perhaps that helped to make him what he was — a man to respect, even to fear, rather than to love. In 1086, after 20 restless years, he sat back for a moment, and embarked upon a mighty survey of English wealth. In 1087 he died, and his kingdom went to William Rufus.

The two magnificent volumes of Domesday Book survive, as well as sundry bits and pieces associated with it (see *D.B.* and *Finn 1973*). The basis of wealth was land; everything else, human, animal, material, was counted with it, and contributed to its gross value. So Domesday information was first divided into shires, and then subdivided under major land-holders (tenants-in-chief) within each shire. The data had been gathered up by itinerant Commissioners (Bishop Remigius was one), with their teams of clerks and scribes. They worked at local centres, taking evidence under oath. All was then summarized, and heavily compressed. Finally it was written up at Winchester.

Beneath its seeming simplicity there are all sorts of teasing perplexities, not least about Eynsham abbey. Here is our first glimpse of the house since 1066, and (as so often in Domesday) it is hedged around with haze and mystery. Information is to be found under Oxfordshire and Gloucestershire.

In the countryside of Oxfordshire (and country material is everywhere paramount) seven bishops and five abbeys are among the tenants-in-chief, each with their own list of lands. Two of each group are from across the water. The bishops are of Canterbury, Winchester, Salisbury, Exeter, Lincoln, Bayeux and Lisieux; the abbeys are at Abingdon, Battle, Winchcombe, Preaux and Paris (St. Denis). The bishop of Lincoln (and here lies our first puzzle) is a tenant-in-chief; Eynsham abbey is not, and all that is left of Eynsham abbey's country estates (in this its home-shire) is on the bishop's list. Eynsham, Shifford, and (in a somewhat different manner) Yarnton remain from 1005, and Little Rollright has been added.

First, in the bishop of Lincoln's Oxfordshire list, come his five ancient estates hereabouts — Dorchester, Thame, Great Milton, Banbury and Cropredy, remnants of the endowment of the one-time bishops of Dorchester. And then:

The Bishop holds EYNSHAM (*Eglesham*) himself and the monk Columban from him. 15½ hides belonging to this church. Land for 18 ploughs; he found as many. In lordship land for 2 ploughs, *inland*.
Now in lordship 3 ploughs.
   3 men-at-arms with 34 villagers and 33 smallholders have 15 ploughs. A mill at 12s. and 450 eels; meadow, 255 acres; pasture, 100 acres; woodland 1½ leagues long and 1 league and 2 furlongs wide; value when stocked 25s.
The value is and was £20.
Columban also holds SHIFFORD (*Scipford*) from the Bishop. 3 hides. Land for 5 ploughs. Now in lordship 1 plough.
   8 villagers with 5 smallholders have 5 ploughs.
   Meadow, 50 acres; pasture 2 furlongs long and 1 furlong wide; [from a fishery] 250 eels and 4s. 4d.
The value was £4; now 100s.
Columban also holds 5 hides in LITTLE ROLLRIGHT (*parva Rollandri*) from the Bishop. It belongs to the Church. Land for 6 ploughs.
In lordship 2 ploughs; 2 slaves.
   12 villagers with 3 smallholders have 6 ploughs. Meadow, 25 acres.
The value is and was 100s.

Next come sub-holdings of each of the bishop's five ancient estates; numerous individuals are named. Then there is what may perhaps be called a sub-holding of Eynsham:

Roger of Ivry holds YARNTON (*Hardintone*) from the Bishop. It is Eynsham Church's. 9½ hides. Land for 9 ploughs. Now in lordship 2 ploughs.
   20 villagers with 3 smallholders have 7 ploughs. Meadow, 200 acres less 20; pasture, 80 acres.
   One Mainou had 1 hide there; he could go where he would.
Total value before 1066 £10; value now, with the fishery and the meadow, £14.[2]

The city of Oxford gets separate treatment, somewhat cursory, but before the countryside. There is a considerable list of property-holders. The bishop of Lincoln and Eynsham abbey are both in it, and they are quite distinct. Here are their entries:

   ... The Bishop of Lincoln has 30 dwellings which pay 18s. 6d. 16 of them are derelict.
   ... Eynsham abbey (*Abbatia de Eglesham*) has 1 church and 13 dwellings which pay 9s.; 7 of them are derelict.

(Eynsham extracts from *D.B.*, *Oxon.*, folios 155b, 155c and 154a.)

So Eynsham abbey had had its own little 'village' within the city bounds before 1066, and possibly as early as in 1005. Later records include two mills and some meadows. An urban toehold of this character was of obvious value to a local country estate.

Turning to Gloucestershire and its countryside, we find no less than five bishops (York, Worcester, Hereford, Exeter and Coutances) and 19 religious houses listed as tenants-in-chief. Eynsham abbey (*Abbatia de Eglesham*) is 12th among the latter. Here is its entry:

Land of the Church of Eynsham.
In Chelthorn Hundred.
The Church of Eynsham holds MICKLETON. 14 hides.

In lordship 5 ploughs;
   20 villagers and 7 smallholders with 10 ploughs. 8 male and 2 female slaves;
   24 measures of salt from Droitwich.
The value is and was £10.
   The Church also held it before 1066.

(From *D.B.*, *Glos.*, folio 166b.)

Those Domesday extracts bristle with questions. Just one of them is of special concern here. Do they, or do they not, demonstrate that Eynsham abbey, destroyed in 1066, was fully functioning again in 1086, with Abbot Columban and his family of monks living the correct Benedictine life together? Salter says that that was the case (see *E.C.*, vol.1, pp.ixf.). In other words he defines the situation by the two positive references to 'Eynsham abbey', one in Oxford city, the other in Gloucestershire. He takes them to imply recognized institutional life at a restored house in Eynsham. His view has, at first sight, held the field, unchallenged, throughout the century (see *E.Cust.*, p.15, *M.R.H. 1971*, p.65, *H.R.H. 1972*, p.48, and *D.B.*, *Oxon.* (Morris, 1978), n.6, 6.)

Surely, however, those two references (one to the city, the other to the next shire) could be regarded as merely formal, technical, legal allusions to a dormant institution? Surely the main body of Eynsham data should decide the issue, rather than those peripheral ones? If Eynsham abbey had really been re-established, surely it would have been a tenant-in-chief, in its own right, in its own shire, just like the other abbeys? No individual monk would have been mentioned, and certainly no bishop. Abbeys were as wary of bishops as they were of earls. The subordination of Eynsham abbey properties to Bishop Remigius must surely mean that they were still under episcopal trusteeship, awaiting a future as yet unsettled. If so, we may think of Columban as an individual monk, rather than as abbot of a community; one strong and trustworthy man, in charge of a temporary situation; a caretaker-monk, resident in Eynsham, looking after abbey interests in general, holding the fort, both for the bishop and for monasticism.

Perhaps he was already paving the way for the removal plan, which was in fact to take effect in 1091, and was to involve himself. What better leader could there be in Eynsham, in the midst of all the tensions surrounding the derelict abbey, than a competent monk, Remigius' appointee, perhaps even trained with him at Fécamp, a man with potential for greater things, a man able to protect the fragile monastic plant, in a disturbed, greedy and often hostile society?

Maybe he had one or two companion monks, not a whole community, but a small 'cell', as they were called. If so, they would assist in general management, and perhaps give some framework of ordered worship. Such cells were a common expedient, and especially in the case of houses that had fallen on bad days. In general, they proved unsatisfactory. They asked too much of human nature (see *Knowles 1963*, pp. 134-6, 686f.). Nevertheless, in 1086, Eynsham may well have had a little group like that, to keep Columban company. It would be distinct, and known to be distinct, from a fully-fledged abbey.

There is just one further alternative, which should be looked at, and almost certainly discarded. Could it be that Eynsham abbey was already, in 1086, a bishop's *Eigenkloster* (own monastery), that is, a piece of his property, entirely under his control, even to the extent of appointing the abbots and conferring their temporalities (their lands and rights) upon them? It was to become such an institution at a later date, and its unusual status was to be defended with might and main by the famous St. Hugh of Lincoln. What is more, the roots of that special status seem to go back as far as William II, the very next king. The idea is attractive, but it is virtually certain that William I, who was very wary of separate power-bases, vested in great land-holders, would not have dreamt of handing Eynsham abbey over to Bishop Remigius in that way. Temporary caretakership of a derelict abbey was one thing; downright ownership was quite another.[3]

From this point onwards this study will assume that at the Domesday survey Eynsham abbey was still in a state of suspended animation, holding one monk, perhaps a tiny cell of monks, certainly not a community. Its revenues would be flowing into episcopal/cathedral/diocesan funds, not as yet as strictly distinguished as would later be the case.[4]

Notes

1. He was the illegitimate son of Robert I, sixth duke of Normandy; his mother was Herlève, of Falaise, later married to Herluin, vicomte of Conteville.
2. The king had a hunting lodge at Woodstock, and it seemed natural for his officials to hold adjoining lands (see E19 for Cassington and E44B for Yarnton); Rôger of Ivry was the royal butler. Eynsham abbey gradually lost its grip upon Yarnton (see Appendix 7).
3. Bishop's *Eigenkloster*: this type of institution, rare in England, is briefly discussed in *Knowles 1963*, pp.402f. and 631.
4. General handbooks, such as *M.R.H. 1971* and *H.R.H. 1972*, defer to Salter's judgement on what I have called Eynsham abbey's wilderness years, 1066-1109. So do specialist studies which do not demand a re-examination of those years, for example, *E.Cust.*, or *D.B., Oxon.* (Morris, 1978). Other books, however, reveal cautious reservations, which have encouraged me in my own doubts about some of Salter's conclusions. Chambers professes to build on Salter, and indeed does, but (in regard to the years after 1066) writes, 'A refoundation of the abbey *may have been contemplated*, but . . . Remigius decided to refound instead another derelict abbey . . .' (see *E.M.*, pp.2f; the italics are mine). Lennard, in discussing Domesday England and choosing Oxfordshire for closer study, comes to Bishop Remigius and Eynsham abbey, and writes, 'The [Domesday] evidence . . . is inconclusive . . .' (see *Lennard 1959*, p.42, n.2). Knowles positively contradicts Salter, but only in *obiter dicta*; of Eynsham abbey in 1086, he writes, 'Here presumably a single monk was holding what had been the abbey of Eynsham'. He includes Eynsham in the list of pre-Conquest houses which had by 1086 ceased to exist. In the table of monastic wealth, as revealed by Domesday, he puts Eynsham alone in brackets. (See *Knowles 1963*, pp.81, n.4, 100, n.1, and 703.)

   If there is substance in the argument of this chapter, Columban was only doing what many Norman Benedictines were told to do in post-Conquest England (see *Matthew 1962, passim*). The Conqueror had given English lands to most abbeys in Normandy. Each abbey managed its new possessions in its own way. Normal practice was to place one monk in their chief English estate, and to charge him with managing their group of lands, and sending as much revenue as possible back to their mother house over the water. Sometimes he had a companion monk, as prescribed by canon law; often he only had domestic and other staff. Sometimes he did local parochial work in the churches on the abbey's lands. Sometimes he was chaplain to a nearby nobleman, who was a patron of his house and wanted his prayers. It is noticeable that in any case he was called prior, and his establishment was called a priory. In effect, however, he was an estates manager, living as such a layman would. A few of such priories became genuine 'conventual priories', with several monks, sharing the regular life, but most did not. In fact, their Norman mother houses really wanted the revenues, for their life and work in Normandy, rather than to use them up in promotion of monasticism here. So these 'alien priories' went their way, until English kings lost their French possessions, and fell into war with France. Then, of course, they became 'security risks'! It is amusing to record that in the 14th century the lay bailiff of Warminghurst (who was by this time looking after the English lands of the abbey of Fécamp) was arrested for sending bows and arrows to Normandy (see *Id.*, p.95)! Bishop Remigius, like all the nobility of 1086, be they ecclesiastical or lay, would have been very familiar with the ways of the alien priories. It is hard to think that he did not treat the derelict Eynsham abbey and its lands just like one of them. He had himself been an important official at Fécamp. He knew what Fécamp was now doing in England. He probably brought Columban from Fécamp to be just such an estates manager in Eynsham. Norman monasticism was ahead of England in current reform; but such practices continued, and were to continue, and were more in accord with recent English practice.

18. (*above*) **Stow Church, near Lincoln: north side, 1793.**
(Lincoln Central Library: Banks, vol. 4, p.13.)

19. (*above*) **Anglo-Saxon archway in north transept: St. Mary's Stow.**

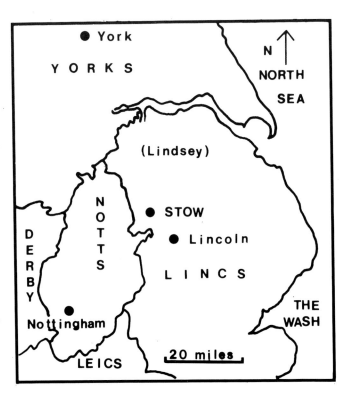

20. (*left*) **St. Mary's Stow: situation.**

St. Mary's Stow

Up at Stow-in-Lindsey, about 10 miles north-west of Lincoln, still standing, and much loved, there is a great church. It is St. Mary's Stow, St. Mary's 'holy place'. Parts of it are Norman, parts Anglo-Saxon. And of the Anglo-Saxon parts the crossing and the transepts, massive, awesome, painstaking, dedicated — the walls of the crossing 4ft. 6in. thick, its arches about 30ft. tall and about 14ft. wide — are late Anglo-Saxon work at its noblest, dating perhaps from the middle of the 11th century, perhaps even earlier (see *Taylor 1965*, vol.2, pp.584-93, and *Fernie 1983*, pp.124-7).[1] No one knows how old is the holiness of the site itself. Perhaps it started with a vision of the Virgin Mother, or a wondrous healing, or the hut of a hermit, good and wise. Some think that the bishops of Lindsey had their cathedral-church here.[2] Whatever the case, the architecture shows that Stow was a very important shrine, before the Conquest, as also afterwards (see illustrations 21 & 22).

For a brief while, towards the end of the 11th century, Eynsham abbey was reborn there, and its prayers were said in that very church. There seems to be no sure evidence of any earlier contact between Eynsham abbey and St. Mary's Stow, and yet, without any warning, the compilers of the Eynsham cartulary take us straight from their first entry, Aethelmaer's Eynsham abbey foundation-charter, to a series of Stow documents, starting in 1053-5. It is a strange and devious story. Edward the Confessor is king; Wulfwig is bishop of Dorchester; the donors are Leofric, earl of Mercia, and his wife, the Lady Godiva, of notable legend; the matter in hand is publicized in Lincoln city, as well as at an annual fair at Stow. Here is the first Stow entry:

> Here it is declared, in this document, how arrangements have been made between bishop Wulfwig and Earl Leofric and Godiva, the earl's wife, with regard to the minster of St. Mary's Stow.
>
> In the first place, they asked the bishop for permission to endow the minster and assign lands to it with his full consent, and the bishop granted their request, and was very glad to have any assistance for that purpose.
>
> Now they have furnished it with priests and desire that divine service should be celebrated there as it is at St. Paul's in London.
>
> And the lands which they assign to it shall provide food and clothing for the brethren who are therein. And the bishop shall have as food-rent for himself everything which Bishop Aethelric and Bishop Eadnoth had before him and which rightly belongs to his bishopric, namely, two-thirds of everything that comes into the minster, and the priests shall have the remaining third, except at the two festivals. The bishop, however, shall have everything that accrues to it for eight

21. **Anglo-Saxon crossing at St. Mary's Stow.** Massive Anglo-Saxon arches embrace later medieval work.

days at the earlier festival of St. Mary, and for eight days at the later festival of St. Mary,[3] except for food alone. The priests, however, shall have the third part of the food which accrues to it. And the lands which the bishop and the earl and Godiva and good men grant to it shall remain for all time in the possession of the holy foundation for the needs of the brethren and the endowment of the minster, so that no bishop who succeeds him shall demand any food-rent from it, except what rightly belongs to his bishopric, as other bishops had before him.

This is done with King Edward's full consent, and with his cognisance, and that of his wife, Edith, and of Archbishop Stigand, and of Archbishop Cynesige . . .

And if anyone increases the community with benefactions, God Almighty shall increase the days of his life, here in this life, and in the future life he shall be allowed to have his dwelling with God's elect. And if anyone expels them and alienates the lands from the holy foundation, he shall be rejected by God and St. Mary and all his saints on the great Judgment Day.

There are three of these documents. One is with the king's relics: the second is in Earl Leofric's possession: and the third is in the possession of the bishop at the holy foundation

(from the O.E. of E1A, based on *Robertson 1956*, pp.212-7, 465-8; see also W.H. Stevenson, in *E.C.*, vol.1, pp.28-30).

22. **Plan of crossing: St. Mary's Stow** (roughly to scale). C-D, with its four semi-circular arches supported by huge rectangular piers, is Anglo-Saxon. A-B, with its four pointed arches supported by polygonal piers, which have been built into the corners of C-D and carry the tower, is of later date.

There is general agreement that that record is authentic.[4] Even if there had once been Benedictine monks at Stow (see *Knowles 1963*, pp:66, 721, and *M.R.H. 1971*, pp.57, 77, and 483), they had by now been replaced by secular canons, and St. Mary's Stow was a 'secular minster' (see *Harmer 1950*, esp. p.358, n.2, and *Barlow 1*, p.56). The reference to St. Paul's, London, clinches the point (see *Brooke 1957*, pp.12-5). These clergy would work together, perhaps to some extent live together, jointly responsible for the work of the minster, but (unlike monks) they could have private property and personal funds, and they would move freely, in and out of 'the world'. Such an arrangement seems to have suited this Danelaw area of England: the archbishop of York had colleges of secular canons at St. Peter's, York, Beverley, Ripon, and Southwell.[5]

St. Mary's Stow was built on an episcopal estate. Bishop and canons shared the miscellaneous offerings brought to the church, as well as the various revenues from the estate. The formula for sharing had been in operation since Bishop Aethelric's time (1016-34), and Leofric and Godiva reveal evident anxiety lest their generous new endowment should tempt future bishops to poach upon the canons' share!

Back now to Eynsham. The monks there were so determined to involve that document (one which made no reference whatsoever to their house) in their own history, that they not only copied it into their new cartulary but almost merged it with their foundation-charter of 1005. The two documents referred to different places, different donors, different styles of religious life, separated by nearly half a century, but they were so entered as to look like two elements of one affair. The number '1' (already put twice by the charter of 1005) was repeated by the Stow charter. No new and separate heading was given to the Stow document. Even its distinctive initial letter was only pencilled in, and never coloured.

Then, as if to settle the issue, they entered a copy of a second document. This one added papal approval of the scheme, and a touching reference to Godiva's disposal of precious heirlooms (reminiscent of Sutton Hoo), and (above all) particulars of the lands and dues which were being given. As the story unfolds, it will be seen that the precise identities and values of those lands and dues would be of considerable economic relevance to Eynsham in later years:

To the most illustrious and most reverend VICTOR, our Pope:
Godiva, wife of Leofric, English earl, (makes her prayer): may all for which you yearn in Christ be yours.
Forasmuch as the worldwide catholic church holds you chiefest over all Christian people, and radiant with all holiness, it is meet that you should lend willing ears, for a while, to the prayers of your handmaid.

I entreat you, therefore, pastor supreme, to confirm with your authority the gifts, which for the redemption of my husband's soul, and of my own, I have now made to Blessed Mary, Mother of God, at Stow, just as the bishops and abbots of our own land, as also the earls, all whose names are written below, have already done.

The lands given are called Newark and Fledborough, with what pertains to them, as also Brampton, and Marton in the wapentake of Well, with what pertains to them.

These gifts, acquired through the disposal of my necklace and ear-rings, the gold ones, inlaid with enamel (*per monile meum & murenulas aureas vermiculatas*),[6] I have now given to the Mother of the Lord.

+ I, EDWARD, king of England, supreme in authority throughout my kingdom, have gladly granted liberty for this gift. + I, Ealdred, Archbishop-elect to the see of Canterbury, have given assent to this royal bounty.
+ I, Wulfwig, bishop. + I, Leofric, earl.
+ I, Harold, earl. + I, Tostig, earl.
+ I, Siward, earl, and many others.

The papal  seal.

Thus I support this gift with all my might, and confirm it with the authority of Rome, and return your charter, duly endorsed with my seal.

If, nevertheless, any man dare to overthrow this gift, let him be numbered with Pilate, and Judas Iscariot, with Caiaphas also, and all their company, and let him be vexed eternally by the fires of hell, unless perchance, before the moment of death, he repent and make due amends (from the Latin of E2).

This second document may well have been developed (in a somewhat imaginative manner!) from authentic material, but in its present form it is almost certainly spurious.[7] Whatever the case, however, it is not disputed that Leofric and Godiva gave valuable lands and dues to St. Mary's Stow, some 10 or 12 years before the Conquest. It is clear also that Stow was no monastery, no abbey, but a secular minster. And yet, in due course, and as a result of their gifts to Stow, Leofric and Godiva were to be named daily, and their souls prayed for, by the monks of Eynsham, centuries afterwards.

Roger de Howden, writing at the end of the 12th century, seems to refer to the same benefaction. Leofric, he says, died, full of years, in 1057. Godiva and he had done great things for Coventry abbey.

They had also lavished rich adornment on the minsters of Leominster and Wenlock, and on St. John Baptist and St. Werburgh Virgin, at Chester, and on the church built by Eadnoth, bishop of Lincoln, at a well-known place, which in English is called St. Mary's Stow, but in Latin St. Mary's Locus (*in loco famoso, qui Sanctae Mariae Stou Anglice, Latine vero Sanctae Mariae Locus appellatur*). They had also enriched Worcester abbey with lands, and Evesham abbey with buildings, and sundry adornments, and lands

(from the Latin of *Howden: Chron.*, vol.1, p.103).

There were two bishops of Dorchester (not Lincoln), named Eadnoth — Eadnoth I, 1006-16, and Eadnoth II, 1034-49. There must have been a firm tradition that one of them built substantially at St. Mary's Stow. Eadnoth I may have welcomed a cell of Benedictine monks to Stow, sent from Eynsham by Aelfric, soon after 1005. If so, there is no other evidence, and the monks must have given way to secular canons, not long afterwards.[8] Eadnoth II, on the other hand, may have built the great mid-11th-century crossing at Stow, assisted liberally by Leofric and Godiva.

From then onwards, until the Conquest, the canons appear to have gone on steadily. In *c.*1066-8 a substantial Lincolnshire landowner, named Ulf, and his wife Madselin, determined upon a journey to Jerusalem, perhaps a pilgrimage, perhaps a penance. It was a hazardous matter, and they made a will. It benefited four abbeys, Peterborough, Crowland, Ramsey and Thorney, but also the canons of Stow:

I have granted . . . the estate at Ormsby and all that I possessed there to St. Mary's Stow (*into Sce MARIAN stowe*)

(from the O.E. of a 12th-century Peterborough cartulary; based on *Whitelock 1930*, pp.94-7, 207-12).

In the end they did not go; probably the Conquest forestalled them. But their surviving will shows that St. Mary's Stow was not only in being, but held in respect.

Notes

1. For 19th-century restoration of St. Mary's Stow, see *Spurrell 1984*.
2. For the see of the bishops of Lindsey, see *Sympson 1905-6, Hill 1948*, pp.22f., 377f., *M.R.H. 1971*, p.469, and *Owen 1984*.
3. Probably the Assumption (15 August) and the Nativity (8 September) of St. Mary.
4. For authenticity of E1A, see *E.C.*, loc.cit., *Harmer 1950*, p.359, *Oleson 1955*, p.155, *Robertson 1956*, loc.cit., *Hart 1966*, p.103, and *Sawyer 1968*, p.413.
5. From *c*.1100 onwards, in England, such bodies often became 'Augustinian or Regular Canons', with lives organized in a somewhat Benedictine manner (see *Dickinson 1950*).
6. Anglo-Saxon women were more free to dispose of personal possessions than were their Norman counterparts; see *Whitelock 1952*, pp.93-5.
7. For spuriousness of E2, see W.H. Stevenson, in *E.C.*, vol.1, p.31, n.1, *Oleson 1955*, p.155, *Hart 1966*, p.103, and *Sawyer 1968*, p.360; but note Anglo-Saxon Latinity, as in *regni totius fastigium tenens* (of the king) and *eternaliter acherontica combustione trudatur* (of punishment in hell).
8. Knowles may have been influenced at this point by a heading in Dugdale, 'Stow in Lincolnshire. Cell of Eynsham (*Cella de Eynesham*)'. Dugdale follows the heading with three short passages from medieval chronicles; all concern the building, the adornment, and the restoration, of St. Mary's Stow, but none link it with Eynsham (see *Dugdale 1817-30*, vol.3, p.13). It seems that Knowles and Dugdale were anxious to explain the sudden appearance of Stow in the Eynsham cartulary. It is probable, in fact, that much more mundane considerations than a mother house/daughter house relationship moved the compilers of the cartulary. Note that, whilst Kennett, in *Parochial Antiquities*, accepts Dugdale's cell-hypothesis without question (see 1695 edn., p.54), Tanner's *Notitia Monastica*, 1744 edn., p.417, note b, makes a charming comment, 'But I don't find that Stow ever was cell to this abby, as 'tis said to have been'.

Domesday again

It seems that by 1086 the canons had vanished from Stow. All that they had shared with the bishop was in his hands alone. That, of course, was just what Leofric and Godiva had feared, but even they could not have foreseen the Norman Conquest, nor the tough Norman bishop of Dorchester, nor the removal of his see to Lincoln.

It is not impossible that the canons had been driven from Stow by fire. It could have happened in 1069-70, when the Norman troops swept north, to dislodge invading Danes from the Isle of Axholme, and to harry Yorkshire. The great Anglo-Saxon crossing of St. Mary's Stow bears evidence of severe burning, followed by rebuilding in a similar style, perhaps Saxo-Norman rather than Anglo-Saxon.

It is perhaps more likely that the bishop and his staff squeezed the canons out, either deliberately or by force of circumstance. Lincoln must have been a stressful place, full of noise and smells, dirt and confusion; and accommodation must have been very cramped. For some 20 years the cathedral and its attendant buildings were being erected. It must have been a joy for the bishop and his entourage — chaplains, clerks, servants of all kinds — to escape from time to time, and live at Stow. There would be little space for canons.

Later on, in 1091, the bishop spoke of them unkindly:

> Through lack of concern, on the part of those in charge, this church (sc. St. Mary's Stow) has lain deserted for a very considerable space of time (*quondam prolixo temporis spatio presidentium incuria desolatam*)

(from E5).

Perhaps he had given them very little chance to do anything else?

Here is the main reference to Stow in Domesday Book. It is first among the bishop of Lincoln's 59 Lincolnshire items:

> In STOW ST. MARY 4 carucates of land taxable. Land for 4 ploughs. Bishop Remigius (has) in lordship 1 plough;
> 20 villagers and 3 Freemen who have $3\frac{1}{2}$ ploughs. A church and a priest; 3 smithies.
> Value before 1066 £32; now £30.
> Of this land 2 men-at-arms have what is valued at 30s.

(from *D.B.*, *Lincs.*, folio 344a.).

So there is just one priest, presumably the village priest, wedged in the property list between the church and the three smithies.

Elsewhere in this shire Domesday has canons of Lincoln and canons of St. Mary's, but the cathedral, as well as Stow minster, was St. Mary's. There are no clear and convincing references to canons of St. Mary's Stow.[1]

One Stow item, in the bishop's list, shows the shape of things to come:

> In this village (sc. Hougham) Robert the priest had 1 carucate of land from the King in alms. Now he has become a monk in St. Mary's Stow with this land (*modo cum eadem terra effectus est monachus in S MARIAE Stou*), but no one may have the land except with the King's consent.
> Value before 1066, 10s.; now the same
>
> (from *D.B., Lincs.*, folio 345a).

We know that a Benedictine abbey was to be founded at Stow five years later. Perhaps Robert was an early recruit, already there? Perhaps he was on the bishop's staff, ready to go? The word 'monk' has been inserted between the lines, but probably by the same hand. The omission seems to have been accidental, but did it reflect some uncertainty as to whether Robert was a canon or a monk?

In a charter whose authenticity some doubt, Eynsham cartulary has it that careful plans for Stow abbey had been formulated some years before 1091. They sound like the business-like work of Archbishop Lanfranc. What was left of the endowments of Eynsham abbey and Stow minster would be merged. The joint funds would support a new Benedictine abbey, and it would be at Stow. The whole monastic intent and inner being of Eynsham abbey would be kindled again at Stow. A single institution, healthily endowed, would replace two derelict ones. It is true that funds expressly meant for secular canons would now support regular monks, but perhaps Remigius comforted himself by remembering that even at that time he was founding an entirely new college of canons at Lincoln cathedral. Here is the text:

> WILLIAM, king of England:
>   to the bishops, and to all his faithful people, throughout England: greeting:
> You are to know that I have confirmed the benefaction, which Earl Leofric and his wife, Godiva, made to the church of St. Mary's Stow, namely, Newark and Fledborough and Well wapentake, together with what pertains to them.[2]
>   Furthermore, I grant to the said church, at the request of Bishop Remigius, the church of Eynsham, together with the lands which it now possesses.
>   It is a condition that the abbot there shall be appointed in consultation with myself: he shall be such as to handle the affairs of the churches wisely: and the abbey shall abide under my lordship, precisely as the rest, throughout England.
>   Moreover, lest any man should have ground for dispute with that same abbey, I am granting the excellent estate of Sleaford to the bishops of Lincoln, in exchange for the altar of Stow and the four carucates of land there, which pertain to their bishopric.[3]
>   And this I do, in consultation with Archbishop Lanfranc, and with his agreement.
>   Witnesses: E., sheriff, and Robert d'Oilly
>
> (from the Latin of E3).

Remigius was to die in 1092, almost on the eve of the consecration of his new cathedral; but he just managed to get Stow abbey floated in 1091. He would have started his cathedral from its east end, working steadily westwards, through the years. It is perhaps significant that there are some stylistic parallels between his cathedral's west front and Ṣtow's rebuilt crossing. Maybe the same planners and craftsmen had been at work.[4]

Notes

1. *D.B., Lincs.*, refers to:

   i. the cathedral, St. Mary of Lincoln, at C 4;17. 7,8 (canons). 51,12. CS,5. CN,6 (numbering, here and below, follows Phillimore edn.)

   Its predecessor (see C 17. CS,5) may well have been a small parish church, by this time swallowed up by the new cathedral, rather than a powerful minster (see *Owen 1984* and *per contra Hill 1948*, pp.64ff.). In that case Stow minster must have been dominant in north Lincolnshire before the Conquest.

   ii. Stow minster, St. Mary of Stow, at T 4. 7,1 et seq.; 55. 12,41. CN,27. CW,9-11.

   In two cases the text may imply 'trusteeship' for the canons as well as the bishopric (see T 4. CN,27).

   iii. In five of the above references the text says simply 'St. Mary's' (C 4. 7,11. CW,9-11). I have ventured to disagree with H.W.C. Davis, who appears to refer CW,9-11 to the cathedral (see *Regesta*, vol.1 (1913), pp.69f.).

   iv. That leaves 7,57, land at Redbourne, now held by 'Bishop Remigius and the canons in St. Mary's'. This may imply the continued presence of canons at Stow, though it would be hard to reconcile with 7,55 — the recruitment of Robert, priest of Hougham, as a monk at Stow. It might only imply a legal interest by non-existent canons of Stow. But might it not refer to cathedral canons?

2. According to *D.B., Notts* (folios 283b-284) Newark and Fledborough were still in Lady Godiva's hands at the Conquest: and yet a whole series of charters (E2, 3, 5, 7, 27, and L3/3) concur in making them part of Leofric and Godiva's gift to Stow some years before. Davis (*loc.cit.*) sees grounds here for questioning the authenticity of E3. See ch.28, below.

3. Sleaford had been part of the initial endowment of Lincoln cathedral (see L2/2, in ch.11, above). How then could Remigius claw it back to the bishopric, in compensation for the offerings of the faithful (the altar of Stow) and the estate there? The answer may lie in the lack of clear boundaries between episcopal/cathedral/diocesan funds, or (just possibly) in some sort of rough justice to Stow which had probably lost much, through cathedral building, for many years past.

4. For *D.B., Lincs.*, see also *The Lincolnshire Domesday and the Lindsey Survey* (Linc. Rec. Soc., vol.19), ed. C.W. Foster & T. Longley, introd. by F.M. Stenton, 1924 (reprinted 1976).

The wrath of St. Mary

The foundation-charter of Stow abbey is an old man's testament — ponderous perhaps, prolix perhaps, even fulsome, but strangely moving. It is fraught with acute apprehension. The bishop must soon meet the Blessed Virgin, face to face, and he had held on to her institutions and their revenues for far too long. St. Mary's Stow was clearly hers, but where were her canons? Eynsham abbey had been given 'to God and Saint Mary' (according to the O.E. charter: see end of E1), but where was her household of monks? His cathedral also was St. Mary's. Her presence and her concern would haunt his prayers.

By this time the Conqueror was dead. Archbishop Lanfranc was dead also. Surviving Norman pioneers were lonely. Perhaps Remigius had intimations that he too would soon die. He would picture St. Mary, seated on her throne, hard by the great white throne of the Lord. How might he fare? Our 'Eynsham Madonna' (as some call her: see frontispiece) speaks vibrantly of Remigius' thinking. The Virgin has crown and sceptre; in her arms she holds the Ancient of Days made flesh; she is good and just, stern, strong, and majestic. What would she say of his taint of simony long ago? And what of his long years of misdirection of her Stow and Eynsham moneys? The bishop would tremble.

In 1091 he reached his solution. Stow abbey was founded. In effect it was the Benedictine abbey of Eynsham, removed to Stow, and supported by the surviving revenues of both houses. William II was king, no lover of churchmen, but greedy for their funds. His adviser in such matters was Ranulf Flambard, a clerk of dubious repute, one day to be rewarded with the bishopric of Durham. To achieve Stow abbey Remigius must have bribed his way. Surprisingly enough William II granted even more than his father would have done. He made Stow a bishop's 'own monastery' (see ch.12, above). One day that rare privilege was to have a profound effect upon the Eynsham story.

The tenants of Stow abbey were told about their new feudal lord:

WILLIAM, king of England:
   to the men of Stow abbey: greeting:
I bid you all, be subject to your lord, Abbot Columban, precisely as you were, in all things, to Bishop Remigius.
   Witness: Richard de Courcy

(from the Latin of E4).

Presumably this was the Columban who had been looking after Eynsham.

To the archbishop of York and other local dignitaries the King was even more

70

direct. He knew full well that the archbishop's claims to Lindsey were still rumbling. The new abbey must be protected:

WILLIAM, king of England:
> to Archbishop Thomas, and to Turold, and to Sheriff Earnwig, and to all his barons of Nottinghamshire and Lincolnshire, both French and English: greeting:
> you are to know that I have granted to Abbot Columban the abbey of Saint Mary's Stow, precisely as I granted it to Bishop Remigius, as his own charter bears witness.
> Witness: Robert, son of Hamon

(from the Latin of E26).[1]

And because the affair could be very contentious, the announcement was made in English also:

King WILLIAM:
> greets Thomas, the archbishop, and Thurold and Earnwig, his sheriffs (sheriff?), and all his thegns in Nottinghamshire and in Lincolnshire, French and English, friendly:
> and I make known to you that I have given to St. Mary at Stow and to the monks Newark and Fledborough and Brampton and Well wapentake, with sake and soke, and toll and team,[2] as fully and most completely as Godiva had them, in the days of King Edward, in all things, and the things that Bishop Remigius can testify rightly belong thereto:
> and I bid that there shall come in again whatsoever has been alienated, and nothing else

(from the O.E. of E27; based on translation by W.H. Stevenson, in *E.C.*, vol.1, p.50).

And so we come towards the full foundation-charter. Long years of hard bargaining lie behind its elegant language. There is a great sense of occasion. The bishop employs his best Latinist. Composition has gone on for days. The earlier parts are marked by a curiously involuted, and almost kaleidoscopic, sexual imagery. Behind it all lies the bishop's conscience about simony and money:

> + Christ Jesus, mediator between God and men, himself man, holds holy church most dear: for she is his bride, prefigured by sundry mysteries from the very beginning of the world, made one with him by the saving waters of baptism, and at the last betrothed utterly to him by the sacrament of his own body, flowing from out the cross (*ac demum proprii lateris e cruce manante*[3] *sacramento prorsus federatam*). And so he wills that she should be enlarged and magnified: and by many an example in the holy fathers that went before us he points the manner of its doing: and ofttimes he encourages his faithful people, and ofttimes inspires them, thus.

> All, therefore, whose hearts long to glorify that same bride of the lamb, that
> · daughter of the king most high, that flawless mother of all peoples, must follow in the steps of the fathers. They too must deal faithfully with her: so, when she stands at the right hand of her deathless spouse, clad about in raiment of gold, she will not turn angrily upon them, nor cast them out, as children of another, children clothed in wickedness and guilt: nay rather, she will look back with thanksgiving, and rejoice that she has nurtured them: she will acknowledge them as her own adopted children, brought forth from her own unsullied womb, suckled indeed with the nectar of her own most sacred breasts.

And, although all faithful people must show this tender care for mother-church, it is more specially appropriate in those who rule and govern her: for they are set apart by God to give her increase: their task is not so much to preside as to profit (*non tam preesse quam prodesse divinitus constituuntur*).[4] They have been born again from her fruitful womb: they have been washed clean by her saving sacraments. It is but fitting that they should bend all their mind and strength to do her good. They should study to endow her in this world, and to make her rich with this world's gifts, and to adorn her, so that, when the day of the great judgment shall come suddenly upon them, her immortal spouse shall reward them, and they may be counted worthy to be adorned with the robe of immortality, and to be made rich eternally with the unthinkable rewards of the saints, together with all who fight the good fight.

Now I, Remigius, bishop of the holy church of Lincoln, long with all my heart, and strive mightily, to share in that inestimable reward: and I press forward, to be worthy to attain that happiness: and so it is that I am undertaking a certain deed. It is for the earthly well-being of my most glorious lord, William II, king of England, and of my own body, and of all who are subject to me, as also for the eternal salvation of both my royal lords, father as well as son, and of my most sweet lady, Queen Matilda,[5] and of my own needy soul, and of each of my parents, and, as before, of all who are committed to my charge.

I have decided to re-establish the church of the holy Mother of God, the ever-virgin Mary, in a place commonly called Stow. Through lack of concern, on the part of those in charge, this church has lain deserted, for a very considerable space of time.

There, with the authority of the aforesaid William, my most victorious lord, king of England, son of the most excellent King William who preceded him, as also of all the bishops and abbots and other magnates, throughout his kingdom, I do now set Columban, a venerable man, a man of no mean experience in the exercises of religion: he shall be abbot, and he shall live by the Rule, he and the monks who are subject to him: and nothing shall alter this decree.

To this church also I make a perpetual grant of all those lands, which, for love of religion, were once conferred upon it by the most noble Earl Leofric, and by his most devout wife, Godiva, namely, Brampton and two-thirds of Well wapentake, together with all that appertains to them, Newark also and Fledborough, similarly. This present charter bears final witness to this grant.

And that the Mother of God herself, the only Virgin Mary, may take of those gifts which her only Son bestows, and may transport me, thirsting as I am for the waters of life, from hope to vision (*me fontem vite sitientem ab spe ad speciem transferat*), where I may be counted worthy to see the King in his glory, I do here and now make a further grant. Whatever rights have until this time appertained to the bishop, at the very centre of the said episcopal estate, in which the said church of Stow is situate (*quecunque in ipso capite prenotate pontificalis mansionis, in qua prefata sita est ecclesia, juris episcopii hactenus extiterant*), namely, the altar-offerings at that church and four carucates of land there, all these also I now grant to the said church, long dedicated to the queen of heaven. These are in addition to its other revenues, already mentioned, which, as law directs, were being credited to the bishopric. They are for the restoration of the same church, and for the use of the brethren who do battle for God therein. They will gather up the fruits of these gifts: they will possess them in like manner for all time: and what I have given, that I now confirm, and nothing will change it.

And lest my successors, the days of my life being ended, do despite to my soul, and assert that I have carelessly diminished the see, or in any wise despoiled them of what is theirs, I have secured another estate for the see, in permanent exchange for the above-mentioned payments now taken away from it. It is

Sleaford, a particularly delightful manor, together with all that properly belongs to it. Its acquisition involved me in immense trouble. It has proved to be a convenient property, not to say essential, and doubtless it will be the same for those who at Christ's bidding succeed me. This I now give to the see, both for myself and for those who come after me. It is a complete and permanent exchange and recompense, now established firmly and inviolably.

Furthermore, I also add to the same church of the most glorious Mother of God at Stow, and to the monks of its household, yet another outstanding benefaction. It is the church of Eynsham, together with those lands in which it has stood from of old and the other estates which go with it: namely, Shifford and Little Rollright, as also Yarnton and Mickleton, and a certain little church of Saint Ebbe, situate in the city of Oxford, with its own small properties, gifts of the faithful: also two mills, long set beside the water-courses of the same city, together with all that rightly appertains to them. All these also I now grant, to be held in like manner in perpetuity, and I link them firmly with the rest.

Thus I have established this house: those are my settled benefactions: the list is here, for all to see. These things are set down irrevocably in this present charter. I have allocated and granted them to the said church of the Mother of Christ at Stow, as also whatever the godly generosity of the faithful may bring to that church in days to come. They are entrusted also to Abbot Columban, that father famed for godliness, and to his successors, duly and canonically appointed there through all the years: they shall preside over them, and by right unchanging receive all customary dues. This is my grant: and may Christ and all his church bear witness that I have granted these things, and set them down in this present deed: and here and now I confirm them strongly with my episcopal authority, and do sign them with my own hand.+

And lest some son of perdition, prompted by our ancient foe, should afterwards bring the gifts of this my establishment to nought, nay rather that they should be preserved intact and firm, I do here and now bestow upon this same church of the most holy Virgin such perpetual freedom, that no mortal man, be he never so swollen and drunk with pride, may exercise any dominion over it, saving only the bishop of Lincoln, holder of this our see. To him this house, together with its pastor, whosoever he may be, and all the other endowments which may be given to it for the healing of many faithful souls, shall for ever be subject, as to its lord and indeed its founder: and thus shall the tradition of our fathers of old be maintained. From him also the gift of the manorial rights and ordination to the holy office of abbot shall be granted in accordance with canon law: it shall be given to such a man as will preside in godly and fatherly wise (*a quo etiam honoris donationem & sacri ordinis consecrationem secundum canonum censuram adepturus est, qui . . . presit*): not such as would ever exact a tribute from this abbey, or any other kind of payment: not such as would yield to some pressure and presume to impose a tax of a fourth of its income upon it: not such as would extort any other customary due whatsoever from it (*ut nunquam tributum vel quemlibet redditum inde exigat, seu tesseram necessitate aliqua ingruente sibi imponere presumat, vel etiam consuetudinem quamlibet aliam ab ea extorqueat*): but rather such a man as will defend his abbey from the attacks of its enemies. So, on the day of retribution, the judge of all the earth shall pay heed to the prayers of his most gentle Mother and reward him abundantly.

If, nevertheless, which God forbid, anyone in days to come shall yield to the wiles of the enemy of all goodness and, with sacrilegious and deceitful purpose, thwart this wholesome scheme of ours: if, filled with the poison of greed, he shall dare to diminish this most sound gift of mine, endorsed as it is by so many and such distinguished men, or even to lay violent hands upon it and blot it out, then let him also be blotted out from the book of life: let not his name be written with the just: nay rather, like the dust which the wind carries away from the face of the earth, let him be borne away with the wicked, lest he behold the glory of God: let him be (as the apostle puts it) anathema maranatha (*sitque juxta apostolum anathema maranatha*):[6] unless perchance he has repented, and made adequate amends to God and to holy church, which he has defrauded and injured. Amen.

> In the year of the incarnation of our Lord, 1091, and in the 14th year of the current indiction, and in the fourth year of the reign of that most noble prince, William II, king of England, and in the 24th year of the episcopate of Remigius, bishop of Lincoln

(from the Latin of E5).

There is an Eynsham legend, picturing boatloads of Eynsham monks, embarking there, going down the Thames, and so by water and by land reaching Stow. In fact there is no evidence, no likelihood indeed, that any but Columban, caretaker-monk at Eynsham, and his domestic and travelling staff, and perhaps a monk or two, made the journey. He faced a daunting task.

Let William of Malmesbury have the last word about the bishop. He died in the following year. And there was a special element of personal tragedy in his end. William gives us one of his delightful thumb-nail sketches, concluding thus:

> In later days he (sc. Remigius) established a monastery at St. Mary's Stow: previously he had restored another at Bardney (*cenobium monachorum apud Sanctam Mariam de Stou ex novo fecit: alterum apud Bardenei ex veteri favore suo innovavit*). His achievements were the more pleasing, because in body he was prodigiously small. His mind was ever striving to reach upwards and stretch outwards: and his strength of character, coming from so slight a frame, was all the more delightful. Nature, it might be thought, had so compacted him, that all should know that a most blessed spirit could dwell in the meanest body. So, when his life had run its happy course, and during the final preparations for consecrating his cathedral at Lincoln, and on the very day before the dedication, death in its envy took him away from such great joys. For also, at the urging of this great-hearted man, the edict of the king had summoned all the bishops from every side. Robert alone, bishop of Hereford, had refused to come: the stars had shown him clearly, that the dedication would not take place in Remigius' time: nor had he been silent in the matter[7]

(from the Latin of *Wm. Malm. G.P.*, pp.312f.).

Notes

1. At this point the cartulary turns to a series of earlier records, starting with E26-8, all from the 11th century.
2. These ancient terms implied full feudal jurisdiction within the bounds of the estates concerned.
3. Salter's *manente* is a misreading of the MS.
4. This patristic jingle is taken up by St. Benedict (see *RB* 1980, ch.64, v.8).
5. William I's widow.
6. The words 'anathema maranatha' are from 1 Cor. 16, 22. The first word is Greek, and means 'accursed'. The second is Aramaic, and means 'The Lord is coming' or 'Lord, come'. The thought of the Lord's return to judge the world is of course particularly apposite. But had the phrase become by this time almost a magic spell?
7. Robert Losinga (of Lorraine), bishop of Hereford, showed sturdy independence. He was famed for his mathematical and astronomical knowledge, but the boundary between astronomy and astrology was as yet ill defined.

Back to Eynsham

The next bishop of Lincoln was Robert Bloet. Stow abbey, so recently established, would now be uprooted. Eynsham abbey would return to Eynsham. That this happened, and that Bishop Bloet was responsible, is certain; but the exact timing of the process is not.

The world of monks shuddered and shook, and thought the whole affair obscene. So William of Malmesbury's account is not only lively and lurid, but also biased, and charged with portents. When the bishop dies at Woodstock, and his viscera are buried at Eynsham, ghosts are seen in Eynsham church, and have to be exorcised. When a young Eynsham monk lies dying, and is harassed in his delirium by hordes of demons, the Virgin Mother drives them off, for she loves her Eynsham house and is loved by it. The famous hermit, Roger of St. Albans, is sheltering the yet more famous Christina of Markyate. Not unnaturally he is questioned by the bishop, but gives blow for blow, and darkly prophesies his coming death, speechless and apoplectic.

Here is William's earlier account:

> The whole affair (sc. the consecration of Lincoln cathedral) had to be postponed: but it was little trouble for his successor to see it through: in fact he had entered comfortably into the labours of another. His name was Robert Bloet.
>
> This man never allowed any consideration to come between his shameful desires and their fulfilment. He had a particular prejudice against all monastic life: so he instructed that the monks of Stow should be moved out and settled at Eynsham. He was a thoroughly bad man, envious of his predecessor's high repute, and alleging that it was inconvenient to have the monks so near him. If then the monks of Eynsham gained a welcome increase of prosperity through their removal, it was by the gift of God, and small thanks to the bishop: his view (and he boasted of it) was that he was doing them a favour by even permitting them to live.
>
> He survived in his bishopric for just under 30 years, and died at Woodstock, far away from his see. He was out riding, with another bishop, at the side of the king, when fate suddenly struck him down.
>
> For the rest, it may be said that he was reasonably good-natured with his own people, and not unduly severe with them. He was second to none in his experience of worldly affairs, but not at all so in church-matters. He adorned his cathedral-church with very precious ornaments. At his death his body was disembowelled, lest evil smells should foul the air (*defuncti corpus exinteratum, ne tetris nidoribus vitiaret aerem*). His entrails were buried at Eynsham, the rest of his body at Lincoln.[1]
>
> And it is well-established that the guardians of Eynsham church were much troubled by shadowy shapes, appearing at night: they were at pains to cleanse the place by offering masses and alms. There were reports also of other visions: I

hardly like to record them here, for fear I seem to press too harshly upon this harasser of monks. When, for example, he expelled the monks from Stow, the Blessed Mother of Our Lord appeared to one of them in a dream: and she was breathing forth no light threats against the bishop: and, on the very night before he died, the same monk saw her again: and she was before her Son, bewailing the injuries which the bishop had done to her: and at break of day, just as the monk was acquainting his fellows of the vision, tidings were brought that the bishop was dead. And there was a certain hermit, a holy man named Roger, who dwelt in a wood, hard by St. Albans: he followed a strict manner of life, one in fact scarce heard of in our own days: this man gave a somewhat obscure prediction of the way in which the bishop would die. The bishop, in his usual abrasive manner, was demanding why the hermit harboured a certain virgin, who had deserted her suitor, and fled to him, wanting to be celibate. The hermit was in course of giving a seemly reply, when the bishop burst out with, 'You are answering in a very impudent and rebellious manner. It's only your cowl that protects you.' The hermit gave as much as he got, 'At the present time you despise the cowl: but the day will come when you will want it greatly: you will wish to pray for it, but words will fail you.' Readers may take that story as they will.

It is well-known, however, that the Eynsham monks were deeply devoted to Our Lady, and deeply beloved by her. Here is one last instance. In the course of the year before the bishop died, one of the Eynsham family, a young man, was lying sick: and it became apparent that Our Lady came to his aid and drove off sundry hordes of devils that had come around him. He was pointing at them with his finger, and showing them to those in attendance, and begging them to rid him of them by sprinkling holy water: but as soon as they were hounded off from one place, they made at him from another. When, however, the mighty Queen of Heaven drew near, one and all they vanished. And forthwith the sick man, just as if he were fit and well, sang out with a tuneful voice, and commenced the Responsory, 'Rejoice, O Virgin Mary.' But, when he was halfway through, he came to a halt, perhaps because of his illness, perhaps he just forgot. Then the monk who was in attendance prompted him, and his memory returned, and with the last word of the Responsory he breathed his last.

So then, with that particular story about that particular house, we will resume our pen, and wander off, amongst the other houses situate in the diocese of Lincoln (from the Latin of *Wm. Malm. G.P.*, pp.313-5).

Bloet was a secular priest, of noble Norman stock, latterly chancellor in William II's court. He would not be predisposed to like monks; but was it their relative holiness that troubled him? Or was it the economic folly of what Remigius had done? He had given so much land to Stow — land near to Lincoln, land strategically placed athwart the Trent, land that challenged the ambitions of the archbishops of York. Remigius had held on to it all for years, then given it away in his dotage, and finally claimed to be honouring the Blessed Virgin. Bloet (we may well believe) would give an episcopal snort!

So he persuaded William II to reverse Remigius' decision. Stow abbey would close, and its great church become an ordinary parish church, situate on an episcopal manor. Its Lincolnshire and Nottinghamshire revenues would go entirely to the bishop. Eynsham abbey would take its place, once again at Eynsham. It would retain its traditional lands. But (and here was the rub) the bishop would have to surrender to it some of his own southern lands, equivalent in worth to what he was now appropriating in the north. This was a stipulation

upon which the king, and presumably the monks, laid great stress. Inevitably
it would cause argument, and in all probability delay.

In the end the Eynsham monks were to prosper from the exchange. Even
William of Malmesbury (as we have seen) admitted it, and Gerald of Wales
portrayed the bishop as fair, business-like, and even liberal:

> Robert Bloet, Norman like Remigius, was a man of eminent ability and integrity
> . . . he transferred the monks of Stow to Eynsham: there was a generous exchange
> of lands: and the arrangement evinced shrewd foresight: for it gave the church of
> Lincoln the convenience of an attractive manor, as also prebends, close at hand
>
> (from the Latin of *Ger. Wales*, pp.31f.).

The king seems to have been reluctant to agree. After all it was a tiresome
problem, unpalatable because ecclesiastical, and he thought that he had already
solved it. And, ungodly as he was, he would hesitate to offend the Virgin
Mother. The scales were already weighted against him. So when Bishop Bloet
dragged his feet, the king wrote sharply:

> WILLIAM, king of England:
>   to Robert, bishop of Lincoln: greeting:
> I bid you treat Abbot Columban in a peaceful and honourable manner. See that
> he gets fair and full exchange for all the lands which he has been holding at Stow.
> The value of what he is given must in no whit fall short of the precise and total
> value of what he has been holding there. And see to it that no further squabbling
> reaches my ear in regard to this affair. Otherwise my consent to your exchange of
> the abbey-site is withdrawn (*quas habebat apud Lestou, ita ut nichil inde desit quin habeat
> totum ad valens sicut habebat illuc, & vide ne inde amplius audiam clamorem, quia aliter
> non consensi te facere mutationem loci*).
>   Witness: William, chancellor, at Eu
>
> (from the Latin of E6).

And there were practical problems at Eynsham as well. Lands were useless
without their labour force — men, women, children, livestock. During the
upheaval many had strayed away, spirited off perhaps by other land-holders.
William II issued another stern notice, this time to local authorities throughout
the land:

> WILLIAM, king of England:
>   to all his sheriffs and thegns in England: greeting:
> I bid you ensure that Eynsham abbey and its abbot receive justice without delay,
> and that they secure all their men, and the men's livestock (*cum pecuniis eorum*),
> wherever the men of that same abbey may be found. And I decree that anyone
> who retains them unlawfully be subject to a fine of £10: for I will that the abbot
> hold both his men and his abbey with a substantial fief (*cum magno honore*).
>   Witness: William, chancellor, at Leigh
>
> (from the Latin of E28).

Salter argued that those two peremptory missives from William II settled
the issue. Eynsham abbey, he wrote, was back in Eynsham during William's
reign, either in 1094, the year of Bishop Bloet's consecration, or at latest by
1100, the year of William II's death. And he drew the attractive conclusion that
'Eynsham can claim to be the one religious house in Oxfordshire which existed

continuously from the eleventh century to the dissolution of the monasteries' (see *E.C.*, vol.1, pp. xif., closely followed by *M.R.H. 1971*, pp.65 & 77, and *H.R.H. 1972*, p.48).

Earlier monastic historians had paid greater attention to Henry I's decisively-phrased and business-like charter of 1109, and especially to its forthright description of Eynsham abbey at that time:

> Right until now it has lain deserted, with its affairs in disarray (*hactenus desolatam & dissipatam*)

> (from the Latin of E7: see *Dugdale 1817-30*, vol.3, p.1, and *Tanner 1744*, pp.417f; followed by Hamilton, in *Wm. Malm. G.P.*, p.312, n.7 (not Wm. Malm. himself, as *E.C.*, vol.1, p.xii), and Elspeth, in *V.C.H., Lincs.*, vol.2, p.118. cf. Chambers, *E.M.*, p.3).

Salter brushed Henry I's charter aside, saying only that it 'seems to have put an end to some years of unsettlement'.

My own feeling is that Salter may have been too optimistic about the effectiveness of William II's two decrees. It was a troubled reign, and especially unpropitious for decisions in church affairs. Archbishop Anselm was at loggerheads with the King, and went into exile. It was a time when all such business dragged on interminably; and in this case there must have been almost endless wrangling between Bishop Bloet and the monks and the network of families who were concerned with the various lands. It is not unlikely that the monks stayed on at Stow until 1109, and indeed went on building there, until the firm hand of Henry I concluded the affair.[2]

If that is true, it may well be reflected in the surviving architecture of Stow church. To each side of the Anglo-Saxon crossing there is Norman work, butted up against it. To the east there is a fine chancel, originally vaulted.[3] Who but monks would have built it so magnificently? It was at the heart of their daily devotions. To the west there is a considerable nave, adequate for the local congregations, which would pour in during the two great Mary festivals. And if all that Norman work was executed between 1091 and 1109, we can assume that, but for the removal of the community to Eynsham in 1109, the (to us) especially precious Anglo-Saxon crossing and transepts would have been demolished, and replaced by more up-to-date 12th-century material. That they got as far as they did, and that they did so with a degree of elaboration, suggests a longer period of occupation than Salter permits. That the Anglo-Saxon work was spared suggests an untimely halt to their work. And, in any case, monks at a new abbey would have been more likely to go to such expense than a bishop at a parish church from which he had just expelled the monks.

One more difficulty remains. The argument of this chapter has rested upon Eynsham charter E7, in which Henry I states, quite unequivocally, that he is re-establishing Eynsham abbey at Eynsham, and endowing it, and that 'right until now (sc. 1109) it has lain deserted, with its affairs in disarray'.

Another document, however, also from Henry I, and clearly issued between 1100 and 1107, seems to contradict E7.

HENRY, king of England:

to W., sheriff of Oxford, and to all his Oxfordshire foresters: greeting.

You are to know that, on behalf of the abbot of Eynsham, I have exempted the men of Eynsham from going to serve the hunt (*ad stabilitatem*), whilst my household is lodged there.

Witness: Robert, bishop of Lincoln, and William de Werelwast: at Hanborough

(from the Latin of E698).

E698, therefore, suggests that, already by 1107, there was a re-established abbey, in full institutional being, at Eynsham. It had an abbot, and therefore a community. It had estates and tenants. It had a guest-house, adequate for important visitors, with their staff and servants; with it would go catering facilities. And when the court accompanied the king to his newly-developed country residence and game-park at Woodstock, guests could overflow to Eynsham abbey.

The English word 'stably', used until *c*.1450, referred to 'besetting' a hunting-area with a ring of men, equipped with bows, nets, dogs etc., and manned by local peasants. Eynsham men would, on such occasions, be excused, because of their more local hospitality duties.

Must we modify, or even forget, the main contention of this chapter? May I suggest that E698, agreed at nearby Hanborough, perhaps on a royal visit to assess progress at Woodstock, was just a minor settlement of one small item in a protracted series of negotiations, and that it cannot nullify the definitive statement that Eynsham abbey was in a very poor state until 1109?[4] What becomes clear, however, is that Henry I's enthusiasm for Eynsham abbey was not unconnected with his enthusiasm for the Woodstock project!

Notes

1. This procedure was, in fact, normal and essential, when burial was at a distance.
2. For such slowness, see *Gibson 1978* (Lanfranc), pp.145, 152, & 157, n.5. Aethelric, bishop of Selsey, was deposed at Easter, 1070, but his case was 'only now being concluded' at Easter, 1076. Lanfranc became archbishop of Canterbury in 1070, but it took him 'at least 10 years' to establish his title to the various estates which pertained to his see. Battle abbey was founded in 1067, but the project 'hung fire for 10 years or more'.

   The provision of local endowment for a daughter of Fécamp abbey, a new Benedictine priory, at Cogges, just a few miles to the west of Eynsham, may well have contributed to the special delays attendant upon Eynsham's return to base. The abbot of Fécamp was present in person at the final inauguration of Cogges priory in 1103, and the preparations must have occupied several years before then.

   The 'alien priory' of Cogges was to have a troubled 12th century and it proved, in the end, to be no serious rival to Eynsham. In fact, it became little more than an estate office for the management of Fécamp's extensive English holdings. See *Blair & Steane 1982*, pp.43ff.; also J. Blair, *Medieval Cogges: An Oxfordshire Landscape in the Making. OLHA Jnl.* vol.2, 1988, pp.298ff.
3. It has been shown that the Norman chancel, like the Anglo-Saxon crossing, was at some time damaged by fire. Perhaps there were two, otherwise unrecorded, fires?
4. Salter deals confusingly with this issue. In *E.C.*, vol.2, p.155, he gives E698 its correct date, viz. 1100-7; but in *Id.*, vol.1, p.xii and p.54, n.3, he gives 1109 or 1110. If my contention is correct, E698 did not actually take effect until 1109 and after.

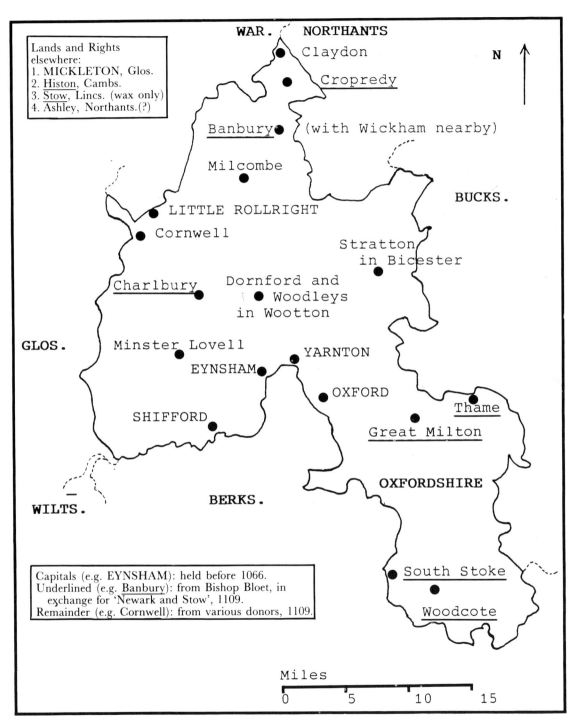

23. Eynsham Abbey: lands and/or rights, 1109.

Settlement

Henry I's charter of 1109 combined practical generosity, straightforward piety, and administrative efficiency. Not a word was wasted. Eynsham abbey — 'the church of Christ and of the most blessed Mary, Mother of God' — is to be re-established at Eynsham. 'Right until now it has lain deserted, with its affairs in disarray.' The settlement is an act of prayer for the King's parents, William the Conqueror and Queen Matilda, as also for the King's brother, William II, and for himself and his wife and children.

The abbey is to be well endowed: first, with its own traditional possessions, including those in Oxford city and just outside its walls; next, with substantial lands and rights, extracted from Bishop Bloet, in exchange for 'Newark and Stow'; lastly, with all kinds of gifts, large and small, from members of the flourishing Norman nobility (see illustration 23).

Eynsham abbey was, in fact, to be richer by far than it had ever been before. Its long travail and its northern sojourn had in the end brought profit. And, what is more, the unusual privilege which William II had given to Stow abbey was now transferred to Eynsham abbey: it became a bishop's *Eigenkloster* (own monastery). Perhaps that was a consolation-prize for the bishop?

Below is the text of Henry's 1109 charter, which was settled at the royal palace and abbey of Westminster, on Christmas Day that year. Such councils had a delightful way of coming together at the great festivals of the church, Easter, Whitsun, and Christmas, and so combining worship, business, and pleasure.

In the name of the holy and undivided Trinity, Father, Son, and Holy Spirit.

I, HENRY, king of England, with the assent and counsel of my bishops and barons, have determined to re-establish and confirm Eynsham abbey, to wit, the church of Christ and of the most blessed Mary, Mother of God, which right until now has lain deserted, with its affairs in disarray. And this shall be for the salvation of the souls of my father and mother, and of my brother William, and for my own salvation, and that of my wife and children. And I have decreed that it shall stand possessed, in all that pertains to it, by right perpetual, according to church-custom (*jure perpetuo ecclesiastico more*), as follows:

The manor of Eynsham, and all that pertains to it, in meadows and fields and woodlands: and Rollright, and whatever pertains to it: and Shifford, likewise: and, in Gloucestershire, Mickleton, and all that pertains to it: and, in Oxford, the church of St. Ebbe, and all that pertains to it: and two mills, hard by Oxford, and the meadows:[1] and Yarnton:

Also, whatever Robert, bishop of Lincoln, has given, in exchange for Newark and Stow: namely, Charlbury, in as settled and unconditional a manner, as it was held by Bishop Robert, in woodlands and meadows and fields and waters: likewise Stoke, and whatever pertains to it: likewise Woodcote, together with the woodland that pertains to it: and in Cambridgeshire, at Histon, 15 hides and three virgates: and the tithe of Thame, to wit, in corn, in beasts and wool and cheeses, as also one smallholder, together with two acres: likewise, the tithe of Banbury and Cropredy, together with the smallholders: likewise, the tithe of Milton: likewise, the tithe of the altar-wax of Stow:

I grant also to the same church all that my faithful people have given to it, or will in future give to it, for the salvation of their souls. Nigel d'Oilly has been holding one hide of land of Eynsham church: he has now quitclaimed and released it to the said church, and this he has done for the salvation of his soul, and by leave of Robert, bishop of Lincoln: he has also set one monk in the same church, and with him 40 shillings' worth of land, namely, $3\frac{1}{2}$ hides at Milcombe: this is for his own soul, as also for those of his wife and children. Richard de Gray has set one son of his in the same monastery, and with him the tithe of Dornford, and of Woodlays, and of Cornwell, that is, of everything that pertains to those same manors, not only the corn, but also the wool and the cheeses and the remaining payments. Roger de Chesney has given to the same church, on behalf of his own soul, the tithe of his land at Minster and of all his wool throughout Oxfordshire. Likewise, Gilbert Basset has given to the same church two-thirds of his tithe from Stratton, and all the tithe from his wool and his cheeses from all his land. Likewise, Ralph Basset has given to the same church his tithe from one hide at Ashley, and the tithe from all his wool, whatever its source. Likewise, Robert, son of Walchelin, has given to the same church all his tithe from Wickham. Geoffrey de Cropredy has given two-thirds of his tithe. Richard de Newark has given two-thirds of his tithe from Claydon. William, son of Nigel, has given one house in Oxford. Harding of Oxford, who went to Jerusalem and there died, has given two houses in Oxford, one inside the walls, the other outside. Gilbert de Damary has given one house outside the walls, subject only to the customary dues payable to the king. William, son of Bernard, has given his tithe to the same church.

Now this abbey is completely in the hands of the bishop of Lincoln, and under his authority, in the matter of appointing an abbot, in conformity with canon law, and with the assent and counsel of the king (*haec autem abbatia tota est in manu & potestate Lincolniensis episcopi constituendi abbatem canonice assensu & consilio regis*).

So then all these endowments, as set out above, I now grant to the same church and abbey, and do confirm them, to be held for ever, by royal authority, in as good a tenure as any abbey enjoys throughout England.

And these arrangements have been confirmed in the year of our Lord, 1109, and in the tenth year of King Henry, at Westminster, on the day of our Lord's Nativity

(from the Latin of E7).[2]

The year 1109 had proved a bad one for Bishop Bloet. In order to prise Eynsham abbey out of Stow he had had to give up far more land in the south than he had hoped. He had also lost a whole shire from his diocese: Cambridgeshire had been separated off, and Ely abbey had become its cathedral. It was a change that was obviously right, but Bloet had been criticized for allowing it too cheaply.

Henry of Huntingdon, who was one of his archdeacons, moralized about his bishop. Once close to William I, he had at first found some favour with William II; but with Henry I it was different.

Of Bloet's initial appointment to Lincoln, Henry had written: 'None other was more good-looking, more even-tempered, more eloquent . . .'. And of his death:

> The king went to Woodstock, a distinguished place, where he had established a dwelling for men and wild creatures alike (*cohabitationem hominum et ferarum*):[3] and there Robert, bishop of Lincoln, ended his days. This is his epitaph:
>
> > . . . rich, yet humble: mighty, yet godly: meting punishment, yet compassionate: gentle, even when hurt: studying rather to be a father to his people than a lord. . .

At a later date, however, he saw Bloet as an outstanding example of the transitoriness of human happiness:

> When I was a small boy, when I was growing up, when I was a young man, I used to take note of the glory of Robert, our bishop: I would see his knights most elegant, his youths most noble, his horses most costly, his vessels both golden and gilded, the number of his dishes, the splendour of those who carried them, their garments of purple and fine linen, and I could imagine no condition more blessed. Thus, when all men, even those in the schools, men who themselves were teaching about contempt of the world, paid court to him, and when he himself was treated as if he were god and father of all men, and when quite clearly he loved and embraced the world, if anyone then had told me that these very lovely things, things which all wondered at, should be despised, how would I have looked, how thought? I would have judged that man madder than Orestes, more churlish than Thersites.[4] I used to think that nothing could possibly come between so great a man and so great a blessedness. But, when I became a man, I heard tell of the vilest possible charges made against him: and, if such charges had been made against myself, against me who had nothing, and if they had been given such wide currency, I would have thought myself half-dead. Then I began to give less weight to that inestimable blessedness.
>
> Time and again, indeed, worldly men chance upon most bitter things before they die. So let me tell you how it was with Bishop Bloet before his end. He who had been justiciar of all England, he whom all men greatly dreaded, even he, in the very last year of his life, was twice brought to court by the king, before some base-born justiciar, and twice visited with loss most grievous and shameful. And this so troubled him, so shook his mind, that, when I was sitting next him at table one day (by this time I was his archdeacon), I noticed that he had been shedding tears, and, when I asked the reason, he replied, 'Time was when those who waited on me were clad in precious stuffs: but now the extortions of the king, the very one whose good will I ever studied, have made me clothe them in lambswool.' Later on, indeed, he fell into such despair of the king's friendship that, when the king spoke special praise of him in his absence, and that praise was reported to him, he sighed and said, 'The king never praises any of his people, unless he is of set intent to destroy them utterly.' For King Henry (if it is right to say so) was a man of very deep duplicity and of a mind inscrutable. Just a few days later, at Woodstock, where the king had summoned a meet of men and wild creatures, and even whilst the bishop was conversing with the king and the bishop of Salisbury (those men who were highest in the land), he was struck down with apoplexy. Yet alive, but unable to speak, he was carried to his lodging-place: soon afterwards, in the very presence of the king, he breathed his last. That great king, whom he had always served, whom he had truly loved and feared, whom he held in such high regard, in whom he ever trusted, that king was, in his hour of greatest need, no more to him than a beggar. Take thought then that it is not said in vain, 'Cursed

is he who puts his trust in men, and makes flesh his arm.' And, when a child, or a growing lad, or a young man, sees those who are blessed, let him note betimes how doubtful may be their end, and how, even in this world, they may be caught up in decay and wretchedness. Although Robert was a kindly and humble bishop, raising many up, oppressing no one, a father to the fatherless, a delight to his own, yet such was his end

(from the Latin of *Hy. Hunt., Historia Anglorum*, pp.216f. & 244f., and *De Contemptu Mundi*, pp.299f.).

Robert's death was in 1123. His lifestyle was probably not untypical of the aristocratic establishment expected of contemporary bishops. His administrative success was probably above the average. But his sudden death, out riding with his earthly king, yet going unshriven to meet the King of kings, was excellent matter for medieval fantasy. This was the man who had sent Eynsham abbey back home.

Notes

1. For these mills, see *V.C.H., Oxon.*, vol.4 (1979), pp.30 (Plan: Oxford 1375) & 329.
2. Eynsham's new lands and rights make an interesting collection (see *E.C.*, vol.2, pp.xx-lxxiv). Stow's altar wax (*decimam cere altaris de Stou*) was a token of spiritual affinity. Histon, Cambridgeshire, was by now in Ely diocese. Charlbury, Oxfordshire, was outstanding in value, and had, in the tenth century, housed the relics of Diuma, first bishop of the Mercians. And there were useful pickings from all five of the ancient episcopal estates in Oxfordshire. Woodcote and South Stoke, for example, between Wallingford and Reading, provided an excellent foothold in Chilterns timber (see P. Preece, *Abbey Wood or College Wood: Chilterns Coppice over the Centuries, OLHA Jnl.*, vol.2, 1988, pp.150-60; some local maps, old and new, speak of Abbots Wood, rather than Abbey Wood). The channelling of tithe from parish clergy to abbeys aroused tensions, as did annual parochial payments to abbeys (pensions), which at this period became payable. Bishop White Kennett comments acidly, 'Note, this was one of the early projects which the Regulars invented to oppress the secular clergy' (*Kennett 1695*, p.86).
3. His palace and his enclosed game-park.
4. Orestes went mad, after killing his mother, Clytaemnestra, and her paramour, Aegisthus, murderers of his father, Agamemnon. Thersites was notorious, amongst the Greeks at Troy, for his impudent talk.

Part Three

The Promised Land

Growth

Eynsham abbey now entered upon four centuries of relative peace. Henry I had tried to give it a good start. During the 12th century it developed steadily. The cartulary charts its progress, and opens window after window into 12th-century England. This chapter touches upon eight of them. Eynsham, of course, had had no association with a famous saint or martyr — these were sure roads to ecclesiastical prosperity — but it did what it could, where opportunity served. In other days Aelfric might by this time have been canonized, but the Norman arrival had swamped and eclipsed potential Anglo-Saxon saints. Items, however, both great and small, flowed in.

First of all, Pentecostal processions from Oxfordshire. These were so important that in the end the Eynsham scribes entered no less than eight charters about them (see E8-12, 51, 705 & 707; also *E.C.*, vol.1, pp.424-30). Here is the first:

ALEXANDER, bishop of Lincoln:
   to all the clergy and laity of Oxfordshire: greeting.
Be it known to you that having taken common counsel with the chapter of Lincoln I now grant to the church of Eynsham that you may resort thither and there receive the same indulgence that you have been receiving at Lincoln. And this I grant you because you are so far removed from your mother-church.
   Nevertheless penitents who are so enjoined, and others who wish to do so, ought to visit their mother: for the more they toil for God so much fuller the indulgence they shall receive. And I make this grant, saving the dignity of the mother-church

(from the Latin of E8: date, *c.*1138).

Parishes made annual offerings to Lincoln cathedral, and took them there during Whitweek. The pilgrims who went with them received special absolution. But Oxfordshire was at the farthest tip of the great diocese, and the holy place at Eynsham was much nearer. So permission was given for Oxfordshire parishes to go there instead, and, in spite of the more modest effort, to receive the same indulgence. The abbey, for its part, received a 'commission' on what it collected. It was warned, however, not to poach upon those who had been told to go to Lincoln, or wanted to go there.

Next, miscellaneous income from sundry parish churches. Sometimes disputes arose: Merton, Oxfordshire, was a case in point. David, king of Scotland, and son of the famous St. Margaret, queen of Scotland, had given it to Eynsham abbey. But the manor of Merton had gone to Guy de Chaingy, and Guy claimed that he owned the church (and therefore its miscellaneous income) as well. The abbey appealed to the bishop. The bishop wrote a strong letter to Guy, threatening a summons to the archdeacon's court. Guy capitulated. Here is the bishop's letter:

> ALEXANDER, bishop of Lincoln:
>> to Guy de Chaingy, his parishioner: greeting.
> It is my bidding and my command that you speedily return to Eynsham church and to Abbot Walter his church of Merton, together with everything that pertains to it in land and in tithe and otherwise, precisely as your predecessor gave and granted it to the said church of Eynsham.
>> Unless you do this quickly, I am instructing Archdeacon Walter to take you to the church-courts on the matter (*inde justiciam Christianitatis faciat*). Then right and justice will be done, and I shall hear no more of this dispute

(from the Latin of E15: date, 1123-48).

Another dispute was at Banbury. The opposing party was 'William the Grammarian', presumably something of a teacher and scholar, certainly able to prepare and argue a case, and perhaps crusty and independent. In 1109 Bishop Bloet had surrendered all the tithe on his home farm (his demesne) at Banbury to Eynsham abbey. William asserted that his particular patch of land was not part of that demesne, and had not been so when the gift was given. Again, the abbey appealed to the bishop. The bishop gave order that a suitable jury of Banbury men be empanelled, to decide the issue. The abbey won. The bishop had written:

> ALEXANDER, by the grace of God, bishop of Lincoln: to William de Boise: greeting.
>> It is our command and solemn bidding that by the oath of law-worthy Banbury men you should cause it to be determined whether that land, concerning whose tithe a dispute has sprung up between the abbot of Eynsham and William the Grammarian, was or was not at one time part of the bishop's demesne, to wit, on that day when Bishop Robert my predecessor gave the tithe of his Banbury demesne to Eynsham abbey as part of an exchange.
>> And if it be established that the said land was at that time part of his demesne, we bid you to see that the abbot has the tithe of the same land quickly and without delay, and that he holds it in peace. And let whatever has been withheld from him on that account be speedily restored to him.
>> And you are to know that this direction is made after consultation with the chapter of Blessed Mary of Lincoln. Farewell

(from the Latin of E15A: date, 1123-48).

One important settlement concerned Cassington church, nearby in Oxford-shire. At this time Geoffrey de Clinton, chamberlain to the King, held the manor there. Presumably he had special responsibilities at Woodstock, and would from time to time come into residence at Cassington, bringing his chaplains with him. Cassington, however, lay in the parochial care of Eynsham abbey.

Geoffrey built a church at Cassington, and a charter had to be drawn up, settling and balancing various rights and responsibilities. The tensions are apparent: the archdeacon of Oxford (representing the bishop); the abbey (ap-pointing the rector, surrendering some dues, receiving others); the rector (to be acceptable both to Geoffrey and to the archdeacon, and to be appropriately supported, and, in particular, to be protected from any encroachment by Geoffrey's chaplains); and, of course, Geoffrey himself and his chaplains. Here is the charter:

ROBERT, bishop of Lincoln:[1]
to the clergy and people of Oxford: greeting and blessing.
Be it known to you that I have consecrated the church of Cassington, in honour of St. Peter, which Geoffrey de Clinton, royal chamberlain, has built in his fief, and in the parish of St. Mary's, Eynsham. He has done this with my consent, and at the plea of the abbot and community of the same church. By this agreement Geoffrey the chamberlain has given to Cassington church one virgate of land, free and quit of all customary due and service in those matters which pertain to him, together with all his tithe of corn and beasts from the same manor. And the abbot for his part has granted to the same church all his tithe which he was receiving in Cassington and Worton, but he has retained in his own hand, for Eynsham church, both the dead of Cassington[2] and half the offerings at the two festivals of St. Peter. And for so long as the said chamberlain or his household be in Cassington, the priest of that manor shall receive half the offerings from his family and household, as against his chaplains. And the abbot shall appoint the priest there, precisely as in the church in his own demesne, but taking thought and counsel with Geoffrey and the archdeacon

(from the Latin of E19: date, before 1123?).

When Henry I died, there was considerable strife between King Stephen and his cousin, the Empress Matilda. Both in their turn gave help to Eynsham abbey. Stephen gave the right to hold a market in Eynsham. This was a precious privilege, bringing fees, levies, prayers, offerings, and general publicity. Henry II was to confirm the market, and to add the privilege of a fair, twice a year, and lasting a week at a time, at Whitsun and the Assumption (see E702). Here is Stephen's grant:

STEPHEN, king of England:
to the bishop of Lincoln, and to his justices and barons and sheriffs and officials and to all his faithful people, both French and English, in Oxfordshire: greeting:
You are to know that I have granted to the abbot and monks of Eynsham that they may hold a market on the Lord's day every week at Eynsham. And I command that all those men who come to it, whether going or returning or there abiding, shall be assured of my strong peace. See to it that in this matter they suffer no unlawful molestation in any respect, on pain of a fine of £10.
Witnesses: Robert d'Oilly and Richard de Lucy and Turgis d'Avranches and Warner de Lusoriis and Hugh de Chesney and William de Elaston: at Oxford

(from the Latin of E30: date, 1135-40, see illustration 24).[3]

Matilda's gift was the church of Combe, hard by Woodstock park. Here also Robert d'Oilly II was a witness; he was constable of Oxford, founder of Oseney abbey, and later buried at Eynsham abbey. Here is Matilda's grant:

MATILDA, empress, daughter of King Henry and Lady of the English (*Anglorum domina*):
to all faithful people of holy church, both French and English: greeting:
You are to know that for the soul of King Henry my father and for my own salvation and that of my sons I have given and granted the church of Combe, together with all that pertains to it, to the monastery and community of St. Mary

24. **Market Cross, Eynsham, c.1790.**

of Eynsham. Wherefore it is my will and my stern command that the same Eynsham community do hold the said church of Combe, together with all things and customary dues that pertain to the same church, soundly and without dispute, freely and without claim upon them, and in due honour, as a perpetual gift to God.

Witnesses: Robert, my brother, earl of Gloucester, John de St. John, Robert d'Oilly, Geoffrey Lovell: at Oxford

(from the Latin of E29: date, 1141-2).

There was even a royal decree to protect the abbot of Eynsham's hares, at his warren on the abbey's ancient estate at Mickleton, Gloucestershire! It is noticeable that the threatened fine is £10, the same massive penalty as for molesting travellers attending Eynsham market.

HENRY, king of England, duke of Normandy and Aquitaine, count of Anjou:
to his justices and sheriffs and officials, and to the men of Gloucestershire: greeting:
I grant that the abbot of Eynsham may hold his warren at Mickleton, precisely as his predecessor held it, on the best terms, in the time of King Henry, my grandfather. And I forbid that any should chase or take a hare therein without his licence, on pain of a fine of £10.
Witness: Manasser Biset, steward: at Wallingford

(from the Latin of E35: date, 1154-66).

And one last item. England had its network of roads and tracks, then as now, but numerous charges might be levied, as you went. Henry II awarded Eynsham abbey with free passage for all its necessaries throughout the land. Thomas Becket, at that time chancellor, and in due course to be archbishop of Canterbury and martyr, was one of the witnesses to this grant:

HENRY, king of England, duke of Normandy and Aquitaine, count of Anjou:
to his justices and sheriffs and officials in England: greeting:
I command that all the food and clothing of the monks of Eynsham, and whatever pertains to their necessities, shall be free of toll and ferry-charge and every customary due, wheresoever they buy them, within or without a town. And I forbid that any man should inflict any injury or insult upon them or their men in this matter.

Witnesses: Nigel, bishop of Ely, and Thomas, chancellor, and Manasser Biset, steward, and Warren Fitzgerald: at Danfront

(from the Latin of E37A: date, 1156).

Notes

1. Salter (ad loc.) suggests that this is Bishop Robert Bloet (d.1123) rather than Bishop Robert de Chesney (1148-66).
2. Payments, often quite considerable, and known as 'mortuaries', were due from the widow and family of a deceased serf to his landowner. Eynsham abbey was to retain such payments, when Cassington men died. See *Bennett 1947*, pp.144ff.
3. Several 12th-century papal documents include a market place (*forum*) amongst Eynsham's assets (see L250/879, L251/880, & L254/882). For its market cross, see W. Bainbridge, *Eynsham Cross*, 1978, & *E.R.*, no.4, pp.17-21.

Fate of a cell

St. Benedict had distinguished four types of monk, two good, two bad. For average men the communal life was best; such men were coenobites. Equally good, but only to be undertaken by rarer spirits was the solitary life of the hermit (the anchorite). These were tougher souls, trained already in the community, and now able to strive in solitude, and to conquer.

The two other types, sarabaites and gyrovagues, were in effect travesties of the first two. Sarabaites were, it seems, normally communal; but their groups were so small, their discipline so lax, or even absent altogether, that their profession was worse than useless. Gyrovagues were individuals, purporting to be holy, but unstable, empty, hypocritical, even fraudulent, wandering from monastery to monastery, claiming hospitality.[1]

This is how the Rule of St. Benedict begins:

It is plain that there are four types of monk. First there are the coenobites, living together in a monastery, doing battle for God under a rule and an abbot.

Secondly there are the anchorites, solitary men, hermits. Theirs is not a way for the fiery enthusiasm of a novice. It is reached only by long proving in the communal life. They have been encouraged and taught by many others, and now they know how to war against the devil. They are well-equipped, and thus step forth from the battle-line of the brotherhood, and go out to single combat in the desert. Confident without the good help of another, sufficient with their own hand and arm alone, aided by God, they fight against evil, be it in their flesh, be it in their thoughts.

Thirdly there are the sarabaites, a most objectionable type of monk: experience has not taught them: they have not been tried by a rule, *like gold in a furnace*:[2] they are soft indeed, like lead: in their works they still keep faith with the world: their tonsure is an obvious lie to God. They live in twos or threes, or even singly, without a shepherd: their sheepfolds are their own, and not the Lord's. Their law is what their own desires want: whatever they think, whatever they choose, that they say is holy: and whatever they have no wish to do, that they deem to be inadmissible.

Fourthly there are the monks called gyrovagues. Throughout their life they wander from this region to that, entertained by these monks or those, for three or four days at a time, always on the move, never settled, serving their own wills, tied to the lusts of their own belly. In every way they are even worse than the sarabaites. Concerning all of them, and their wretched manner of life, it is better to be silent than to speak.

So let us leave them aside, and come to the coenobites, the main type of monks, and with God our aid consider how their life should be ordered

(from the Latin text of *RB 1980*, pp.168 & 170).

St. Benedict was writing in the sixth century, and drawing upon the experience and writings of his predecessors. In all the centuries that followed, and not least in England after the Norman conquest, small 'cells' of monks were a problem. Morale could grow slack, standards could drop, eccentric or misguided leadership could prevail. The world was too near. The cells might be remnants of a decayed house, or pioneers for a new one. They might be managers of property, with their abbey far away, perhaps even in Normandy. They might be a little flock, gathered around some charismatic individual. Sometimes perhaps they were unruly monks, sent off into semi-exile, and luxuriating in unwonted liberty. Whatever the case, thus isolated, they were often unsatisfactory. They were not as bad perhaps as the somewhat elusive sarabaites, so deplored by Benedict, but they posed similar problems.

One such cell comes into Eynsham's story. It was at Pheleleie, a site about which authorities differ, but some miles north of Eynsham, and deep in the Wychwood forest. Its land belonged to the manor of Bloxham, still further north. It was known as St. John of the Forest. Henry I had authorized the venture, and had attached it to Eynsham abbey. Now Stephen endorses the arrangement, and adds more land. Here is his charter:

STEPHEN, king of England:
  to the bishop of Lincoln, the justices, the sheriffs, the barons, and all his officials and faithful subjects: greeting:
You are to know that, for the soul of King Henry and for my own salvation, I have given and granted, in charitable benefaction, to God and to the church of St. John of the Forest of Bloxham and to the monks who serve God there seven acres of land, in the said forest, for the increase of the same place. Wherefore it is my will and stern command that the said church and monks hold the said seven acres securely and in peace and freely and quit of claims, in as sound and free a manner as they have ever held their other land in the time of King Henry, with all the liberties and quittances and free customary dues with which they held them then.
  Witnesses: William d'Ypres, and William Martel, and Richard de Camville, and Richard de Lucy, and Bernard de Clairmont: at Oxford

(from the Latin of E32: date, 1142-8).

In due course the manor of Bloxham, and with it Pheleleie, passed to the count of Meulan. He accepted the existing arrangements:

G., count of Meulan:
  to all sons of holy church: greeting:
Be it known to you that, when King Stephen gave me Bloxham, together with all that pertains to it, I found the church of Eynsham already canonically vested with the hermitage of Pheleleie[3] and its forest-clearings, by gift of King Henry and with the assent of Alexander, bishop of Lincoln, subsequently endorsed by King Stephen, and that I have therefore granted to the said church of Eynsham that same hermitage of Pheleleie, which by gift of King Stephen is in my jurisdiction, and have confirmed it with this charter.
  Witness: Henry of Newbury, and William de Pinu, and Roger, chaplain

(from the Latin of E33: date, 1142-8).

So far so good; but (as the next charter makes abundantly plain) leadership at Pheleleie began to falter, and sights were lowered. It became necessary for the count to approve of a new prior. His own sister, the countess of Pembroke, commended a Tewkesbury monk, named Roger de Auco. The count wrote off to the abbot of Tewkesbury, enquiring about Roger, but received no reply. We are left with the impression that silence implied disapproval. It seems also that others had warned the count about Roger's inadequacy. Hugh, the last prior, had been unsatisfactory, and Roger was no better. What is more, the bishop had had some misgivings about Pheleleie, and had pressed the abbot of Eynsham to take firm action there. With all this in mind, the count writes to the remnant of monks at Pheleleie. Here is his model of quiet diplomacy:

> G., count of Meulan:
>> to Godric and the other brethren of Pheleleie: greeting in the Lord:
>
> My sister, the countess of Pembroke, sent me a letter on behalf of Brother Roger de Auco. Your place is in my woodland, and she asked me to consider granting it to him. The said Roger is a monk of Tewkesbury: so I sent a letter to the abbot there, asking him to write and give me his advice in the matter. I have not yet had a reply. Meanwhile I have learned through some reliable people, well-known to me, that the said Brother Roger, as indeed was the case with Hugh, your last prior, would be inadequate for the care of your place (*didici predictum fratrem Rogerum, vel Hugonem, qui vester prelatus fuit, minus utiles esse ad curam loci vestri optinendam*). I have therefore requested my very dear friend, Father Walter, abbot of Eynsham, that for love of God and of myself he would assume charge of your place in all matters which pertain to me. I have heard that the lord bishop of Lincoln gave the abbot similar instructions some time ago with regard to his own interests there. So I charge you to give heed to the abbot from now onwards in all your affairs that concern me. And whatever the fatherly arrangement he may make, with regard to you or your possessions, it has my complete approval, and I here and now determine that it is thus settled and ratified with my warm goodwill
>
> (from the Latin of E34: date, *c*.1142-50).

Thus Pheleleie became a part of Eynsham abbey's lands, and its men were dispersed as the abbot thought best. The church as a whole would be that much healthier, Eynsham abbey would be that much wealthier, and a few monks (it would appear) had failed in an unseemly intrigue.[4]

Notes

1. The terms coenobite, anchorite, sarabaite and gyrovague are essentially Greek; but sarabaite has Coptic (that is, Egyptian) origins and gyrovague is partially Latin.
2. See Prov. 27, 21.
3. *De heremo de Pheleleie*: it sounds as if the title 'hermitage' had continued in use, after an original solitary had been joined by others.
4. Salter (see *E.C.*, vol.1, p.xiv & vol.2, p.xxxv) equates Pheleleie with La Forsaken Ho (see E535-6: 1315), and places it between Fawler and Stonesfield, Oxon. *Steed 1963* distinguishes Pheleleie from La Forsaken Ho, and places it somewhat further north, but still in Oxon. Its remains, she states, 'are quite visible just above Spurnell's Well, to the south of Ditchley Park'. She associates it with *Felleyshegg* or *Felleye Hegge* (see E649: 1298 & *Steed 1961/2*). In 1235 Henry III extended Eynsham's Pheleleie holding by adding 2½ acres of adjacent grassy forest glade (*landa*; see E717).

Buildings

As monks prospered, so they built. Each abbey needed a whole complex of buildings, but its church was central to everything, and symbolic of purpose. It was a matter of delight and pride to make it greater and more elaborate, more richly furnished, more daring in design. Fires were frequent; precarious structures collapsed; older buildings grew rickety. Those were good enough reasons for rebuilding, but the main ones were increasing wealth and changing fashion.

Monasteries can rarely have been free from the sight and sound of building — dust, clatter, songs, shouts, accidents, trucks, hoists, piles of material, carts, horses. Monks, especially their chief officials (*obedientiaries*), would supervise the work, and pay for it, but would not do it themselves. Architects, artists and craftsmen of all kinds travelled to where they were wanted, selling their skills and circulating their ideas. Overspending was all too frequent, so were debts; but a staggering amount of sheer beauty and sensitive devotion was poured into it all.

Motives, it need hardly be said, were often mixed. Human pride entered in. So did human rivalry. At times it must have seemed that monks worshipped buildings and lovely contents rather than the God to whose glory they were raised. Sometimes the Son of Man, who had not where to lay his head, appeared strangely remote. Monks like the rest of us were fallen creatures.

But, say what we will, their structures expressed two great and godlike insights. One was the spirit of sacrifice. Giving that hurts is like God's giving in Christ. The woman who poured the alabaster box of ointment, very precious, over the head of Jesus was praised by him; the bystanders who said, 'What waste!', were rebuked (Mark 14, 3-9). Nothing can be too good for God.

The other insight, surviving through the troubled centuries from the Graeco-Roman world, a part of the lingering stream of classical culture, something resistant to iconoclasts of whatever creed, was that beauty is of God, and is by its very nature a steady bridge between God and man. Loveliness of form and line, colour and sound, design and scent, movement and word, lifts man into eternities, and breathes the eternal into him. Such things are not mere frills to life, not the nonsenses of affected aesthetes, but part of the very being of God and an element in the essential nourishment of man. If so, then the monks were fortified by things deep and true, and sang God's praises by what they built and rebuilt, as well as by their worship within it.

The Eynsham monks can have inherited very little, when they settled down again in 1109. There is, however, evidence that the 12th century saw them building busily. The evidence is twofold: on the one hand, a drawing made in 1657; on the other, miscellaneous pieces of worked and carved stone, surviving in Eynsham village.

The drawing was by Anthony Wood, young at the time, and bursting with new-found antiquarian curiosity, an enthusiasm which would last until his death in 1695. Apart from heraldic sketches he left only a few drawings. His natural artistry lay in word rather than in line. But on a visit to Eynsham, one autumn day in 1657, he went into the abbey ruins, and was much moved, and drew what he saw.

Wood lived in Oxford, but often rambled up and down the shire, visiting old churches, and taking notes of monuments, families, houses etc. He jotted down what he saw, and his jottings grew into his *Oxfordshire Monuments* (as he called them).[1] Meanwhile he was gathering similar material about Oxford city and university, as also about distinguished writers who had been educated there.

It seems that his forebears had come down from Lancashire to Eynsham, working for the earls of Derby, at the time when the earls added Eynsham manor to their many possessions. Anthony's own branch of the family had prospered more than the others, but he sustained a concern for an older, and somewhat impoverished, cousin, Thomas Barncote by name, who lived in Eynsham. Thomas was a freemason by trade, and also somewhat of a free-thinker. Here is what Wood wrote in his autobiography. He calls himself 'AW', joining the letters together:

25. **Portrait of Anthony Wood, printed in 1711.** Frontispiece to Richard Rawlinson, *The Life of Mr. Anthony à Wood, Bodl. 8° Rawl., 594.*

Sept.16 AW went to Einsham to see an old Kinsman called Thom. Barncote — He was there wonderfully strucken with a veneration of the stately yet much lamented ruins of the Abbey there, built before the Norman Conquest — He saw then there two high Towers at the west end of the church, and some of the north

The ruines of the Abbey church of Einsham. 1657. Taken from ye S. E.

The long w-window

Einsham

These two towers were at the W. End of the church

north Ile

w. dore

Body of the

S. Ile

26. **Ruins of Eynsham Abbey: drawn by Anthony Wood, 1657.** This was what Anthony Wood drew 'with a melancholy delight' on 16 September 1657. *Bodl. MS. Wood E1, f.45R.*

27. **Romanesque fragments of Eynsham Abbey (photographs by William Bainbridge)**: a. (*left*) scalloped capital; b. (*below left*) beak-head voussoir; c. (*below right*) voussoir with zigzag; d. (*bottom right*) nail-head moulding.

e. (*right*) capital, Agnus Dei;
f. (*below left*) corbel head; g. (*below
right*) small head; h. (*bottom right*)
gargoyle.

walls of the church standing: He spent some time with a melancholy Delight in taking a prospect of the ruins of that place. All which, together with the Entrance or Lodg, were soon after pul'd downe, and the stones sold to build Houses in that Towne and neare it — The place hath yet some Ruins to shew, and to instruct the pensive Beholder with an Exemplary Frailty

(from *Bodl. Tanner MS.* 102(1), f.26).[2]

Wood was an Anglican, with Roman Catholic friends, but under Cromwell neither Anglican nor Roman Catholic worship was permissible. Wood regretted much of what had been lost with the monasteries, and he certainly longed for something warmer, more colourful, less austere, than what Cromwell allowed. His heart shows clearly in what he wrote about Charles II's return a few years later:

The day of restoration of King Charles 2 observed in all or most places in England, particularly at Oxon which did exceed any place of its bigness. Many from all parts flocked to London to see his entrie: but A.W. was not there, but at Oxon, where the jollity of the day continued till next morning. The world of England was perfectly mad. They were freed from the chaines of darkness and confusion which the presbyterians and phanaticks had brought upon them; yet some of them seeing then what mischief they had done, tack'd about to participate of the universal joy, and at length clos'd with the royal partie

(from *Wood: Life*, vol.1, p.317).

Wood's drawing is the only contemporary visual record of Eynsham abbey that we have. It shows the west end of the abbey-church, together with remnants on the north side, and a short length of battlemented wall on the south. It would appear that all else had vanished (see illustration 26).

What is abundantly clear (with a clarity dimmed by some later representations of the drawing) is that the bulk of what Wood saw was in Romanesque (that is, Norman) style, and that it therefore fitted precisely into that later 12th century, the very time when (to judge by the records) we would have expected to find Eynsham monks building hard, and trying to finish their great church.

There are two substantial towers at the west end. They are balanced in style, but different in detail. Each has a fine Norman arch, leading back into the former aisles of the nave. Each is diversified, on the outside, by Norman window-openings, or by Norman arches used as surface decoration. The northern tower is slightly higher, and carries more ornamentation. We may conjecture that in their usual order the 12th-century monks had started from their own special areas of worship, in the eastern parts of the church, and then worked westwards, to accommodate congregations. We can imagine them finishing triumphantly with the north-western tower. On that tower Wood draws a small human figure, behind the battlements, with arms akimbo. Was this Thomas Barncote? Was it just a scale? Does it indicate that that tower still had its stairs? Between the towers there is a large Gothic window, presumably a later replacement of Norman work. Beneath it there is a small Norman doorway.

And, just as exciting, there are also 13 dumpy little pillars, close to each other, seemingly unattached to anything else, standing in a somewhat shaky and woebegone row, parallel to where the nave columns had once been, but to

The Ruins of the Abby church of Eynesham Co: Oxford taken by A wood from the South East 1657

Cloysters

West Door inside the church

S Isle

Body of the Church

North Isle

28. **Ruins of Eynsham Abbey: purported copy of Wood's drawing, by Browne Willis.** *Bodl. MS. Willis 46, f.96R.* Willis has written on his drawing: 'The Ruins of the Abby church of Eynesham Co: Oxford taken by A. Wood from the South East 1657', 'This was somewhat like Landaff & the last Abbat of Eynsham was Bp Kitchen of Landaff who I doubt was a worse Abbat than Bp. A good draughtsman may easily show how this Building was', 'Cloysters', 'West Door inside the church', 'North Isle', 'Body of the Church', 'S Isle'.

29. **Ruins of Eynsham Abbey: engraving by S. & N. Buck, 1729.** The bottom line of the inscription reads: 'Delin. et Sculp. from a drawing taken Anno 1657, which now is in the possession of the Learned & Curious Antiquary Brown Willis Esqr. by S. & N. Buck 1729'. There is no mention of Anthony Wood. It looks as if the Bucks relied upon Willis, and followed his errors!

their northern side. Some have interpreted them as remains of a cloister, but they are too short and too close to one another for that. And in any case cloisters were normally on the southern side of an abbey, for the sake of sun and shelter; and they would be on that side from which drainage flowed away naturally, in Eynsham's case, southwards towards the Thames. It is perhaps more likely that these little pillars were remains of small arches, possibly interlacing in characteristic Norman style, and attached to and running along the inner wall surface of the north wall of the nave.[3]

Numerous fragments, found and still being found in Eynsham village, also point to late 12th-century Romanesque work. Henry VIII's officials took the abbey over on 4 December 1538.[4] Its buildings and their contents would gradually be dispersed and broken up. Pieces, large and small, found their way into local houses, barns etc.

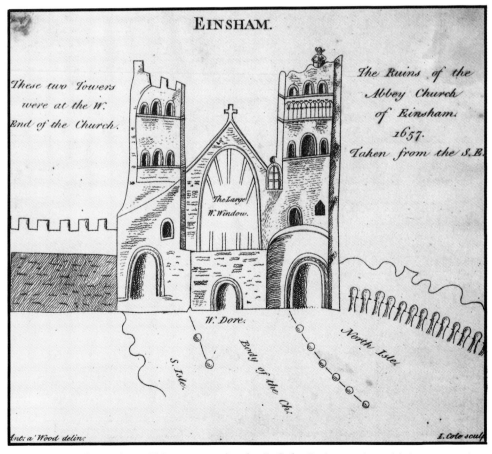

30. **Ruins of Eynsham Abbey: engraving by I. Cole.** Inelegant, but with its own crude charm, this is infinitely more accurate than Willis/Buck.

Of those found in Eynsham a very considerable proportion have Norman characteristics. They are clearly the axed work of late Norman builders. They are bold and strong, sometimes crude, always assertive. They bear the hallmarks of a style which was to melt away at about the end of the 12th century. There are the familiar mouldings — zigzag, beak, roll, diamond, nailhead. There are capitals with fluting and scalloping. There are corbel heads, vigorous, ungracious, powerful, speaking of imagination that must burst into art, be it never so inadequate. They spring from the same rude energy that splashed its great grooves around the columns of Durham cathedral (see illustration 27).

Eynsham abbey never grew outstandingly rich. Had it done so, it might have done more to replace the Norman aspects of its church. All the evidence, such as it is, points to the building of a complete church, a substantial one, in the English Romanesque style of the second half of the 12th century. Both the drawing and the fragments suggest that it was brought up to date, here and there, in sundry centuries, but never totally replaced.

Notes

1. His Oxfordshire material was still in MS. form, and incomplete, when he died. It is *Bodl. Wood MS.*, E.1; for Eynsham drawing, see f.45, & for Eynsham notes, ff.43f.
2. Wood left two MS. versions of his autobiography. This is from the second. The earlier is *Brit. Libr. Harl. MS.*, 5409 (for Eynsham visit, see ff.48f.), copied in *Bodl. Rawl. MS.*, D.97 (for Eynsham visit, see f.30). *Bodl. Wood MS.*, B.15 is the notebook which he had with him that day (see ff.41f.).
3. Reproductions of Wood's drawing; see collotype in *Wood: Life*, vol.1, p.228, and Salter, *E.C.*, vol.2, p.xlviii; the latter seems to be the same plate, by now somewhat worn. Browne Willis made a rough and inaccurate copy of Wood, and then drew wrong conclusions about the architecture; see *Bodl. Willis MS.*, 46, f.96, and my ch.7, n.4, above. In 1729 S. & N. Buck published an elegant engraving, which purported to be based upon Wood, but in fact adopted and developed Willis' errors. This appears to have misled Sherwood/Pevsner 1974, p.603. The total effect has been to obscure the Romanesque character of the Eynsham abbey remains. A different engraving from Wood, by J. or I. Cole, and undated, is bound in *Lives of Leland, Hearne and Wood*, vol.2 (1772), at p.104; it is less elegant than Buck, but more accurate. Chambers, in *E.M.*, p.41, dates Cole in 1690, but I have not been able to ascertain his authority.
4. 1538: as Chambers, in *E.M.*, p.40; not 1539, as *Willis 1718-9*, vol.2, p.178, *Dugdale 1817-30*, vol. 3, p.3, Salter, in *E.C.*, vol.1, p.xxxi, & *M.R.H. 1971*, p.65. (See my ch.29, below, for relevant *Letters & Papers: Henry VIII*.)

Customs

Eynsham abbey did not wish to forget that its roots were in pre-Conquest England, and that they involved Leofric and Godiva, as well as Aethelmaer. So it took pains to enshrine the fact in its regular prayers, as well as in its official records.

We have seen how the first eight documents of the cartulary (El, ElA, & E2-7) were so chosen, and arranged, and perhaps manipulated, as to make this point. The Norman Church tended to denigrate its predecessors, devaluing their saints, demoting their leaders, and depreciating their art and their culture. Eynsham abbey, however, could not but recognize that Anglo-Saxon generosity had paved the way for Norman prosperity. It had twin Anglo-Saxon foundations, Aethelmaer first, and later, by a circuitous route, and unknown to the donors themselves, Leofric and Godiva as well.

There is no reason to doubt the main golden thread of the Eynsham argument. Bishop Robert Bloet had had to surrender valuable estates and rights to Eynsham, and especially Charlbury, Oxfordshire, and Histon, Cambridgeshire. And he had had to do so, because he had purloined what Leofric and Godiva had once given to Stow minster. They, therefore, as well as Aethelmaer, had helped Eynsham abbey.

The same point is stressed in a little-studied customary, written in an early 14th-century hand, and for more than 350 years in the Bodleian library, Oxford. Customaries (or Consuetudinaries) were, in effect, local by-laws for monastic houses. The Rule of St. Benedict was basic, but it needed expansion, to cover all sorts of details of the common life. Such house rules could, of course, become niggling, irksome, and fussy, but you could not do without them. They comprehended elementary matters of discipline and respect, even of good manners, as well as major concerns of procedure in the church and the cloister, the chapter-house and the infirmary, and so on.

Our Eynsham Customary was compiled by John of Wood Eaton, a village just north of Oxford. He was a monk of Eynsham, and did his work between 1229 and the early part of the 14th century. It survives as Bodl. MS. 435. Salter mentions it briefly (see *E.C.*, vol.1, p.xiii, & vol.2, p.vii), and it is clear that he had little time to go deeply (see his working papers, *Bodl. MS. Top. Oxon.*, C.448, *Notes on Oxfordshire Monasteries*, vol.2, pp.1-16). The Latin text, edited by Antonia Gransden, was published in Germany in 1963 (see *E.Cust.*) The MS. comprises 131 leaves of vellum, each about 10½in. x 7in. in size, and mostly covered with 26 lines of writing, in two columns, on each side.

Brother John probably did his work in Eynsham's *scriptorium* (its writing-rooms; see illustration 8), little studies, located in the quieter recesses of the establishment, and more suitable for concentration than the carrels, that is the cubicles set aside, in the cloister, for 'spiritual reading (*lectio divina*)'.

His concluding words, in the contemporary MS., have their own moving dignity:

> This is the end of the customary of the monks of Eynsham, written by Brother John of Wood Eaton, Eynsham monk, for the salvation of all who read it through and observe it well. Readers, pray for the writer. As the end of the Apocalypse has it, The grace of our Lord Jesus Christ be with you all. Amen[1]

(from the Latin of *E.Cust.*, ff.130f.).

His somewhat loose 'sprawly' Latin gives insights into many sides of medieval life. Colds, for example, and catarrh, and wheezy chests, must have been common in monks, as they moved about their large draughty quarters, often during the night. So the instructions for novices include the following:

> HOW TO BEHAVE WHEN EXPELLING PHLEGM, OR UNABLE TO STOP COUGHING . . ..
>
> When he has expelled phlegm, whether from his nose or his chest, he should behave with care and consideration, casting it in front or to one side or behind his back, and (so far as necessary) treading on what he casts. Otherwise he may make more sensitive spirits (*infirmis mentibus*) feel sick, or he may soil the garments of brethren who are bowed in prayer. This is the decent way to behave, not only in the church, but throughout the community . . .[2]
>
> If, however, he is unable to stop coughing, or is overwhelmed by excessive phlegm, then, lest he do hurt to sensitive spirits, he should go out of the company, together with his guardian, and wait awhile, until his trouble is relieved. But he should not presume to go out without permission or without his guardian. And, if this happens at night-time, he should kindle a lantern, when going out with his guardian, and bring it back, still alight, and put it out in the choir . . .

(from the Latin of *E.Cust.*, f.16).

And sometimes, but only with authority, and after many precautions, monks travelled outside their enclosed domain. That, of course, involved moral and spiritual dangers, as well as physical ones. Psalms, and other devotional material, are suggested, in considerable quantity. There is much reference to St. Julian the Hospitaller (of the *Golden Legend*), patron saint of ferrymen, innkeepers etc. And we can see the vital importance of healthy animals, carrying men and baggage securely. Here is a prayer:

> O God, who hast for his hospitality lifted up on high thy confessor, Blessed Julian, grant to us, we beseech thee, that by his merits and prayers we may find a hospice appropriate to our frailty and acceptable to thy majesty.
>
> O God, who hast by brute beasts provided solace for mankind, grant to us, we beseech thee, that what our human state cannot do without thou wilt not permit to perish from our service.
>
> May our everlasting guide look upon us, and in all places give us his angel to guard us: may he rule our souls, may he lift up our minds, may he direct our ways, may he bring our vows to fulfilment, may he plant in us holy thoughts, may he forgive what is past, may he amend what is present, may he control what

is to come, and may he think meet to bless us from heaven, even he who thought meet to redeem us on earth, our Lord Jesus Christ, who with the Father and the Holy Spirit liveth and reigneth, one God, for ever and ever. Amen

(from the Latin of *E.Cust.*, f.126; see Appendix 8, 1).

It is in the chapter prayers, however, that the link with Leofric and Godiva is stressed. All the daily business of the chapter meeting concluded with prayers, and all the prayers concluded with one for founders and benefactors. And, because times were changing, this Customary provided two alternatives, a traditional form and a revised one. And, because young novices were still coming from noble homes, where French was still their native speech, these two prayers (like others in the Customary, where it was important that even the youngest recruit should fully comprehend) were in French. Here is the whole passage, moving (as it does) from Latin to French, and back again:

(Latin) Next, if any stand in special need of absolution, as when prayer is made for the absolution of a departed member of the household, let such prayer be made now. Then let general prayer be offered, as follows:

(French) May God in his grace absolve our Lord Aethelmaer who founded this place, his wife, Earl Leofric, Lady Godiva, and all our other founders and benefactors, all the abbots and the monks of this house, our fathers, our mothers, our brothers, our sisters, all who have done good to us, and all those for whom we ought to pray, and who rest in us their hope, and all the souls whose bodies rest in this cemetery:

(Latin) May their souls, and the souls of all the faithful departed, by the mercy of God, rest in peace. Amen.

But, if anyone prefers to use the ancient and customary prayer for absolution, he shall pray thus (*qui autem secundum antiquam consuetudinem absolucionem facere maluerit, sic faciet*):

(French) May God in his grace absolve our Lord Aethelmaer, who founded this place, his wife, *labbe vel*, Abbot Columban, Abbot Walter, the other Walter, Abbot William, Abbot Godfrey, Abbot Robert, *et cetera*,[3] Earl Leofric, Lady Godiva, King Henry, Henry de Oxford, Hugh de Mortimer, Ralph de Chesney, Ralph Murdac, Walkelin Hareng, Lady Ida, Lady Matilda de Chesney, Master Nicholas, Geoffrey the Chamberlain,[4] *et cetera*, and all our brethren who have departed this life since this house was founded

(from the Latin of *E.Cust.*, ff.38f.).

The resounding list of Norman names rolled out in noble sequence. They must have meant much to those who knew their Eynsham past. But a younger generation was growing up. To them the names meant little. They preferred the newer prayer, and its more human and contemporary references. Old or young, however, none were allowed to forget Aethelmaer, Leofric, and Godiva (see illustrations 31 & 32 and Appendix 8, 2-3).

31. & 32. **Extracts from Eynsham Customary, 13th/early 14th centuries.** (*Left*) The more traditional of the two French prayers for founders and benefactors. *Bodl. MS. 435, f.38V.* (*Right*) A prayer in English, for use by monks and their staff when travelling outside their walls. The word *Anglice* appears in the margin. *Id., f.126R.*

Notes

1. See Rev. 22, 21.
2. The instruction appears to reflect time-honoured procedures — in the absence of handker-
chieves: a finger, a thumb, a squeeze, and a throw . . .
3. Columban sounds like Columban of Eynsham (in 1086), Stow (in 1091), and perhaps Eynsham
again (as late as in 1109). Abbot Robert (1197-1208) was followed, in 1213, by Abbot Adam,
who was deposed in 1228. The absence of Adam's name from this prayer suggests that he was
still alive, in retirement, when it reached the form given in the Customary.
4. See *E.Cust.*, p.77, footnote, for these names.

Part Four

Great Occasions

Reluctant bishop

Years came, years went, and Eynsham abbey pottered on — saying its prayers, running its village, managing its estates, going its undramatic way — until, in 1538, its doors were closed for ever, and its buildings fell apart. During those centuries, and especially at first, there were just a few exciting moments. This essay will now touch upon some of them.

The first is in the year 1186. From 25 May to 2 June King Henry II and his council met daily in Eynsham abbey. The setting was probably the nave of the great Romanesque church, completed not so long ago. Day by day the King and his entourage rode over from his palace at Woodstock. Baldwin, archbishop of Canterbury, was housed in the abbey itself, probably in the abbot's lodging. The others — bishops, abbots, and lay barons — must have stayed with the King, or in the abbey, or with notabilities nearby. The mass of staff — chaplains, clerks, guards, cooks, grooms, valets, and so on — can be imagined. The expense to the abbey, and the administrative effort, must have been enormous. The very fact that the event could be staged at all at Eynsham shows how much the abbey had recovered its status.

The council had miscellaneous business, and amongst it the question of a new bishop for Lincoln. The huge diocese was sorely neglected, and in great need of sound leadership. It had been hurt by years of dispute between King and Church. There had been the murder of Archbishop Becket in 1170; four years later the King had done penance at his tomb. But in 1173 he had engineered the election of his illegitimate son, Geoffrey Plantagenet, to the see of Lincoln. The Church had resisted stoutly, and Geoffrey had never been consecrated, but it was not until 1182 that he had resigned. Then, in 1183, a good man went to Lincoln, Walter de Coutances, only to be translated to the archbishopric of Rouen, the senior see in Normandy, in the following year. The great rambling diocese of Lincoln was still in disarray.

By 1186 the King had another outstanding man in mind, and the canons of Lincoln had travelled down to Eynsham to discuss the affair and to make an election. The story of the council looks like a petty squabble about the correct venue for an episcopal election. Its hero, Hugh of Avalon, appears to be splitting hairs. In fact, all of them were handling a great and lasting issue: where lay the proper independence of the people, and especially of the Church and its leadership, from the King? In essence the question is with us still.

As part of his penance, in connection with Becket's death, the King had undertaken to found and endow new monasteries in England. One had been at

Witham in Somerset. It had become the first Charterhouse (that is, Carthusian monastery) in this country. But neither of its first two priors had been very successful. Carthusians were reformed Benedictines, so stern, so austere, so much engaged in solitary prayer and meditation and study in their cells, that they made no quick appeal. Then it was that the King discovered Hugh of Avalon, and brought him over from Burgundy to England, and saw to it that he was made prior of Witham. Soon the wilting little house began to grow and flourish. And, by 1186, the King felt sure that Hugh was the man for the see of Lincoln.

The story of his election comes from the pen of an Eynsham monk, named Adam. He had already written the *Vision of the Monk of Eynsham*, an account of a mystic experience that had befallen his younger brother, Edmund, also an Eynsham monk. Soon after 1212 he was to write the *Life of St. Hugh*.

It seems that Adam had come into the Eynsham cloister, when quite young, from an Oxford family. He was probably present, a shrewd and amused observer, when Hugh's election took place. Later, he became subprior of Eynsham, perhaps prior, later still abbot. Between 1197 and 1200, the last three years of Bishop Hugh's life, Adam was with him, as his chaplain and intimate companion. No one could know his subject better, and Adam was a well-read man, with a gifted pen. (For Carthusians and St. Hugh, see *Knowles 1963*, pp.375-91, *Farmer 1985*, *Vita Hugonis 1864* & *1985*, *Ger. Wales*, pp.39-42, 67ff., 89ff., and *The Metrical Life of Saint Hugh*, ed. C. Garton, Lincoln Cathl., 1986.) Here is his story about Eynsham in 1186:

Of Hugh's election as bishop, and of the wide extent of the diocese of Lincoln.
After the preferment of that godly man, Walter, bishop of Lincoln, to the archbishopric of Rouen, Henry II, King of England, held a council at Eynsham. It went on for almost eight days without a break: it dealt with sundry matters of state: the bishops and magnates of the land were there. In that same abbey, as guests during the council, there were Baldwin, of holy memory, archbishop of Canterbury,[1] and some of his suffragans.[2] Day by day the King arrived there in the morning, and at the close of the discussion returned to his palace at Woodstock. During the council at Eynsham the elections of certain bishops and abbots were held. The canons of Lincoln had also come down to elect their bishop, or perhaps rather to receive their bishop, chosen from on high (*electuri, seu potius suscepturi episcopum coelitus electum*).

Now at that time some of the leading figures of that church, not a few of them in fact, were bound up with the intrigues and values of palaces. They were famed in matters secular, mighty in their store of worldly learning, not to say worldly riches. A number of them were of the opinion that no bishopric, however ample, was too great for greatness like theirs. And small wonder, since they were loaded up with ampler revenues than any bishopric, however huge. Some of them indeed, whether for the sake of the good work of a bishop (as the apostle would have it), or for the sake of the glory, honour and power of a bishop (as worldly ambition might judge), would by no means have refused to be bishops, if there had been someone there to compel them.

But the Lord was holding the King's heart in his hand, and bending it where he willed: and the archbishop of Canterbury, and some other men of God, were in agreement: but especially Reginald, bishop of Bath, mentioned above, was pressing hard: and thus the King strove to see that an adequate pastor was provided for the care of so many of the Lord's sheep. For that diocese contains eight archdeaconries, and is spread through nine, or even more, shires: it embraces very great cities, and countless people: and it is hard to find another diocese which is larger or more populous. What is more, that splendid see had only recently been empty for about 18 years, two and a half of them since the last bishop had been translated, and 15 of them before he had been consecrated. That field of the Lord had lain uncultivated for so many years that it was small wonder that it was sick with the brambles of wickedness, dense and rank with seeds of abuse.

Now the King was aware that the blame for such great ill was being laid at his own door: for it was obvious that he had himself caused the harmful vacancy. So he strove with all his might to make good the long neglect of cultivation by the appointment of a vigorous and outstanding cultivator now.

Meanwhile those canons were struggling on in vain: they could not agree on a choice: it was commonly said that each one of them, deep down in his heart, was only wanting his own elevation. Many counselled them, and indeed pressed the case, that they should try to get hold of the prior of Witham as their pastor. His goodness, they said, was beyond compare. He was a man of holiness. His common sense, his approachability, his devotion to monasticism, were lauded to the skies. It was said indeed that every excellence of character, the very fourfoldness of all virtues (*omnis virtutum quadratura*), was compacted together in that one man. No one, cried many, with a single voice, could be more worthy of that high-priesthood than he.

At first, when they heard all this, you could see something like a shiver of horror spread amongst those men. And small wonder, for these men felt for fleshly things. Even in the cause of God, they sought after the things of men rather than those of God. In the end they began to argue that that man's practice of religion, his ways of worship, and his manner of speech, were clean contrary to their own, and utterly unfamiliar. And they were even laughing him to scorn (*non sine derisionis cachinno*). Fortunately for them, however, this laughter of theirs was met with laughter, wholesome laughter, by the wiser of those present. And they themselves (to the great glory of all the holy church of God, as well as of their own church) suddenly changed their minds, and at length with one accord elected the man whom at first they had childishly despised. And so the man chosen by the Lord from all eternity was at God's appointed time chosen also by men. Those who knew him gave thanks: those who knew nothing about him marvelled: and one and all conjoined in high-sounding praise to God the Lord.

Of Hugh's definition of the places in which the election of a bishop ought and ought not to be held. And how he set aside his own election, because it had not been held in the chapter-house at Lincoln.

So then the clergy were asking for this man, and the King approved, and the magnates and the bishops acclaimed the choice: very soon his election was confirmed by the archbishop. Meanwhile the man himself was tucked away in his cell (*ipso interim in sua eremo latente*). He was completely unaware of what was being settled about him in that far-away council. But from that very place where the election was held some of the senior electors were sent off to him. In hope they were already his sons and his clergy. They carried with them the mandate of the lord archbishop, as well as letters from the King. Coming to him, they gave an account of his call to higher office. He heard them out, and examined the letters they had brought. These said that he should present himself, with all speed, to the King and the archbishop, and there deal with the business of his consecration. Here is the reply which he gave forthwith to what he heard and read.

'It is not surprising that the lord archbishop or even our lord the King, would be glad to see someone like me advanced to higher office, though I am unworthy of such an honour, and far unequal to so great a burden. For who can doubt that it would please our lord the King to see men, whom he has himself brought here from distant parts for the advancement of religion, flourish and prosper in his kingdom? And it is just so with the lord archbishop of Canterbury: he is now almost alone amongst the bishops of this land in favouring the religious habit: who can be ignorant of his prayer for men trained and disciplined in the regular life as colleagues in his pastoral office and ministry?

'But neither their prayers nor their desires should prevail to warp your judgement. Yours is the duty to elect your ruler freely. And, what is more, it is you who will have to put up with his disciplines and his character. Except therefore when some disastrous difference or division occurs (*dummodo schismatis vel alterius non interveniat noxa discriminis*), the election of the ruler of a church ought to be held in the chapter-house of that same church, and not in a royal palace, nor yet an episcopal council. So be quite clear about my humble opinion. You are to know that I hold that whatever has been done about this particular election is utterly null and void. Consider as undone whatever a certain section of your assembly is thought to have achieved in this matter. Wend your way back to your own church, going with the blessing of God. Supported there by the counsel and aid of the Holy Spirit, set in motion a solemn and canonical election of your pastor. And, that you may do this worthily, hold before your eyes the will, the grace, the favour, not of the King, nor yet of a bishop, nor of any man soever, but of God Almighty alone. Carry back no other message from this small man. Go therefore, and may the good angel of the Lord keep you company.'

He persisted in this way of thinking. For such a business no manner of argument could induce him to present himself, either to the King or to the archbishop. So they went back with all speed to those who had sent them. They were wondrously inspired by all that they had heard from him and seen around him. And not they only, but all who heard, were astounded, and mightily made glad. And one and all they praised and magnified his integrity of mind, his wisdom exceeding strong, his lively counsel, and his zeal for the liberty of the church.

How he was unwilling to agree to his election without the authority of the prior of the Grande Chartreuse, even after he had been duly elected in the chapter-house of Lincoln.

Tidings of this were carried to the notice of the chapter of Lincoln. And the whole college was the more thankful that its elect had already shown an earnest of his future vigour, and firstfruits of his great qualities. And those who before were grumbling that they had been badly led, not to say manipulated, into electing as their ruler and lord a man whose savage nature, and harsh and rustic ways, they dreaded, now turned right about. They had discovered the strength of his goodness and wisdom. They made haste to hold a new election, and to choose him again, and to beg earnestly that he would deign to undertake to minister to their pastoral care. Messengers were sent again, more in number than the first, with letters from the chapter, as well as from King and archbishop. Everyone thought that the business was now settled. He could have no other excuse for delay. Representatives therefore, fully instructed, light of heart, and joyful, came to him. Now that blessed man had foreseen from long ago that at some or other time God would lead him to the office of a bishop: he was sad therefore that what could not be avoided was at last happening: and with all that was in him he wanted it not to happen too quickly.

So he looked at the letters which the messengers brought, and listened to what they had to say, and spoke as follows:

'It is very remarkable that men as wise as you, and so cultured, should so much want a rustic and uncultured man like me (*me hominem incultum et idiotam tantopere solicitatis*), and be at pains to take from me the solitude and quiet, which have been my familiar friends from my youth up, and labour to plunge me into public gatherings and tangled business, things which are quite foreign to my experience. Since it is plain, however, that the arguments I have put forward cannot prevail to make you change your minds, know this for certain. The goal for which you strive is not in my power to assist. I cannot conceal from you that I am a man set under another's authority. You are to know that I am a monk, subject to the decisions of my prior, and bound to obedience until my dying day. In all places and at all times I am tied to the bidding of him who sent me to these lands. The care of this house has been entrusted to me by my superior. There can be no excuse for me to set it aside and undertake the governance of any other house or church whatsoever. My lord of Canterbury is indeed primate and head of the English church, subject only to the supreme pontiff: but in matters of this kind another stands between us. Either, therefore, you must desist from pressing this request upon me, or you must undertake the wearisome and burdensome journey to the Grande Chartreuse. For without the direct command of our prior no man shall put so heavy a load upon my shoulders.'

How representatives were sent off to the Grande Chartreuse, to request that Hugh should be granted to the church which had invited him . . .

Having received this response, and seeing that nothing whatever would make him change his mind, they went back. They were sad because they had not done the business for which they came: but they were glad, because they had had no small evidence of the outstanding determination and the sterling qualities of their future pastor. So then (to cut a long story short) distinguished representatives were sent, with all haste, to the Grande Chartreuse. Arrived there, they presented the petition of the church of Lincoln, and the King's plea, and the archbishop's counsel: they did so both in word and in writing. As was due, they were honourably received, and favourably heard to the end. Then they hurried back, bringing to Hugh the command of the prior and the brethren that from now on he should give canonical obedience to my lord of Canterbury, and in the present matter obey him humbly. He should set aside all hesitation and delay, and accept that yoke which the Lord God was clearly laying upon him . . .

(from the Latin of *Vita Hugonis 1864*, pp.102-9).

Notes

1. Baldwin had been an archdeacon, in the diocese of Exeter, then a Cistercian monk at Ford, in Devon, then abbot there, next bishop of Worcester, and finally archbishop of Canterbury (1185-90). For his mixed repute, see *Knowles 1963*, pp.316ff., as well as his special place in the *Vision of the Monk of Eynsham*, ch.36 (see *E.C.*, vol.2, pp.342-5). In 1190, whilst on Crusade, he died at Acre. For an excellent summary of his life and work, see C. Holdsworth, in *Friends of Lambeth Library Annual Report*, 1989.
2. In this usage the term 'suffragans' embraces all other bishops in the province of Canterbury.

Purgatory unveiled

It was 10 years after Hugh's election, when Eynsham abbey burst into history again. The occasion was a vision, seen there by a young monk, named Edmund. The story was put into writing by his brother Adam, the same Adam who was later to write the *Life of St. Hugh.* News of the event spread rapidly across Europe, and may even have affected Dante. When printing began in London, one of its earliest products was an English translation of the *Vision* (see illustrations 33 and 34).

Adam's account has all the vividness of an eyewitness. But we must, of course, remember that its pictures had first been shaped and moulded by Edmund's mind, and then by Adam's, and that (when he came to write it) Adam was the constant associate of Bishop Hugh, and inevitably much influenced by him.

Edmund had been ill for some 15 months, and growing steadily weaker. By Holy Week in 1196 his condition seemed hopeless. On the Wednesday and Thursday, however, he rallied, and was able to join the common worship, and even to make his confession. But early on Good Friday morning he lapsed into unconsciousness, and remained so (seemingly almost dead) until late on Easter Even. Then, to everyone's astonishment, he came back to life, and piece by piece the others probed his experience.

During those long hours he had been led away by St. Nicholas, and conducted by him around the next world. For much of the journey they traversed purgatory. Edmund saw, and met, and talked with, many many souls there. They were at various stages in their cleansing pains. At the end, though only briefly, Edmund had come to the very gates of paradise, and entered in, and glimpsed its wondrous glories. Then he had returned to tell the tale.

Attempts have been made to identify this Edmund with Edmund Rich of Abingdon, future archbishop of Canterbury, and in due course to be canonized. And medieval handwriting has caused confusion between Eynsham abbey and Evesham abbey. It seems likely, however, that Edmund of Eynsham was in fact the monk in question.

In the sundry sections of purgatory, he had had a remarkable series of encounters, some with groups, others with individuals. Of some he had personal and intimate knowledge, for he had known them in Oxford or in Eynsham. Some indeed had only died recently, and were newly experiencing their purgatorial disciplines. They craved his prayers, and sent urgent warnings to those who were still alive. Thumbnail sketches follow one another. Many contemporaries would recognize them, and perhaps take note, and ponder, and light a candle for them, and amend their own ways.

33. & 34. **The Vision of the Monk of Eynsham.**
English translation, printed by William de Machlinia in
London in c.1483. (*Left*) The Prologue. *Bodl. Auct. 1.
Q.5.28, f.2R.* (*Below*) Ch. 18: reaching Paradise. *Id., f.62R.*

❡ The prologe of this reuelacion

He reuelacion that foloweth þͭ
in this boke treteth how a certeyn de=
uoute person the whiche was a monke
in the abbey of Euisßamme was rapte
in spirite by the wille of god and lade by the hand
of seint Nicholas the space of . ii . dayes and . ii .
nyghtes to see and knowe the peynys of purgato=
rye and the ioyys of paradyse and in what state
the sowlis ware that ware in purgatorye and also
in paradyse . Sothly in bothe this placis þe sawe ʒ
knewe many persons bothe men ʒ woomen the whi=
che þe knewe welle before when they lyued in thes
worlde and spake with þͫ there mowthe to mowth
in bothe the placys as þe founde þͫ as hit folowith
wele aftir in this boke . This reuelacion was not
shewede to hym only for hym butte also for the con=
fort and pfetyng of all cristen peuŗlle that none
man shulde doubte or mystruste of anothir life and
worlde the whiche euery man and woman moste go
to ʒ lyke as they deserue here in this worlde by here
lyuyng so there to be rewardyd . And as for the
trowithe of this reuelacyon no man noithͫ woomaͳ
ought to doubte in any wise ✛ for and a man wele
rede and vndirstonde the begynnyng with the ending
he shalle so largely see hit approued in grete myra=
clis by almyghty god shewed vnto the same . per=
son that same tyme that alle resons and moeyons
of infidelite the whiche risith ofte tymes of mannis

---

ageyne euerichon to her owne places with ioy and
gladnes Treuly þ folowed euimore my duke ʒ lo=
disman sent Nicholas that went forthe farthir and
farther repletyd now with grete ioye ʒ gladnes a=
monge the ful brighte ʒ light mansyons of blessid
sowlys . ʒ the whitnes of hͤ þͭ were here i this pla
ce ʒ the swetnes of sauer ʒ also the melodye of syn=
gyng laudes to god wes iestymable ʒ onethe to ma
nys vndirstondeng credeble

❡ Of the entryng of the gate of paradyse and of the ioy that appered withinforth   ❡ Ca 18

F   Ourthermore nowe whenne we were paste all
              these placys ʒ sightes aforeseyd ʒ had gone
a good space more inward ʒ euer grew to vs more
ʒ more ioye ʒ feyernes of placys . also at the laste
we sawe aferre a ful glorious walle of crystal bope
heythe no man might see . and lenthe no man might
asidͬ . ʒ when we came theder þ sawe within forthe
a ful feyre brighte shenyng gate ʒ stod opyn sa=
ue hit was signed ʒ leide ouer with a crosse Treuly
theder came flockemele the multytude of the blessed
sowlys that were next to hyt . and wold cum in at
that feyre gate The crosse was sette in the myddys
of that gate . and nowe sche was lyfte vpe an hye
and so gaue to hem that came theder an opyn and
a fre entryng . and afterwarde sche was leityn do
ne ageyne . and so spared other oute that wold ha
ue comen in But howe ioyful they were that wente

There was Baldwin, archbishop of Canterbury, whom we have already met at Eynsham in 1186. There was an alcoholic goldsmith from Oxford, and an abbess of Godstow, and King Henry II himself, all jumbled together in levelling misery, just as you see them in medieval wall paintings. There was a group of three bishops, and a band of poisoners and abortionists, and another of homosexuals. There were monks and nuns who had broken their vows; there was a crusader who had turned back; there was a knight who was too fond of hawking; there was a sacrist who was careless about his lights, and so on. Murderers, perjurers, slanderers, were all there.[1] Some were in need of little treatment, others of much. All of them (at least in hope) were moving steadily through their sufferings to that paradise, where at last the pure in heart would see God. Meanwhile vicious demons would come and go, darting in and out, tormenting them as they travelled.

One of those victims is of special consequence for our Eynsham story. He was Godfrey, abbot of Eynsham for no less than 44 years, right through the crucial period from 1150/1 to 1195.[2] So long a reign, at such a formative time, must have left an indelible mark upon Eynsham tradition and personnel. This was the period of massive building, and of expanding business enterprise, at Eynsham. Standards of worship and qualities of morale were being established. Generations in any community overlap, and a spirit once formed tends to survive. Godfrey's influence must have permeated everywhere, touching young and old for almost half a century. And doubtless it was Abbot Godfrey who began the gathering of records which was the basis of the Eynsham cartulary.

It is the more sad to learn (if the *Vision* has substance) that he was a man of dubious qualities. Growing up in the cloister from early boyhood, he had but little strength of character for ruling his near contemporaries. He was a man of this world, moving more easily with magnates than with God. Here is how Edmund found him:

Concerning those whom the monk saw in the first place of torment.
There was the head of a certain religious house, and I had known him well. To his own great cost, as also to his flock's, he had held his charge of souls too long. And now at last, this very year, the kindly hand of death had set him free (*mortis benefitio tandem absolutus*).

And I was aware that much had already been written about his ways, whether as man or pastor, and that those who had read took warning and were helped. And for this, it seems, he had himself merited some easing of his pain, and likewise certain comfort. But I have no wish to weary my reader: so I shall not tarry with what I had before seen and heard about this man and some others.

I recognized him amongst the first to whom we came within that place of pain. There he was, with the very first we saw. And great indeed were his torments. And now in fire, now in foulest pools, seething alike with sulphur and with pitch, he passed through grievous suffering. And his cheeks were wan, and his face distraught.

And seeing me, forthwith he spoke, and hailed me in a gentle voice, and suppliant: and in return I greeted him, and moved with deep compassion spoke with him, and he with me.

I asked him of his sufferings. Why such, and why so great? Were they shaped, I said, by the sins of youth? He had embarked upon that sacred rule of life, when yet a boy (*ordinis sacri, quem in infantia susceperat*). Was it then perchance that he had been neglectful?

But he made reply, 'My pains are hard indeed, and most bitter. And truly I have myself offended much. But these my present torments spring from the sins and wicked deeds of those who were my subjects, rather than from my own.[3]

'Much as I sinned, great as is the punishment due, I could endure all, and with a quiet mind. For with frequent confession, and with faithful penance, and with prayers ofttimes, and much else, I had schooled myself to redeem my sins and to chastise.

'And yet, from out of all those sins, there is one that does oppress me still. It was my undue concern for my own kindred. For some of them, and they unworthy men, I secured a benefice in the church. To all of them I made large gifts from out the goods of the church I was serving. And that was very wrong. Yet, now that I am in this strait, not one of them cares one jot.

'And there is another love, which has wrought chief harm upon me. And that was pride of place, and greed of honour, and care for the favour of men. And that my fault is laid to my account. But also now are laid the faults of those whose sin I caused. And now, unless God pities me, that pain can reach nor bound nor end. For such was my lust for honour, such my greed, so great my fear of losing it, that the eyes of my heart grew blind. And I let loose the reins of discipline: and, just as if my eyes were shut, my subjects had their way. Whatever they pleased, whatever they wanted, that they could enjoy. And all of that, lest, feeling the strength of my hand opposed to their frivolities, they might seek to undermine my prelacy.

'And what is more, the men who were sound, and full of zeal, and burning with love for our way of life — these men I did not help at all. Nor did I even take their side. Indeed (and this was exceeding shameful) I used to go with those who envied them. I would in secret decry their ways, and favour those who broke our holy vows. And this was most damnable. In part my own frivolity led me thus, in part the pretext of my own authority. For my custom was also to devise and show some empty foolish things. And I would wander idly amongst the seculars. What was right for them was right for me.

'And that leniency of mine, cruel as it was, was abused by some of them. They went on to undertake deeds cursed and unspeakably wicked (*execranda et nefanda*). And for this also I am desperately tormented. For I knew full well, and disapproved, yet for empty fear dissimulated. And some of them went forward in their impudence and their corruptions, and turned from worse to worse. And some indeed, whilst I was yet alive, met death, still persisting in their wicked ways, and thus they perished. And others, yet alive, but busied in the works of death, are growing worse. And this I fear: unending sin does kindle inextinguishable fires not only for themselves, but me.

'And thus it is, that from that hour when I left the flesh, I have endured pain unspeakable. And yet, what then I bore seems light indeed, compared with what now I suffer. And that first day was easier far than all that have come thereafter. For those evil customs of theirs outlive my death, yet were caused by my neglect. And therefore, every time they sin, the torments of my punishment increase.

'And some of them have committed deeds most hateful to their God, and most detestable to men, deeds surpassing all their other sins, deeds which it is even wrong to name (*in crimine singulariter odibili deo et omnibus hominibus detestabili, quod nec nominare licet*): and some have gone already to destruction: and some live on, yet ever deeper in their wickedness: and of those deeds I knew, yet stayed my hand: and so I dread that, as they sin the more, my torment will increase the more: until perhaps I have to bear that fearful stench by which such sinners groan. For of all the pains that guilty sinners bear I know that none is worse. And, whenever those I left behind do something very damnable, from them to me come demons hurrying, and bringing deep reproach and insult vile, and loading me with torments fresh, and more than ever cruel.'

He spoke of sins done after he had died: he knew the day, the place, the hour: he knew the person, and his sin: and told me much concerning many: as soon, he said, as his disciples did those things, then Satan's angels brought reproach, and ever added to his pains.

Report, however, tells that, ere he died, some friends and brethren, in that same community, afire with zeal for righteousness, burning for true religion, took pains to remove indiscipline, and to restore due order in all its wholeness. And this I knew: and so I said to him:

'Such dreadful tidings come to you about the dwellers in that place. How then does rumour spread so far and wide that, ere your term in that your house, a mighty reformation came to pass?'

But he replied, 'I know that what you tell is very true: nor is it false that customs there have grown more correct, and more commendable. But none the less the ills themselves still call for punishment of me. No fruit is due to me, and no reward, for that amendment of the house, but only torment, ever more and more. For I was hostile to their reforms, and hindered them: and obstructed all they did, and all they tried to do. Unwisdom went before my feet: and negligence and sinfulness pressed on behind: and I was wrapped in that confusion (Scripture says) which leads the way to sin. I feared lest all the crowd might hear of shameful things: and blushed at manifest correction of what, when uncorrected, caused no blush. And such was my obstructiveness in certain things, that plants from vilest seed grew strong: so much that now I think the sinners past constraint: and those my deeds (if God's almighty power come not to aid his servants who oppose their sins) may bring to nought the rumoured reformation there. Oh, woe is me! Why ever did I trust the counsels of such men? Woe, that I lifted such so high, and thus offended God the King, whilst all the field I left to them, that they and their accomplices might work whatever wickedness they willed!

'And to those four men (whose names he uttered now) you may tell my words, that in the pit of hell eternal pains abide for them, pains utterly inexpressible: unless for all their wicked deeds and plans, by which they brought to nought themselves and all who followed them, they offer swift and worthy satisfaction to their God. And, truth to say, if ever by their toiling how they will they come by satisfaction to that last assize, their total offering will be modest still, when set against such vast and such enduring wickedness, by which they make me perilled with the last calamity, and almost all my house is done away by manifold iniquity. For at their nod I let them have their way, scarce ever ready to restrain.

'And what is worse, the prayers and intercessions due to me, the masses and the psalms they owe, scarce any of the congregation pay in full: and many indeed, for whom I suffer pains the most, do not a whit of all those things.

'And so, for all those ills, my present grief, my dread of things to come, they hem me in on every side.'

Such was his situation: such I saw: and so he spoke with me

(from the Latin of *E.C.*, vol.2, pp.330-4) (see Appendix 9).

Notes

1. These examples have been drawn from chs. 36, 19-23, 44, 41, 35, 38, 25, 40, 32, 33, 47, 37 of the *Vision*, and in that order.
2. For Abbot Godfrey and his cronies, see *E.C.*, vol. 1, pp.xvf.
3. We are reminded of Matt. 18, 7, 'Woe unto the world because of offences! For it must needs be that offences come: but woe to that man by whom the offence cometh!'

Bishop versus King

In theory Benedictine abbots were elected by the community they were to rule, or, failing general agreement, by some sort of sub-committee:

> When an abbot is to be appointed, the following considerations should always be borne in mind. Either he should be the man chosen unanimously by the whole community, acting together in the fear of God, or, failing such consensus, by a section of the community, even a very small section, which is accounted to have a more balanced judgement (*sive etiam pars quamvis parva congregationis saniore consilio*)

(from the Latin text of *RB 1980*, p.280).

In practice other forces came into the discussion, and were often dominant.

Abbots, like bishops, were ecclesiastical barons, controlling substantial lands and dues. Their identity, their personal qualities, their capabilities, mattered greatly to the King and his advisers, as well as to the Church at large (see *Knowles 1963*, pp.395-401).

In Eynsham's case there was a further complication. Like Selby in Yorkshire, it was a bishop's *Eigenkloster*, 'own monastery'. Elsewhere the King conferred upon a new abbot his 'temporalities', that is, his lands and dues, his power and wealth in this world, the means to maintain his household and to look after his guests. And, when there was a vacancy in an abbacy, those temporalities reverted (for the time being) to the King, and were later conferred upon the next abbot. Eynsham abbey, however, was entirely episcopal property. The bishop of Lincoln conferred the temporalities, and also held them during vacancies. Naturally enough, Kings did not like this limitation of their authority and wealth.

Somewhat surprisingly it was William II who had given this privilege to Lincoln. That was in 1091, when Eynsham was merged with Stow at Stow (see E5, in ch.15, above). In 1109, when Eynsham abbey re-appeared at Eynsham, Henry I had maintained the special arrangement (see E7, in ch.17, above). The whole matter came to a head in 1195, when, after his long and unsatisfactory reign of 44 years, Abbot Godfrey died. It was clear that Eynsham needed a particularly good successor. Here, if anywhere, was a chance for Bishop Hugh to defend the proper rights of the Church, including his own peculiar rights at Eynsham.

The passage translated below tells how the bishop took the King of England to the King's own courts, and won his case. It was decided that Eynsham abbey was in truth a bishop's *Eigenkloster*. Armed with that settlement, Bishop Hugh came down to Eynsham abbey in person, in 1197, and spent a week there, whilst the monks chose their abbot. Doubtless he influenced them, but the final choice was theirs. Then he went back to Lincoln, and there the new abbot, Robert, formerly prior of Dover, was blessed in the cathedral-church. How wise it was to introduce new blood! The passage ends with a glowing scene, where Hugh's 'own monks' sit down to feast at Lincoln, cheek by jowl with Hugh's 'own secular canons'. Such brotherly accord between regular and secular clergy was somewhat rare. The account is accordingly both rapturous and poetic.

With what sweat and toil (multo sudore*) Hugh maintained his right of patronage at Eynsham abbey against the King of England himself, and in the King's own court.*

The snare of the hunters was broken, and the saint delivered: God had decreed it. But wicked men, however often beaten back, knew not to lie still: for envy was their way, and malice their skill. So they strewed fresh traps about, and toiled away at new devices: and as the saint went on his way, single of heart, they dug more tunnels of deceit. For now they tried to undermine his church's ancient rights, and to do them no small harm.

Ever since the Normans had come to England, and subdued it by right of battle, the church of Lincoln had exercised the patronage of Eynsham abbey without a single break. That was for 100 years and more. And now some of these bad men strove to snatch that privilege away. In point of fact Remigius, that same bishop of blessed memory, who to his great glory soon after the Conquest founded the cathedral-church of Lincoln, had also re-established Eynsham abbey. It had been laid waste at the Conquest, and its brethren had fled away, frightened of the enemy. At its re-establishment William the Conqueror, of famous memory, had confirmed it as the bishop's own abbey, his by royal authority.[1] No person, be they clerical or lay, excepting only the bishop of Lincoln and his successors, might presume to claim any dominion over it whatsoever.

Now it so happened that, in the tenth year of Blessed Hugh's episcopate, a certain venerable ruler and abbot of this abbey departed to the Lord. His name was Godfrey.[2] He is known to have presided over that same house for some 44 years, right from the days of King Stephen to the later years of King Richard, son of King Henry. Hearing of the abbot's death the bishop followed traditional practice, and sent one of his clergy there. That man was to receive the custody of the abbey on behalf of the bishop, and to cooperate with the brethren there, in taking diligent care of abbey-business, until such time as a canonical election might be held and a new abbot appointed. Those, however, who were responsible for the King's interests in England made a vigorous attempt to deprive the bishop of his rights. They disputed his custody of the vacant abbey, as well as his lawful right to appoint the next abbot (*tam vacantis custodiam abbatiae, quam substituendi abbatis debitam facultatem*). The King himself, you should know, was over the water at that time, at war against the King of France.

Upon this, a number of level-headed men, honest friends of the bishop, did their best to persuade him not to swim against the tide (as the saying goes): his arms would not be strong enough: he would wear himself out for nothing: his opponents were so numerous, so powerful, that his efforts would be in vain. What was more, Henry, the King's father, had made a decree, which applied to every abbey in his kingdom: all of them were to remain in his gift (*generali constitutione decrevisse, ut universae regni sui abbatiae in sua manerent donatione*). It would be unlikely, they judged, that the son would go against his father's decree, especially as in many matters he seemed to be even more tenacious than his father. He would not be likely to let the bishop rejoice in such a privilege, even if it had been granted in his predecessors' times. The business, they advised, would be very troublesome: its benefits would be minimal, its risks innumerable: in no way ought it to be attempted. And, even if their labours bore fruit, it was questionable whether the fruit would be proportional to the labour. They could foresee huge expense in every direction: the bishop, and his friends also, would be heavily involved in it: that was plain: there was virtually no hope of success: and, even if they got what they wanted, would it really be of much value?

That was the tenor of their advice. Hugh, however, was a man of singular confidence and astonishing judgement. He replied forthwith, 'God forbid that any mortal man should presume to make a decree, which could deprive both God and the most blessed Queen of heaven of what is theirs! Even if such a law were just, it could only shape things to come. It would not tear asunder earlier decisions. Which of my predecessors would have subscribed to a decree, by whose sole authority he could be justly deprived of what he had till then possessed? God forbid that the decree of any lay person soever should infringe the privileged liberty of the church! May it never befall that, in fear of any power, or dread of any difficulty, I should (so far as in me lies) permit the rights of my lady, the church, to perish! Shame enough if we do not increase the dignities and freedoms of holy church, things won by our fathers, things defended by men of old! A diligent steward should add to them, and pass them on in better shape. How shameful then, if his rule is so unprofitable, so slothful, so idle, that they decrease, and wither, and perish!'

Such was his cause: and he pursued it ceaselessly for two years and a half: he spared no expense, nor yet the sweat of his own brow. Now he was assuring the special liberty of Eynsham abbey: now he was watchful for the rights of his see. He fought on at his case, both this side of the sea, and that: he fought it against the King himself: he fought it against all sorts of crafty and underhand adversaries: he refused to yield. And at the last, by the favour of the Lord God, he gained a famous victory. The rights which his predecessors had exercised in that monastery were recognized: upon the oath of 24 trustworthy men, half of them clergy, half laymen, those rights were determined: judgement was passed, in the King's own court, that the patronage of that same abbey was his. Thus the custody of the vacant abbey was restored to him, as also complete and absolute authority to appoint the abbot (*hinc ei restituitur abbatiae vacantis custodia, praeficiendi quoque abbatis jurisdictio plena et absoluta*).

Then he went to Eynsham abbey, in his own person, and for eight days he stayed there with the brethren of the place. He was like the most loving of fathers with the dearest of his children: he went in and out with them: he ate and drank with them in their common refectory: he refreshed them generously with the wine of his pleasantness and the good fare of his largeness of heart. And at his command, whilst he was there, they met together, and put in train the choice of the next abbot. At the close of the week, abbots from nearby, and other men of religion, were called together: and the name chosen by the monks was put before the bishop, and by the bishop solemnly confirmed. And when all was rightly done, that splendid pastor set forth for Lincoln.

There, in the cathedral-church, the abbot-elect of Eynsham received the sacred blessing of the bishop, and was with all due honour elevated to the abbacy: and all thought well: and all were glad. And a solemn banquet was arranged: and there was the bishop, sitting with his cathedral-clergy, as also with his abbot and his monks: of either cohort he was their noble general: and he sat in their midst, rejoicing wondrously and exulting in the Lord, for that like the most high shepherd, the good shepherd himself, he had brought in other sheep, sheep from another fold, that those sheep and these be made one flock, and he of both one shepherd[3] for he had bound both cathedral-church and abbey to himself, that both should be for ever one. He also presented to the new abbot a pastoral staff, beauteously inlaid with silver and ivory, and with it a great and noble chalice. And the place, now firmly committed to his authority, he enlarged with yet further benefactions and adorned with yet more gifts: and with ever-fatherly affection he loved and cherished both his abbot and the flock now subject to him

(from the Latin of *Vita Hugonis 1864*, pp.188-92).

Notes

1. Nothing in Eynsham's cartulary carries their *Eigenkloster* status back to William I. It would not have been in character for him to grant it, and the Eynsham/Stow plans attributed to him (see E3, in ch.14 above) appear to exclude it. On the other hand, a somewhat untrustworthy Lincoln text (see L3/3, and Stenton, ad loc.) seems to make William II say that, in making Stow a bishop's *Eigenkloster*, he was following in his father's footsteps. It is likely that both Hugh's biographer and the compiler behind L3/3 have been influenced by the later controversy, and have carried the rare privilege one reign too far back.
2. *Godefridus*: Godfrey, as in *E.C.*, vol.1, pp.xvf. & *H.R.H.* 1972, p.49; cp. *O.D.E.C.N. 1950*; not Geoffrey, as *Vita Hugonis 1864*.
3. See John 10, 16.

The hanging of the clerks

Oxford university (*studium generale*) had grown rapidly during the 12th century. By the year 1209 it was said to contain about 3,000 teachers and students. Tensions between town and gown were inevitable, and they now reached breaking-point. The extraordinary events which followed were to affect Eynsham abbey until 1538, and the British exchequer until 1984.

Here is Anthony Wood's delightfully phrased account of the hanging of the clerks (*suspendium clericorum*) in 1209:

> A most unfortunate and unhappy accident fell out at Oxford, which was this. A certain Clerk, as he was recreating himself, killed by chance a woman: which being done, he fled away for fear of punishment, that he thought must necessarily follow. But the fact being soon spread throughout the Town, the Mayor and several Burghers made search after him, and having at length received intelligence in what Inn or Hall he was resident, made their repair thither, and finding three other Clerks laid hold on them, and though innocent of the fact, yet cast them into prison. After they had remained there certain days, King John (no great lover of the Clergy) being then in his Manor of Woodstock, commanded the said three (some say only two) Scholars to be led out of the Town, and there to be hanged by the neck 'in contempt of ecclesiastical liberty'. Whereupon the Scholars in the University being much displeased at this unworthy act, they, to the number of three thousand (as well Masters as Juniors) left Oxford, so that not one (as some say) remained behind, but either went some to Cambridge,[1] some to Reading, and others Maydestone in Kent, to make a farther progress in their studies
>
> (from A. Wood, ed. J. Gutch, *The History and Antiquities of the University of Oxford*, vol.1 (1792), p.182).

The accidental killing of the woman was bad enough. The mob-law which hanged the students was worse. But to church politicians of the day the 'contempt of ecclesiastical liberty' was almost worst.

Universities were, as yet, preserves of the Church. Many, perhaps most, of the students were in major or minor orders, and were therefore 'clerks (*clerici*)'. Others, it seems, were tonsured, and wore clerical dress, and counted as 'clerks'. All of them, if occasion arose, would be dealt with by church courts, rather than by those of the State; and such courts, supervised by the archdeacon and his staff, on behalf of the bishop, tended to be more lenient. What was more, the profits of justice, as well as the prestige and power, accrued to the Church. The Mayor of Oxford, therefore, and his colleagues, egged on by King John, had not only done injustice to guiltless students, but had offended the Church.

The immediate effect upon the town itself was catastrophic. Eynsham abbey must have suffered with the rest. Not only had it a group of small properties in the town, but, already perhaps, its own 'Schools', that is, a small residential and teaching hostel (*scholae*) for students.[2] When the whole university population packed up and went, so did all the trade they brought. And as the whole country was already at odds with the Pope, ministrations of grace were also in very short supply. Oxford became a special victim of the long-running dispute between our somewhat unprincipled King John and Innocent III, one of the most upright and powerful Popes that had been.

Time went by, but in the end the town had to capitulate, and to accept whatever penance might be imposed upon it. The Pope dispatched Nicholas, bishop of Tusculum, as his apostolic delegate. The verdict — costly, humiliating, picturesque, medieval — came in 1214. The Mayor and his fellow-bigwigs had to bite the dust. The man in the street must have chuckled.

The leading citizens had to go in absurd procession to each parish church in turn. They must go barefoot, and with garments stripped off, presumably barebacked, and carrying scourges in their hands (*depositis indumentis pedibusque nudis*; from *Matthew Paris*, vol.2, p.569, here based upon *Roger of Wendover*).[3] They could only go to one church each day. Arrived there, they would crave the parish priest for absolution, saying Psalm 51, with its repeated pleas for mercy.

Those responsible for the barbarous executions were to have the bodies of the students exhumed. Again they would go barefoot and half-stripped, and thus they would with due solemnity conduct the bodies for seemly burial in consecrated ground.

What was more, the town was to mend its ways in all treatment of students. Charges for board and lodging were to be curtailed and regulated, and there was to be special care for needy students.

It was that last item which was to affect Eynsham abbey for many years to come. The town agreed to pay one shilling per week (26s. paid half-yearly, a considerable sum) into the bishop's university funds. It was to be used for grants to poorer students. And, in addition, once a year, on 6 December, St. Nicholas' day, 100 of them were to be given a special feast of bread and ale, vegetables, and a portion of fish or meat (*in pane, et cervisia, potagio et uno ferculo piscium vel carnium*; see *Salter, Archives*, vol.1, pp.2ff.). Almost at once (if not at once) Eynsham abbey took over the payment of 52s., as also the provision of the feast. In the latter case it paid two pence per head to the selected 100 students, 16s. 8d. in all, in lieu of an actual meal.

The citizens of Oxford were thus delivered from their annual pantomime of concern, and doubtless they made it worth the abbey's while to relieve them of it.

In 1538, when the abbey was dissolved, the making of those payments, on behalf of the town of Oxford, fell to the King, and in due course to the British exchequer. It was only in 1984 that the whole affair was finally tidied away and swept under the carpet.[4] Here is what Eynsham abbey undertook:

> ADAM, by the grace of God abbot of Eynsham, and the community of that same place: to all Christ's faithful people to whom this present writing comes: greeting in the Lord.

Be it known to all of you that, forasmuch as the citizens of Oxford had sworn to submit themselves entirely to the judgement of the Church, in recompense for the hanging of the clerks, as determined by the venerable father, Nicholas, lord bishop of Tusculum, legate of the apostolic see, and when, amongst other things, it had been laid upon them by that same bishop that year by year, for ever, they should pay out 52s. for the needs of poor scholars, as advised by the venerable Father Hugh, then bishop of Lincoln, and his successors, or by the archdeacon of the place, or by his official, or by the chancellor whom the bishop of Lincoln shall set over the scholars there, so indeed that year by year 26s. shall be paid at the Feast of All Saints, and 26s. at the beginning of Lent, and furthermore that, on St. Nicholas' day, every year for ever, they should also feed 100 poor scholars, whom the bishop of Lincoln would present, or the archdeacon of the place, or his official, or the chancellor himself, or some other person nominated for this purpose by the bishop of Lincoln himself, now we make known that we have taken this burden entirely upon ourselves, to do each and every year for ever according to the plan laid down, so however that instead of feeding the 100 poor clerks on St. Nicholas' day we shall on that selfsame day each year give 16s. 8d., to be shared out amongst the selfsame people who would have been fed from it, so that each one receives his two pence, at the hands of those whom the bishop of Lincoln has appointed for this task. To this end, therefore, we have by this our present charter bound ourselves for ever to the bishop and church of Lincoln, and we have affixed our seals to this present document. Witness: the Chapter

(from the Latin of E712 & L336/227).

Notes

1. Rashdall sees this exodus from Oxford as the origin of Cambridge University, and makes the wry comment, 'What attracted them to that distant marsh-town we know not' (see H. Rashdall, *The Universities of Europe in the Middle Ages*, ed. F.M. Powicke & R.B. Emden, Oxford, 1936, vol.3, pp.33ff.).
2. Eynsham 'Schools' in Oxford: see Wood/Gutch, *op. cit.*, vol.2 (1796), pp.741f.
3. A 'gentleman' of this period would wear a linen shirt and a pair of short baggy linen drawers (*braies*) as underwear. Over them might be three layers, a 'tunic', reaching more or less to the ankles, then a 'supertunic', also long, and finally a shorter cloak or wrap. Various words were used and various fashions followed in the case of each of these garments. It sounds as if the chief citizens of Oxford were reduced to their drawers. See F.M. Kelly & R. Schwabe, *A Short History of Costume and Armour: chiefly in England*, Batsford, 1931, vol.1 (1066-1485).
4. See *Statuta Antiqua Universitatis Oxoniensis*, ed. S. Gibson, Oxford, 1931, pp.72f.; *E.C.*, vol.1, pp.xxf.; *Oxford Times*, 29 June 1984.

XXVI

Speculation

Abbot Adam had agreed to paying part of Oxford's penalty for the hanging of the clerks. As he was a native of Oxford, and must have had many friends and contemporaries there, he probably made an excellent bargain. That was in 1214.

In the next year, however, he embarked upon a somewhat speculative venture. This was a scheme for 'property development' in Eynsham itself. In this case his advisers may have been much less sound. Adam had been chaplain to Bishop Hugh; he had proved himself an excellent man of letters; but neither experience was a guarantee of business acumen.

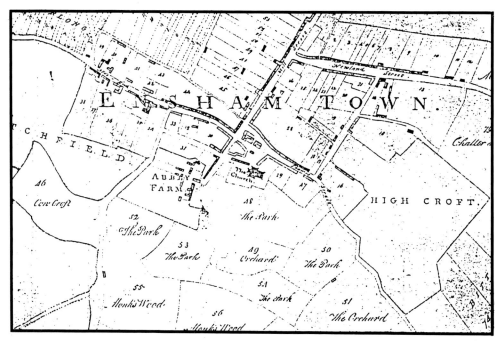

35. **Eynsham, 1782: map by Thomas Pride.** This 18th-century map shows Abbot Adam's town planning of five centuries before. Twentieth-century maps still show it. Note New Land, with its parallel plots, at the north-east of the village, as well as the severance of the Stanton Harcourt road, below Abbey Farm, to the south-west. (For a more extensive reproduction of this map, see *E.M.* (inside back cover), and for New Land, see *E.C.*, vol. 2, p.xii.) (*Oxon. Archives, CH XIX/I.*)

He hived off quite a substantial part of the abbey's 'demesne' (its home-farm) in Eynsham, and put it on the market for residential tenancies. The area in question, adjacent to the existing village, and to the north and east of it, lay along each side of the main road to Oxford (see illustration 10). It came to be called New Land (*nova terra*), and was in effect a small 'new town'. Today's Newland Street, leading on into Cassington Road, is the actual backbone of New Land of 1215. Many parallel boundaries, stretching back, on either side of it, still follow the lines laid down for plots in 1215 (see illustration 35).

Abbot Adam's new town was not large, and it probably did not grow as much as he had hoped. But it did come into being, as a more or less independent community, a small borough. It had its own headman, its own court (numerous court rolls survive),[1] its own boundaries, its own administrative rules, and its own terms of tenancy. According to Adam's 'prospectus' the terms were as good as any in Oxfordshire, and on a par with those prevailing in Oxford itself. The document was as persuasive and tempting as such documents always are. Holdings, for example, entailed no feudal labour for the abbey; they were subject only to ground rent and to fees upon a change of tenant; they could be sold, or given away, or inherited, though (not unnaturally) they could not be passed to another ecclesiastical body; and if and when civic service was required by the State, it would be no more onerous than that from the remaining part of the demesne.

Perhaps some of the discredited burgesses of Oxford, their wings clipped by the papal delegate, their lives hemmed around by dominant teachers and scholars, were only too glad to leave the crowded streets and insanitary alleys of the medieval town, and set up house in the Eynsham countryside, there to pursue their craft and cultivate their plot at a slower tempo and in a cleaner air. Here is the text of Adam's published plan:

ADAM, by the grace of God abbot of Eynsham, and the community (*conventus*) of the same place: to all sons of holy mother church, to whom this writing shall come: greetings in the Lord:

You are to know that, for the benefit and advancement of our house, and after consultation with our friends, we have allocated some of our land for tenancies, to wit, all that land, which was part of our demesne, lying outside the village of Eynsham, between the village itself and the south side of the great street towards Cassington bridge, and likewise all that land, which was part of our demesne, stretching for a distance of 110 yards to the north of the same street (*locasse totam terram que fuit de dominico nostro et jacet extra willam Egnesham, scilicet inter ipsam villam et magnam stratam versus pontem de Kersintone ad austrum, et similiter totam illam terram, que fuit de dominico nostro versus north in longitudine viginti perticarum ab eadem strata versus north*).

The conditions are that whoever shall hold one acre of those lands shall pay us four shillings per annum: at the Nativity of our Lord 12d., and at the Annunciation of the blessed Virgin 12d., and at the Nativity of blessed John Baptist 12d., and at the festival of St. Michael 12d. And he who shall hold three-quarters of an acre shall pay us three shillings at the said dates. And he who shall hold half an acre shall pay us two shillings at the same dates: and he who shall hold a fourth part shall pay us 12d. at the dates mentioned.

And whoever shall take any part of those lands let them hold it, no man gainsaying them, in return for the said service of payment (*pro predicto servicio*): let them hold it with right of inheritance, they and their heirs for ever: let them hold it, as well in roads and paths as in entrances and exits, within the designated bounds of the said lands: let them hold it freely, and quit of all other service and secular payment (*ab omni servicio & seculari exaccione*) that pertains to us: let them also remain as free and quit of all external service (*ab omni forinseco servicio*) as is our demesne in Eynsham. And if tenants wish to give or sell their holding to any secular party (*cuilibet seculari persone*), let them do so freely, but so as the seller shall give us two pence, and the buyer four pence, in acknowledgement of our fief (*in recognicionem feoudi nostri*).

These tenants shall also have a headman, one of themselves (*prepositum de seipsis*),[2] chosen by them freely: he shall swear fidelity both to us and to them.

And if any tenant of that land (*aliquis de illa terra tentus*) (*sic*) shall do wrong, or make complaint about another, then let a court be held upon that same land. And if he be judged worthy of punishment, then he shall make amends to us for his wrongdoing, according to the measure of his fault, and in the sight of his peers, so however that his punishment shall not exceed a fine of 10s.

And if perchance it shall happen that any of those burgesses (*aliquis istorum burgencium*) shall die, having already made his own division of his things that are contained in this fief, his arrangement shall stand. But if he dies without having made a division, then let his chattels be divided into three parts, one part for his children, and another for his wife, and let the third part be divided amongst his closer relatives for the good of his soul.

These liberties, and all other good customary rights which we could possibly give them, comparable to the liberties of the burgesses of Oxford and of others, in the county of Oxford, who hold on better and freer terms (*qui melius & liberius tenent*), these we do now grant and confirm.

And in witness to this matter we have delivered this charter, marked and fortified by our seals, to the community of those, who shall have the said holding (*commune illorum, qui predictum tenementum habebunt*). Settled in A.D. 1215. Witness: the Chapter

(from the Latin of E44A).

In effect the abbot and his staff had chosen to exploit this section of their demesne for ground-rents, fees, and miscellaneous income, rather than for the agricultural produce of earlier years. The choice was certainly adventurous, and possibly unwise. It may indeed have contributed to the disastrous termination of Abbot Adam's reign.[3]

Notes

1. Amongst over 150 Harleian Rolls, concerning Eynsham abbey, in the British Library; see *E.C.*, vol.2, pp.viiff. & xl-xlviii. These Rolls, like the Customary, deserve more attention than Salter was able to give.

2. Salter has *de seppis*, a misreading of the contracted *de seipsis* in the MS; hence sundry local theories that the headman was essentially the official in charge of gates and boundaries.

3. *Postan 1972*, p.240, speaks of several 'new towns' at Eynsham, all stillborn. New Land, though weak, was not stillborn (see E615 & 729). Were there others?

Inglorious tragedy

Tragedy is often dramatic, sometimes heroic: Abbot Adam's was neither. Nevertheless, its cautionary tale must have sounded up and down the cloisters of England.

He had been a promising young monk, and then a trusted official, a witness of his brother's vision, a teller of its lessons, a chaplain and daily companion of St. Hugh, and his brilliant biographer, as also a traveller overseas whilst King John was brought to his knees. Finally, he was abbot in the house where he had begun. There were all the ingredients for a great abbacy. In fact, he became abbot in *c.*1213, was deposed from office in 1228, and more or less sank into oblivion.

It is fair to say that in 1213 Eynsham abbey was an awkward inheritance. For the last five years it had had no abbot at all. Its priors (in Benedictine houses, the seconds in command) had ruled, according to their lights. It is not unlikely that all of them had been tinged with the feeble disciplines of Abbot Godfrey's 44 years.

What was more, the bishop of Lincoln, true owner and guardian of Eynsham abbey, his *Eigenkloster*, had been in exile for four years. In spite of St. Hugh's famous victory, King John had appointed a layman, Roger de Neville, as guardian of Eynsham.

In the end the Church won, and King John lost. And so, in the summer of 1213, he wrote from Portsmouth, as follows:

> JOHN, by the grace of God, King of England, lord of Ireland, duke of Normandy and of Aquitaine, count of Anjou, to the prior and convent of Eynsham, greeting:
> You are to know that we have restored his abbey of Eynsham, together with what pertains to it, to our venerable father, Hugh,[1] lord bishop of Lincoln. And accordingly we bid you pay heed to him from now onwards. And in witness to this matter we send you these our letters patent concerning it:
> Witness, myself: at Portsmouth: 14 July: in the 15th year of our reign

(from the Latin of E710 = L203/162).

Three days later he had moved on to Portchester, and wrote in similar vein to the knights (the men-at-arms, available for royal service), the free tenants (those exempt from compulsory local service), and 'the men' (those tied to certain feudal duties on their manor), on the various Eynsham abbey estates (see E711 = L202/161). And three days later still, by now at Winchester, he wrote in somewhat testy tones to Roger de Neville, his lay guardian of Eynsham abbey:

THE KING: to Roger de Neville etc:

We bid you put behind you every delay and excuse, and restore to our venerable father, Hugh, bishop of Lincoln, all the issue, whether in cash or otherwise (*omnes exitus in denariis et aliis*), which you have taken from Eynsham abbey, since we took possession of it:

Witness, myself: at Winchester: 20 July

(from the Latin of *Close Rolls*, vol.1, p.138).

Upon that crest of new-found liberty Brother Adam became abbot of Eynsham. He seemed an excellent choice, but he led his abbey into debt and appears to have pursued over-ambitious, and perhaps grasping, policies. A whole series of records survives from his time, or from just after it. They tell of extensive litigation, and they suggest mismanagement. Here is a summary:

a. 1214. An abortive attempt to gain full authority over Luffield priory. The result was a payment by Luffield of 10s. per annum (see E229-31 & *Luffield 1975*).

b. 1215. The elaborate scheme for New Land, Eynsham — a new town instead of farm-land. It never really flourished (see ch.26).

c. 1217. The diversion of the road which led due south from Eynsham centre — an expensive and inessential extension of the abbey-surrounds (see illustration 35 & *E.M.*, pp.76-8).

d. 1219. Aid to Stephen of Fretwell and his family — but at a price (see E186 & 716 and *E.R.*, no.5, pp.8-14).

e. 1227. Debts, adding up to £152. 15s., to David the Jew, of Lincoln (see E340 & *E.R.*, no.4, p.10).

f. 1228-31. An apparently harsh effort to dispossess Robert of Norfolk, an ex-crusader, from his late wife's land at Histon (see E342-8).

g. *c.*1230. A fine of five marks for over-extraction of timber from royal woodlands near Charlbury (see E339-339A).

h. *c.*1230. A fine of 40s. for raising the mill-dam, and disturbing the use of certain meadows by the men of Hanborough (see E659-60).

It is a significant catalogue, and we cannot be surprised at Adam's deposition. The Barnwell Chronicle put it down to 'many and various causes' (*ob multas et varias causas, College of Arms, Arundel MS 10*, f.110, also *Walter Cov.*, vol.1, p.xli, n.2). The Tewkesbury Annals are more specific, referring to mismanagement (*propter dilapidationem, Ann. Tewk.*, RS36a, p.70). *The Dunstable Annals* speak also of

36. **From a misericord in New College chapel, Oxford: drawing by Gwynneth Holt, 1986.** Sins are forgiven; grace is sought; but the devil continues to inhabit the scene.

perjury (*tanquam perjurus et dilapidator, Ann. Dunst.*, RS36c, p.109). If that meant straightforward lying, when under oath, it was serious indeed. But it may have meant breaking his promise to be an efficient abbot — bad enough, but not so grim.

It is likely that Adam, when deposed, continued to live in Eynsham abbey.[2] As a Benedictine monk he had sworn to lifelong stability in one house, as well as absolute obedience to whoever was in charge. The situation would clearly require much tact on every side. At this period abbots normally enjoyed a higher standard of living than the cloister monks. They would have their own quarters within the precinct. Adam's quarters would now be there also, and presumably midway in quality between the abbot and the rest. He would probably have a companion monk and domestic staff, as well as an allowance of money. The manor of Little Rollright seems to have been allotted to him. (See *E.R.*, no.3, pp.6-11).

It remains to note that, just when Adam's crisis was reaching its head, the Chapter of Eynsham abbey had anxious discussions about access to its official seals. It is clear that there had been instances of misuse.[3] Here are the new regulations:

Concerning the seal of the convent: how it should be kept, and how to proceed when applying the great or the small seal.

There is one chest, set aside under three locks, and kept for the deposit of records about worldly affairs. Its keys are held by the prior and by two other brethren, appointed in Chapter. The box in which the greater seal of the convent is put away is in this chest, and is fitted with two locks. And one key is held by the lord abbot, the second by another brother, appointed (exactly as the other two brethren mentioned above) by common consent of the Chapter. So that greater seal is guarded by five keys.

It shall never be applied to any document, unless it has been read out in General Chapter, and approved, and there and then sealed, in the presence of everybody, with the consent of all.

And they shall not seal with this seal any but great and difficult pieces of church-business, and those requiring permanent validity, such as charters, or documents like charters, or those destined for more important people, in whose cases, because of their high standing in society, the lesser seal could not fittingly be applied.

And a record shall be kept of all those documents, whatever have been sealed with that same seal, for the greater security and information of those who come after, that men to come may know what men today have done. And if perchance some doubt arise, concerning the genuineness of a seal, or of some or other document, then let the truth be ascertained by reference to the record.

And let not that greater seal ever be sent forth without the lesser seal always being applied on the reverse of the document.

Now, concerning the lesser seal, let it be understood, that it also is kept in the chest where the charters are stored, and under the three locks, two of whose keys are held by the two reliable brethren appointed in Chapter to that task: and the prior holds the key of the box wherein the lesser seal itself is kept: thus, without his presence and the placing of his personal seal on the reverse of a document (if it is not counter-sealed with the abbot's personal seal), and only with the knowledge and agreement of as many brethren as can be present, nothing is sealed.

And, whatever document has been sealed, let its purport be made plain to all the brethren in Chapter, beforehand if possible, or afterwards, if there has been negligence in this respect.

And let a summary be made of all documents that are sealed, lest anything sealed with that seal also is consigned to oblivion.

These provisions were made in the year of grace, 1227, on the day of the Nativity of the Blessed Virgin. But the arrangements made concerning counter-sealing with the small seal of the convent and the abbot's or the prior's personal seal were instituted in the year of grace, 1228, on the eve of the Conversion of St. Paul

(from the Latin of *E.Cust.*, pp.80f.).[4]

Those tedious, but necessary, rules for the management of Eynsham abbey's seals were a lasting memorial to Adam's economic unease; but two great and delightful books, *The Life of St. Hugh* and *The Vision of the Monk of Eynsham* are an even more lasting memorial to a literary skill which few could emulate.

Notes

1. Hugh II: Hugh of Wells, bishop of Lincoln, 1209-35.
2. *H.R.H. 1972*, p.49, states that Adam, after his deposition, became a monk of Crowland. The editors, however, have misread *Walter Cov.*, loc. cit., which refers to a statement in the *Barnwell Chronicle*, loc. cit. In fact, the latter says that Adam was succeeded at Eynsham, as abbot, by Nicholas, a monk of Crowland.
3. For a similar state of affairs at Bury St. Edmunds, see *Jocelin*.
4. It is clear that, during the autumn and winter of 1227-8, Eynsham's crisis of management was steadily worsening. Its regulations for the safety and the correct handling of its seals were made in two stages. Counter-sealing was part of the second stage. Documents important enough to have the greater seal were also to have the lesser seal on the back. Those needing only the lesser seal on the front were to have the abbot's or the prior's seal on the back.

Part Five

A Niggling Question

If you find the next chapter tedious, then skip it, and move on to the Epilogue, and to the Appendices, some of which are full of fascinating material which was too discursive for the main story.

You will value this next chapter, 'How true?', if you have been vexed, all along the course, by doubts about the reliability of what you have read. Here you will find a summary, partly repetitious, of relevant considerations. It has been hard to put it together, hard to assess, hard to compress into a manageable form. I felt, however, that the attempt ought to be made.

So here it is, with much modesty, even with apologies. It raises doubts about some details of our story; but do not forget that you will encounter such doubts about any story, even of events 10 years ago, let alone nearly 1,000! I would be very sorry if the result of your reading it were to make you close the Eynsham records and never look at them again.

They are about men and women, vibrant with life, wrestling with things intractable, both in themselves and in their world, and finding it just as hard to love God and to love their neighbour as do we. Sit with them on their journey. Think with them in their puzzling. Trace out the maze of life with them. And (dare I say?) see the ultimate dawn, and journey's end, and travelling mercies, as they did, in the Light of the world. Johnny Head-in-Air must alwys be Johnny Feet-on-Earth, and vice versa.

How true?

This story has leaned heavily upon the earliest section of the Eynsham Cartulary, and therefore upon material which was set down within the walls of the abbey itself in *c*.1196. But how far can we really trust it? When the compilers chose this to copy and rejected that, was their judgement sound? And, more important still, were they men of complete integrity? Were they impartial recorders of the truth as they saw it? Monks of that day sometimes manipulated their records, or even fabricated new ones, to fill up gaps (see Appendix 10). What then of the Eynsham brethren at the end of the 12th century?

In any case the whole line of evidence, reaching from the year 1000 to the year 1200, is slight and tenuous; and we have already noted points where it is suspect. Such suspicion can only be deepened, when we recollect that about one-third of our earlier cartulary was planned and written out in a single extended operation, and at a particularly critical moment in the history of the house. There may well have been special temptation, as well as clear opportunity, to doctor the story.

Let it be said at once that many of the problems in our manuscript concern Leofric, earl of Mercia, his wife, the Lady Godiva, and the gifts that (jointly or individually) they made to Stow minster, its secular canons, and their bishop. Stow minster was a famous shrine, set on an episcopal estate, not far from Lincoln, at the north-eastern corner of ancient Mercia. What those Anglo-Saxon benefactors gave to Stow before the Conquest was to prove of immense importance to Eynsham abbey, many miles away and many years later.

It will be convenient to tabulate the difficulties, which are presented by the manuscript of our earlier cartulary. Some are great, some small, but taken together they pose curious questions:

i. The compilers reveal an excessive anxiety to underline their tradition that Eynsham abbey had two distinct Anglo-Saxon roots, not one, and that both mattered. Their first document concerned Aethelmaer of Wessex and Eynsham abbey, their second Leofric of Mercia, Lady Godiva, and Stow minster. Each text appears to be authentic, but they had been entirely separate in origin and in concern. Nevertheless, our cartulary runs them together, and puts the number '1' in the margin by them three times (see ch.13, with charters E1 & E1A). Why this strange device, one which can hardly have impressed anyone but themselves?

ii. That first Stow charter (E1A) said that Leofric and Godiva had given 'lands' to Stow minster and to its bishop, but it did not name them. The next charter (E2) named the lands, made Godiva alone the giver, and recorded the Pope's personal endorsement of the affair:

> Newark and Fledborough, with what pertains to them, as also Brampton, and Marton in the wapentake of Well, with what pertains to them.

So the lands were of considerable extent, stretching for many miles, up and down the Trent, mainly on its east bank, some in Nottinghamshire, some in Lincolnshire (see illustration 37).

Popes, however, did not then endorse other people's charters in this manner, and the charter names an archbishop of Canterbury who never existed. Although the reference to Godiva's jewellery has a touching realism, and some of the charter's Anglo-Latin expressions sound very genuine, the list of lands given is most difficult to reconcile with other lists of the same benefaction.

It is generally agreed that, although this text may embody some accurate traditions, it is so spurious, in its present form, that it cannot be trusted. Did the compilers make it up entirely? Or did they adjust an existing text?

iii. There appears to be a special conflict between those Stow property lists and the records set down by the King's Commissioners in Domesday Book in 1086. And we must remember that all Domesday evidence was certified by local juries under oath.

According to the Nottinghamshire Domesday Newark and Fledborough were both in Lady Godiva's hands until 1066 (see ch.14). In what way then, if any, had she given them to Stow some 10 years earlier?

iv. The same Domesday item throws doubt upon the next Eynsham charter as well (see ch.14, esp. n.2, with E3). The Conquest is now well past. Both religious communities, the monks of Eynsham and the canons of Stow, seem dormant. William I authorizes a plan to merge the surviving resources of both houses in support of a new Benedictine foundation at Stow. The charter names Leofric, as well as Godiva, as donors to Stow minster:

> The benefaction, which Earl Leofric and his wife, Godiva, made to the church of St. Mary's Stow, namely, Newark and Fledborough and Well wapentake, together with what pertains to them.

How can we reconcile the royal charter and the royal survey?

v. There are other disturbing elements in the first part of our Eynsham manuscript. One concerns the system of lettering by which each folio is distinguished. From the 7th to the 49th folio the markings are as follows: *aa, aa, aa, aa, ae, ai, ao, au, ba, be, bi, bo, bu, ca* etc., right through to *hu*. It is clear that the markings are carefully planned. They are in the first hand, and go beyond the actual documents entered by that hand. And those first four folios, all marked with *aa*, embrace charters E1, E1A, E2 and part of E3.

Were those confusing marks caused by careless secretarial work, or do they perhaps reveal some monastic manipulation of Eynsham's available material, at a very early stage of the compilation?

vi. Parchment was costly, and medieval scribes often erased documents and wrote others in their places. At E13 this happens in our cartulary. Was it really

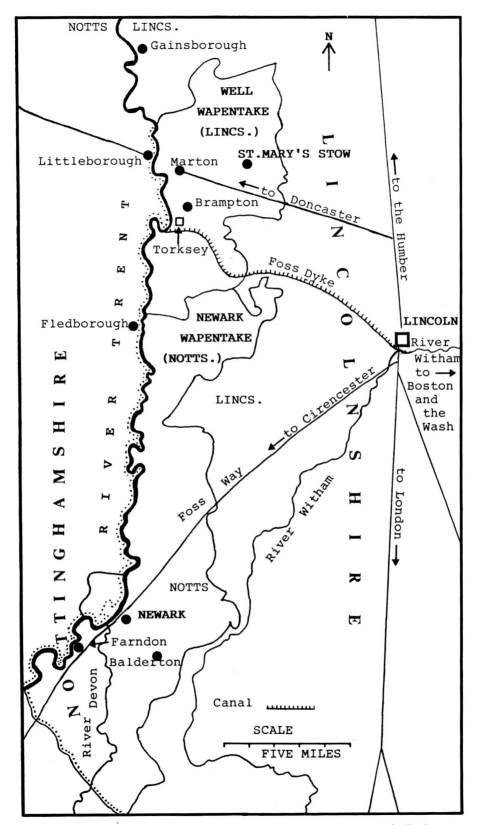

37. **St. Mary's Stow: endowments** (associated with Leofric and Godiva).

the removal of something obsolete and useless? Or was it the erasure of something inconvenient to Eynsham's later claims?

vii. Most of the earlier records are in related groups, and arranged by date within their group (see Appendix 11). One group (E20-28), however, breaks the sequence. To each side of it there is 12th-century material, mostly from the earlier part of that century but, when we reach E20, we plunge into a strange mixture.

It begins with five charters of Bishop Hugh's time (1186-1200), the time when the cartulary was being compiled. Then it moves to two 13th-century charters, written in a later hand, and using up a gap. And then, quite suddenly, we find ourselves two centuries back: three 11th-century charters appear, all of them concerning aspects of the vexatious Eynsham/Stow affair (see chs.15-16, with charters E26-28).

Is that confusing group an accident or part of a design? Is it possible that those last three charters had been mislaid, and then mercifully found, and hastily inserted? Or can it be that, having reached this point in their story, the monks of Eynsham felt that their much-prized links with Stow needed reinforcement, and that the concoction of suitable documents might help?

So much for the evidence of the manuscript itself; it is cumulative and it is puzzling. First we must ask, What was the likely 'climate of integrity' at Eynsham abbey, when work on its cartulary began? Was it the sort of place that might be expected to resort to adjustments of its records?

The key to an answer probably lies in the fact that Abbot Godfrey had just died; he had reigned for some 44 years (1150/1-95: see *E.C.*, vol.1, pp.xv-xvi). They were years when Eynsham abbey was building and establishing traditions. Men come, men go, but not all at the same time; they overlap, they influence each other, they transmit ways of living and patterns of praying. Abbot Godfrey had been weak in discipline and deplorable in personal example.

Small wonder that in his famous vision Brother Edmund met the late abbot in purgatory! Small wonder that he told Edmund of experiences that were grim, lugubrious, and agonizing! And emphasis was laid upon his evil influence upon his subjects. And every time they sinned anew, because of what they had seen in Godfrey, fresh relays of demons pounced upon him, and made purgatory even harsher (see ch.23).

Now Adam, who wrote of the vision, was Edmund's brother, and both had been under Abbot Godfrey. By 1196 Adam had risen to be subprior, or even prior, at Eynsham abbey; as such he was probably responsible for the initial compilation of our cartulary. He was a gifted man, humorous, intelligent, well-read, able to write with charm and colour, attractive enough for Bishop Hugh to take him away as his chaplain and companion. But such qualities do not always sit comfortably with integrity.

It is all too easy to moralize, but it is sadly true that some 30 years later this same Adam, by now returned to Eynsham abbey as its abbot, was to be deposed for 'serious mismanagement and for oath-breaking'. However we interpret the latter charge, it suggests lack of integrity, a lack which may well have been rooted in Godfrey's time, a lack which could readily have touched the compilation of the cartulary. There is talk in the *Vision* of some reform after Godfrey's death, but Adam could have inherited a tradition of duplicity, and been affected by it. Is it fanciful to think that, when he spoke of Godfrey's pains for the sins of his successors, Adam was perhaps massaging his own conscience and assuaging his own fears of agonies to come?

And so we are led to another question. Adam and his fellow-officials were together responsible for the economic stability of their house. In an age of increasing litigation sound records, well-maintained, were of obvious value. Had Eynsham abbey any particular .anxiety which might have led them to tamper with their records at the close of the 12th century? The broad outline of the tangled Eynsham/Stow story suggests that in fact it had.

Bishop Remigius had founded Stow abbey in 1091. He had given it all that survived of the erstwhile resources of the Stow canons and the Eynsham monks; he had, it seems, been holding all of them for years. At the same time he had relinquished the whole of his pecuniary interest in the ancient episcopal estate of Stow, and recompensed his successors in the see by giving them the estate of Sleaford. Thus, it seems, he had died in peace, ready to meet the Blessed Virgin, as she stood beside her Son at the Last Judgement.

Bishop Robert Bloet, Remigius' successor, thought otherwise. It was probably his opinion that Remigius, in his dotage, had acted with extreme unwisdom in parting with what we may perhaps call 'Newark etc.' (full lists may be found in Appendix 12). Those lands and rights were both valuable and local. Not only that, but they were a useful buffer-zone against the ambitions of the archbishops of York. Lincolnshire (and especially Lindsey, its northern part, hedged in by the Trent, the Humber, and the sea) was a northward promontory of the diocese of Lincoln and of the province of Canterbury. Nottinghamshire, mostly to the west of the Trent, was a southward promontory of the diocese and province of York. 'Newark etc.' fortified the bishop of Lincoln's westward flank. So Bishop Bloet took them all back, and sent Stow abbey (as an institution) back to Eynsham. Monastic forces expressed horror. Probably most men saw his wisdom.

As we know, of course, Bishop Bloet had to pay heavily. He had to surrender to Eynsham abbey episcopal lands in its neighbourhood, precisely equivalent in value to 'Newark etc.', which he had commandeered in the north. We may call what he surrendered 'Charlbury etc.' (the full list is in E7, beginning with Charlbury, and ending with Milton; see ch.17).

It seems likely that throughout the 12th century that whole Bishop Bloet/ Stow affair left the Eynsham monks uneasy. They would have a lingering fear that what one bishop had been forced to surrender another bishop might recover. Then they would lose part, perhaps all, of 'Charlbury etc.', lands and rights that were at the very heart of their growing prosperity. That would have been a calamity. It was essential to maintain, and strengthen, the chain of events which wound its way back from 'Charlbury etc.' to 'Newark etc.', and thus to Stow minster and Leofric and Godiva. Nothing must weaken it.

If such fears existed, they were likely to come to a head when Abbot Godfrey died whilst Hugh of Avalon was bishop; for Hugh (one day to be St. Hugh of Lincoln) had taken the King of England to law, and won his claim that Eynsham abbey (unlike almost all other Benedictine houses in England) was a bishop's 'own monastery', his *Eigenkloster* (see ch.24).

The thunderings of the case had probably hastened the compilation of our cartulary. For therein was Henry I's explicit grant:

> Now this abbey is completely in the hands of the bishop of Lincoln, and under his authority, in the matter of appointing an abbot, in conformity with canon law, and with the assent and counsel of the king

(from E7).

Hugh's very saintliness, coupled with his newly-confirmed ownership of Eynsham abbey, may well have seemed a special threat to the brethren there. For saintliness has an awkward way of concerning itself with justice, as well as with prayer and compassion. And for a bishop of Lincoln justice included care for the proper interests of his successors in the see. Perhaps Hugh would feel it right to question Eynsham's hold upon 'Charlbury etc.', and to seek to diminish it? Here then was good reason for Eynsham to check its records, and to weave more strongly the thread of gratitude that led back to Leofric and Godiva in that pre-Conquest world.

Day by day, when they met in chapter, they prayed for the souls of founders and benefactors, still wending their painful way (like Abbot Godfrey) through the perils of purgatory. Day by day they named outstanding benefactors. It is likely that Leofric and Godiva were already included, side by side with Aethelmaer and his wife (see ch.21). Their names were a continual reminder and an ever-renewed claim that, in the long run, 'Charlbury etc.' were Eynsham's, because 'Newark etc.' had been given by them to Stow.

Documentary evidence was even more urgent. So it gave special pleasure to Eynsham officials to record the express wishes of Leofric and Godiva when they gave lands to Stow. They wished to support a community of men of religion; they were to model their life on St. Paul's in London; they were to receive their traditional share of Stow minster revenues; and bishops, now and in all days to come, were to be content with their own traditional share:

> And the lands which the bishop and the earl and Godiva and good men grant to it shall remain for all time in the possession of the holy foundation for the needs of the brethren and the endowment of the minster, so that no bishop who succeeds him shall demand any food-rent from it, except what by rights belongs to the bishopric, as other bishops had before him

(from E1A).

And Godiva herself, they recorded, had given the whole of 'Newark etc.' to St. Mary's Stow, not to the bishop. She had done so at no small personal sacrifice, and the Pope himself had approved the scheme (see E2, in ch.13). And after the Conquest William I himself had maintained the momentum, planning for another community of men of religion (Benedictine monks now, not secular canons) to inherit Stow minster, and that the bishop should relinquish all financial claims upon the place (see E3, in ch.14). And Bishop Remigius had fulfilled that plan with precision, making clear that Stow church and all its attached revenues were to belong to the monks there, and to the monks alone, and at the same time compensating his successors for their loss (see E5, in ch.15). And the ultimate transfer to Eynsham had been simply a removal of the project from one place to another, and the substitution of 'Charlbury etc.' for 'Newark etc.' (see E7, in ch.17). It was as simple as that![1]

That was the Eynsham story. Nothing, however, could obscure the fact that, according to Domesday, Lady Godiva had still held Newark and Fledborough, Nottinghamshire, at the Conquest, and that, according to the Eynsham cartulary, she had given them away to Stow minster some years earlier.

Cornelius Brown, in his monumental *History of Newark-on-Trent* (2 vols., 1904-7), vol.1, p.18,[2] admits the conflict with Domesday, but makes the tentative suggestion that Godiva had during her lifetime passed the revenues of Newark to Stow minster, but retained her hold upon the actual property. The idea is ingenious, but hardly accounts for the spurious character of Eynsham's charter no.2 (that is, Godiva's total donation of all 'Newark etc.' to Stow, with papal blessing), or for the other anomalies which we have noted in the Eynsham manuscript.

We ought, it seems, to hold on to the Domesday statement, whilst looking for some post-Conquest explanation and occasion for the transfer of 'Newark etc.' from the Leofric/Godiva family and their heirs to Bishop Remigius and to Stow minster/abbey. It is clear that by 1086 all of it was in the bishop's hands, and that by 1091 he had allocated it all to his new Stow abbey. At a later date, and for their own business reasons, the Eynsham monks will then have pushed the whole benefaction back in time, to a date before the Conquest, and attributed it all to Lady Godiva rather than to her husband.

The solution to the problem may possibly lie in a combination of two factors: one, the decaying fortunes of the house of the earls of Mercia; the other, the utterly confused state of England, as it gradually came to terms with its new Norman order.

The influence and status of the earls of Mercia had long been waning. Once they had been dominant in England, controlling London, demanding an archbishopric at Lichfield, stronger than Wessex to their south and Northumbria to their north. But things had changed. Earl Leofric remained important, first under King Cnut, then under King Edward the Confessor; but in 1057 he died. He was succeeded in the earldom by his son Aelfgar; but in 1062 he too died. He left two sons, Edwin and Morcar, and Edwin became earl. He was young, however, he was inexperienced, and he was torn this way and that, between the sullen and resentful south of England and the openly turbulent and rebellious north. And when the Conqueror travelled northwards to scourge Northumbria and crush it into submission, his way lay through Nottinghamshire. In the end Edwin fled towards Scotland, and was treacherously murdered on the way.

What then of the Dowager Lady Godiva, and of her lands at Newark and Fledborough? For they were in fact her own. They had been given to her by her brother Thorold of Bucknall, sheriff of Lincolnshire. We do not know when she died, but we can picture her growing old and tired and very sad. She may well have lived through all the initial troubles that followed the Conquest. Towards the end of the worst of them Bishop Remigius moved his see from Dorchester to Lincoln. He had once been a monk at Fécamp; now he was a bishop and a statesman in England, but with something of a monk's conscience.

It is tempting to speculate that at that point — with the house of Mercia in ruins, and the years creeping on, and with Bishop Remigius much in need of economic and ecclesiastical support in Lincoln — Godiva may have been glad to part with Newark, and to let the bishop have it, for the monastery which he was now planning at Stow. Her husband and she had always had a deep concern for the Church, and especially for religious houses. Here at Stow was a project near to her heart. And, in any case, far better to let Newark go there than (like so many Anglo-Saxon heritages, all over the country) to some upstart Norman noble!

So much then for that part of our Eynsham cartulary. Let me add that I do not think that these conclusions need shake our general confidence in the main body of its evidence. The monks in question were men of their day. Their records were frail, and had survived through troubled times. Their facilities for copying, for storing, for communication, were slender and inadequate. And those compilers (whether we admit or not) were busy men. On the one side, like all clerks in holy orders, they were almost the sole exponents of reading and writing; on the other was a routine which combined long periods in prayer and worship with tedious and tiring conditions of life. We may reasonably assume that they did their best.

Notes

1. I have omitted from this summary any reference to the three somewhat suspect 11th-century charters, E26-28. The first two appear to be alternative versions, one in Latin, the other in O.E., of the same proclamation by William II. The second is reminiscent of the spurious E2, both in its list of lands and in its concentration upon Godiva. If authentic, these two charters would appear to date from *c.*1091, when Remigius was at last founding Stow abbey. They seem to reflect uncertainty about the stance of Thomas, archbishop of York (1070-1100), who was definitely bishop in Nottinghamshire, and (as we know from elsewhere) still hungering to add Lindsey, in Lincolnshire, to his vast diocese, although by now Remigius had his see at Lincoln. E27 spells out Godiva's firm hold upon the whole of 'Newark etc.' before the Conquest, but, in contrast to E2, does not assert that she gave any of it to Stow church before 1066.

2. Brown refers to E.A. Freeman, *The History of the Norman Conquest*, 6 vols., 1867-79 (see vol.4, pp.195-201); for Nottinghamshire, see also R. Thoroton, *The Antiquities of Nottinghamshire*, 1677, ed. J. Throsby, 3 vols., 1790-6 (republished 1972); Thoroton Society *Transactions & Record Series*; A.C. Wood, *A History of Nottinghamshire*, 1947 (republished 1971); for Newark, see also R.P. Shilton, *The History of the Town of Newark upon Trent*, 2 vols., 1820; *V.C.H., Notts.*, vol.1 (1906), pp.220f. (F.M. Stenton); *Documents relating to the Manor and Soke of Newark on Trent*, ed. M.W. Barley (Thor. Soc. Rec. Ser., vol.16, 1955).

Part Six

Epilogue

38. **Jacob and the Angel: alabaster by Epstein, 1940-41.**

Wrestlers

If prayer is the most strenuous and penetrating of human exercises — and that, of course, is the insight of 'Wrestling Jacob' (see Gen. 32, 22-32), and of Epstein's great block of stone at Liverpool, and perhaps also of Michelangelo's 'Prisoners', struggling out of their rocks of mystery, at Florence — if prayer is any or all of that, if indeed it recalls the bloody sweat of Jesus, in Gethsemane (see Luke 22, 44), then that was the course upon which Eynsham abbey had been well and truly launched by the year 1200. The religious life, honestly lived, is no easy option. Who are we to say what went on within those seemingly placid, and secure, and comfortable men?

We do well to turn again and again to Charles Wesley's delving into Jacob's experience, on that lonely tremulous night, by the Brook Jabbok:

> Come, O thou Traveller unknown,
> Whom still I hold, but cannot see;
> My company before is gone,
> And I am left alone with thee;
> With thee all night I mean to stay,
> And wrestle till the break of day.

(From *Songs of Praise Enlarged* (Oxford, 1931), no.476.)

We may set the wrestling monk by wrestling Jacob.

Some would say that the world was too much with those monks, and that getting and spending they laid waste their powers; others, that they cared too little for those beaten, and robbed, and left to die, by the roadsides of life; others, that they should have adventured into the world, building empires, as Elizabeth's men were to do, or searching for Spanish gold and commercial glory; or perhaps they should have turned to dropping weights from Leaning Towers of Pisa, and sought to understand the world of physics. Maybe they should have done so. But, in fact, like many many others, before and since, and in every land, they chose the secluded place and prayer. Better to leave the assessment to God!

Eynsham abbey now continued for over 300 years, never very conspicuous on the stage of history, but mindful of the still small voice at its heart (see 1 Kings 19, 12f.). And then, one day in 1538, and not unexpectedly, there came the knock at the door, and the royal official, demanding possession. Willy-nilly they must surrender their keys, vacate their premises and their lands, hand over their papers, and go. Here is the laconic summary of the royal annal:

No.989 Eynsham Abbey

Surrender to John London, clerk, of the site, etc., of the house, and all its possessions in England, to the King's use. 4 Dec. 30 Hen. VIII. Signed by Anthony the abbot, S.T.P., Edm. Etun, prior, Geo. Brodhurst, sub-prior, and seven others.

Enrolled as acknowledged same day before John Williams, King's commissioner.

(from *Letters & Papers, Foreign & Domestic: Henry VIII*, Vol.13, Pt.2, 1538, ed. J. Gairdner, 1893, p.425.)

Probably there had never been more than 25 or 30 monks, and with them perhaps a similar number of 'staff and servants'. By 1538 there was only a small remnant. For the abbot the future was to bring preferment and security: he became bishop of Llandaff. For the rest perhaps there was hardship, and a penurious path to the grave.

Some abbeys, such as Gloucester, became cathedrals. The naves of others, Malmesbury, for example, long used by parishioners, were sold as parish churches. Others were, in one way or another, incorporated into country houses. In most cases the lead was at once stripped off the roof, and given to the King; the English climate and purchasers of building-material did the rest. The accounts of Mr.Thomas Day, for 1546, make the story come alive: he was demolishing Oseney abbey, Oxford. An Eynsham man dealt with 'Great Tom':

Item, paid to Willouby of Einsham for carriage of the great bell to Frydeswide's, 26 Sept., 20s. . . .

To Popingjaye the joyner for taking downe the stalls and sides of the quire and high altar and other things in the church, 5s. 4d. . . .

To the said Popingjaye for himselfe 3 dayes at taking downe the roof of the church, 18d. . . .

To Mr. Raynolds for melting the lead of the church and casting it into sowes, £16 18s. 8d. . . .

To Jeffry Vyne, 4 dayes, about taking downe the battlements of the church and upon the porche . . .

(from *Wood's History of the City of Oxford*, ed. A. Clark, vol.2, pp.227f.).

In 1657 Anthony Wood visited the stricken ruins of Eynsham abbey, and sat amongst them, and made his drawing, and was 'melancholy'. Natural enough! Many of us feel the same. 'Ichabod!' — 'The glory has departed' (see 1 Sam. 4, 21). All that beauty! All that skill! All that craftsmanship! All that patience and devotion! Yes, but of course, we must look ahead, and do better.

39. **Example: bronze by Gwynneth Holt, c.1970.** In the Methodist East End Mission, London. 'If I then, your Lord and Master, have washed your feet, ye also ought to wash one another's feet. For I have given you an example, that ye should do as I have done to you.' *John xiii, 14f.* Love God. Love your neighbour. Both commands matter.

Manx Cross

the pagan darkness
and the dragons
and the weary cross
the ancient mystics
coiled their riddles
on the patient slate
the watery death
lay close to hand
the ague and the fever
wormed within
the wild witch woman
cried her wares
vervain and fennel
sloe and musk
and tiny skulls
of new-born mice
the dust of corpses
and forgotten things
meet mystery
with mystery
but strange wild men
cry death is dead
the beginning of the end
is come
set swords aside
and let the thorns of love
sweep in

Eric Gordon
1978

40. **The Dragon Cross: Kirk Michael, Isle of Man.** Below the arms of the cross, back and front, and to either side, Satan's dragons writhe upwards, their eyes glowering and their jaws snapping. This may reflect the Norse mythology of the kings who held the Isle of Man from 1079 to 1266 — Siegfried (Sigurd) slaying the dragon Fafnir (see E. H. Stenning, *Isle of Man*, Hale, London, 1950, pp.136-45). Drawing by Gwynneth Holt, from an old photograph.

Appendix 1

London to Gloucester

The estuaries of the Thames and the Severn lie opposite one another. Each of them bites deeply into England. The cities of London and Gloucester grew up naturally, at the first good crossing-points, as you pushed upstream from east and west. Inevitably they became focuses for trade and for travel, and the road between them (both its route and its quality) mattered greatly.

Hills, and even more so rivers, determined roads. There were the Chilterns and the Cotswolds, and there was the Thames, with all its tributaries, sprawling its way across the land. Pack-horses, heavy waggons, and (later) coaches, would be guided by gradients, and fords, and (still more) by bridges. And other towns, such as Oxford, would spring up at critical points. And so the London/Gloucester road was not always the same.

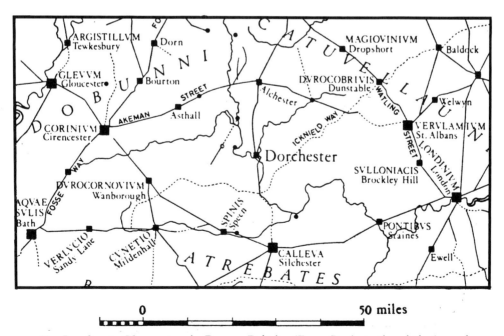

41. **London to Gloucester: in Roman Britain.** (From *Dorchester through the Ages*, ed. J. Cook & T. Rowley (Oxf. Univ. Dept. for External Studies, 1985), p.25.)

151

i. The Romans had their own solution. Their roads were, of course, links between garrisons, and they managed to avoid the Thames almost entirely. One road went northwards from London to St. Albans, and then swung across to Alchester, down to Cirencester, and up again to Gloucester. The other went south-westwards to Silchester, involving a Thames bridge at Staines, and then north-westwards to Cirencester and Gloucester.

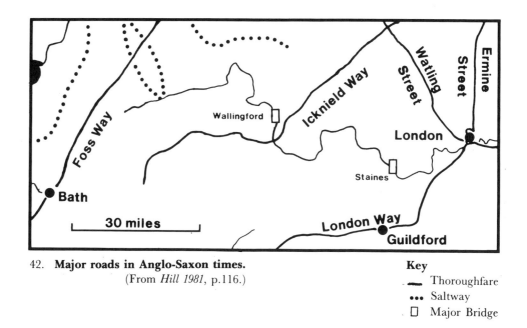

42. **Major roads in Anglo-Saxon times.**
(From *Hill 1981*, p.116.)

Key

━━ Thoroughfare
••• Saltway
▢ Major Bridge

ii. The Anglo-Saxons inherited and used the Roman road system, together with other ancient trackways. In their later days they had their four Royal Roads — Ermine Street, Watling Street, Icknield Way, and Foss Way — none of them linking London and Gloucester.

It seems, however, that they had many other long-distance tracks. These were well-established, familiar, and much frequented, but their routes are difficult to assess accurately today (see *Hill 1981*, p.115). On this issue Hill is probably more reliable than Stenton, who (in his otherwise vital examination of the problem) characterizes Anglo-Saxon road planning as haphazard and locally centred (see F.M. Stenton, *The Road-System of Medieval England, Econ. Hist. Rvw.*, vol.7 (1936), pp.1-21).

iii. The famous Gough map, of *c*.1360, shows a main London/Gloucester road, going through Oxford. It is not unlikely that, as it wound its way westwards from Oxford to Witney, it went through Eynsham. If so, it had probably done so for centuries, including the late Anglo-Saxon period when Eynsham abbey took firm shape (see illustrations 10 & 11).

Salter seems to have this in mind, when, writing of 12th-century Eynsham abbey, he says:

> Eynsham . . . was . . . situated on the main road which led from London to Wales, whether the traveller went through Abingdon or Oxford

(from *E.C.*, vol.1, p.xvi).

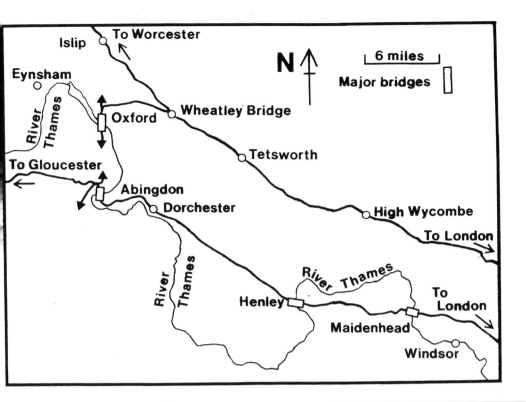

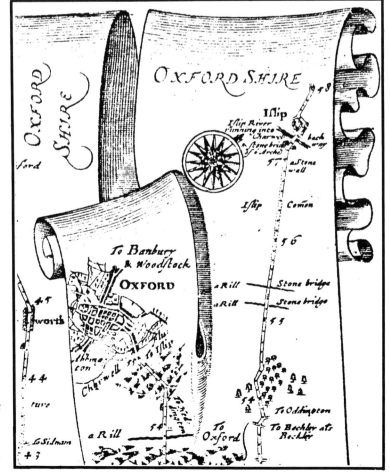

43. **London to Gloucester and Worcester, 17th century** (according to Ogilby's *Britannia*, 1675).

44. **Ogilby's London/Worcester road, leaving Oxford to one side.** (From Ogilby's *Britannia*, 1675. *Bodl. Gough Maps 101*.) Main roads are displayed in continuous strips, winding up and down the pages; distances are from London, in miles and furlongs; side-turnings, bridges, woodlands, villages etc. mark the way.

So also Postan, speaking of the next century:

The new towns which the Priors of Eynsham founded along the Oxford-Gloucester road

(from *Postan 1972*, p.240).

iv. In the latter half of the 17th century there was a well-defined national system of roads, but Oxford was at a dead end. The London/Gloucester road passed south of Oxford. It used the three vital bridges at Maidenhead, Henley, and Abingdon; it went on from Abingdon to Faringdon and Lechlade, and from there to Gloucester, and on to St. David's. The London/Worcester road came nearly to Oxford, through High Wycombe, but then veered north of the city to Islip, and so on to Worcester and Aberystwyth. A short turning branched off to Oxford, but ended there. Doubtless some or other track led on to Eynsham, but not a main through-road (see *Ogilby's Road Maps of England & Wales, from Ogilby's 'Britannia', 1675*, facsimile, ed. R. Cleeve, Reading, 1971).

v. From that time onwards building of roads and bridges went on apace, funded for the most part by tolls, and serving a developing network of stage coaches. In 1769 the building of Swinford bridge (near Eynsham), together with sundry improvements to roads and bridges between Swinford and Oxford, made Eynsham/Swinford/Oxford part of an attractive coach-route:

The main highway from London to Gloucester and South Wales, the precursor of the modern A40

(from E. de Villiers, *Swinford Bridge 1769-1969*, Eynsham Hist. Grp., 1969).

As with the Gough map in *c*.1360, so with the coming of Swinford bridge in 1769, London/Gloucester traffic went through Oxford and Eynsham; but now the route was different.

For further reading: about Roman roads, see *Salway 1981*; about medieval transport, see J.F. Willard, *Inland Transportation in England during the 14th century, Speculum*, no.1 (1926), pp.361-74; about the Gough map, see E.J.S. Parsons, *The Map of Great Britain circa A.D. 1360, known as The Gough Map. An Introduction to the Facsimile*, with F.M. Stenton, *The Roads of the Gough Map*, rev. edn., 1970.

Appendix 2

Aethelmaer's gifts: why those?

i. Salt-traffic?

Anglo-Saxon England got its salt by evaporating salty water, either from underground supplies in brine pits or from the sea. It used much timber for the necessary fires. The rock-salt mines of Cheshire were not exploited until the 17th century.

Distribution was by pack animals, using traditional salt-ways (see illustration 12 and *Hill 1981*, p.109). Men slaughtered most of their flocks each autumn, and salted down the meat. So salt was essential for food preservation, as well as for flavouring.

One salt-way came down from Droitwich, and its famous brine springs, to Lechlade, on the Thames. Eynsham abbey may have received salt by boat from there. But another salt-way was probably more important to it. This one ran eastwards from Droitwich, dropping across the confines of Warwickshire and Gloucestershire, entering Oxfordshire, passing close to Eynsham, and petering out in Buckinghamshire. At that point it could probably not compete with sea-salt from the coasts. It seems likely that Eynsham abbey had more than one useful contact with this route.

a. *Bentley, in Holt, Worcs.* If this Bentley was Eynsham's Bentley, then its salt supplies may well have been very useful to our monks. By the river Severn, and not far from Droitwich, it was, at a later date, almost eclipsed by Holt (see *D.B., Worcs.*, folio 172b). In the 9th and 10th centuries, however, bishops of Worcester had held valuable land there, land to which were attached four vessels, used for evaporating brine, at one of the Droitwich springs (*quattuor vascula ad coctionem salis on Upwic*), as also some woodlands for the fires (*silvam necessariam*). (See *C.S.*, vol.3, no.1087 (*Beonetlaeage*) and vol.2, no.487 (*Beonetlege*); also *V.C.H., Worcs.*, vol.3, p.405 and vol.4, p.437.)

b. *Droitwich, Worcs.* The land which Eynsham abbey held at Mickleton, Gloucs., entitled it to 24 measures of salt from Droitwich (*XXIIII mensurae salis de Wich*; see *D.B., Glos.*, folio 166). The ancient Droitwich/Oxfordshire salt-way passed close to Mickleton, and probably brought Eynsham's salt. The same route is likely to have served two other Oxfordshire estates, which are known to have had rights in Droitwich salt. They were Bampton and Great Rollright (see *D.B., Oxon.*, folios 154c & 160c).

c. *Marlcliff, in Bidford-on-Avon, War.*[1] (also in the 1005 endowment) and *Little Rollright* (added to Eynsham endowment between 1005 and 1066) were near to that same salt-way.

Perhaps salt-traffic along that vital ancient route was a special commercial concern of Eynsham abbey's?

(For salt-production in general, see publications of Cheshire Salt Museum, Northwich, and for Droitwich salt, *V.C.H., Worcs.*, vol.1, pp.268-70, vol.2, pp.256-63, & vol.3, pp.72-89.)

ii. Mercian links?

Aethelmaer's string of Eynsham endowments stretched across England in a curiously straight line, and, although he was a distinguished Wessex layman, those gifts to Eynsham almost missed traditional Wessex territory.

It was not long since the great Midland power of Mercia had been predominant in England (see ch.7, above, and illustration 14). Stronger than Northumbria, it had overshadowed Wessex; and even London, and Kent and Sussex beyond it, had been subservient. By 1005 Wessex had achieved dominance, but (very roughly speaking) it was with former Mercian lands that Aethelmaer now endowed Eynsham abbey.

Was it just an accident that those particular lands were at Aethelmaer's disposal at that moment? Or had he been helped by the very powerful Wulfstan I, archbishop of York, holder of the see of Worcester in plurality (see *Barlow I*, pp.68ff.& 226ff.), friend and admirer of Aelfric, and a man of great influence in the south-west Midlands?

Could it even be that Aethelmaer was picking up and re-attaching to a formerly great church of Eynsham what had once belonged to it? One bishop of Worcester had certainly had a slender link with the church of *Egenes homme* in 864. Was Aethelmaer re-assembling pieces of Eynsham's golden past?

Notes

1. *Aet Maranaclive* seems to be Marlcliff. *Aet Beonetlege* is Bentley, a common English place-name, meaning 'a clearing overgrown with bent-grass' (see *Ekwall 1960*).

   Salter seems correct, in placing Marlcliff in Bidford-on-Avon, War. (see *E.C.*, vol.1, p.21, nn.7f.), and Sawyer correct, in placing Bentley in Holt, Worcs. (see *Sawyer 1968*, no.911).

   V.C.H., War., vol.3, pp.52 & 55, includes Marlcliff, as a hamlet, in Bidford-on-Avon. Bidford (as its name implies) is at a river-crossing, where the Roman Ryknield Street crosses the Avon. The road is coming down from Alcester, and going south to meet Foss Way, near to Bourton-on-the-Water.

   Bidford itself is on the north side of the river, and Marlcliff on the south. The shire boundary with Worcestershire winds about below it, and Cleeve Prior, Worcs., is just beyond the boundary.

Appendix 3

Eynsham Abbey Library

The two cartularies survive; so also the customary. What then of other books? The Rule required that periods should be set aside each day for *lectio divina* (spiritual reading; see *Knowles 1963*, pp.5f.). What had Eynsham abbey on its shelves?

One such book has been mentioned already. Marked B9, it was a work by Augustine of Hippo, entitled *De vera et falsa penitentia* (Concerning genuine and sham repentance). It is part of Bodleian *MS. Laud Lat. 31*, and it dates from the 12th century. It carries the shelf-mark, and also a reference to Eynsham abbey as its owner (see ch.6, above, and *Ker 1964*, p.86).

Ker notes three other MSS., which have closely similar shelf-marks — B4, C15 and D20. In these instances, however, there is no reference to Eynsham abbey.

B4 (*B IIII*) is another work by Augustine, and it seems likely that it stood on the Eynsham abbey shelves, not far from B9. It dates from the same century, but was not necessarily written and illuminated in Eynsham. It is *Bodleian MS. 269*, and it is a *Commentary on Psalms 101-150*.

It contains a very beautiful painted drawing of the Virgin Mary with her infant Son, a drawing which would always be of special significance in St. Mary's, Eynsham (see ch.15, above). It is discussed at length in C.M. Kauffmann, *Romanesque Manuscripts 1066-1190 (A Survey of Manuscripts Illuminated in the British Isles, vol.3)*, 1975, p.86, and in M. Rickert, *Painting in Britain: the Middle Ages (Pelican History of Art)*, 1954, pp.92f.

Probably executed in *c*.1130-40, and more than 10in. by 6in. in size, the crowned and enthroned Virgin, bearing on her arm the Lord incarnate, is full of delicate beauty, deep authority, and rich symbolism. Its challenge would confront, and check, and inspire, each reader. It speaks at once of Marian teaching of that day, and it is in itself an apt commentary upon Bishop Remigius' dilemma of 1091 (see E5, in ch.15, above).

John Leland, King's antiquary, was dispatched by Henry VIII to report upon old manuscripts in English religious houses. He found three in Eynsham:

i. Prosper of Aquitaine, *Concerning the Contemplative and the Active Life*. This was a favourite monastic theme. In effect, it concerned two sides of one Benedictine coin (see *Butler 1924*, pp.93-110).

ii. Henry of Huntingdon, *History of the English*. Henry was one of Bishop Bloet's archdeacons (see ch.17, above).

iii. William of Malmesbury, *Concerning the Lamentations of Jeremiah*. Leland calls William *Meldunensis*, after Mailduibh, 7th-century Celtic hermit, founding father of Malmesbury abbey, and teacher of Aldhelm.

Leland's work, left in manuscript, was published by Thomas Hearne, early in the 18th century.

For Eynsham, see J.Leland, *De Rebus Britannicis Collectanea*, ed. T. Hearne, 2nd edn., 6 vols., 1774, vol.4, p.161.

For Leland himself, see *Lives of Leland, Hearne and Wood*, ed. W. Huddesford, 2 vols., 1772. (Note that in vol.2, at p.104, this work embraces Cole's somewhat crude, but comparatively accurate, engraving of Anthony Wood's 1657 drawing of Eynsham abbey ruins.)

Appendix 4

Anglo-Saxon Latinity

The ordinary Anglo-Saxon, like most men of Germanic stock, prized skill in hunting and fighting, rather than in reading and writing. Literary excellence was for clergy, or women, or (so far as necessary) for kings and princes. Each one, of course, had his own tribal tongue, but, over and above it, and pervasive in western Europe, was Latin. This was the *lingua franca* of culture, scholarship, and education. Inherited from the ancient classical world, it served to transmit civilizing ideas from older Mediterranean teachers, as well as to provide a flexible and precise medium for expressing, analysing, and codifying fresh thought about new problems in the medieval world. Aelfric, as we have seen, perceived the need to communicate deeper things to wider audiences by means of their daily speech, but, in matters of general scholarship, he, like all the rest, used Latin.

Some English writers, such as William of Malmesbury, maintained a sound style of classical Latin — economical in words, unadorned, austere, and firm. Others, like Aldhelm, at the end of the seventh century, abbot of Malmesbury, afterwards bishop of Sherborne, a teacher widely read in pre-Conquest England, used a Latin, which was more florid, more imaginative, at times more affected and extravagant. New words were strained after, especially Greek ones. Archaic words were searched out and played with. Variety was prized for variety's sake. There was something fanciful, and almost deliberately obscure.

This style, sometimes called 'hermeneutic', may well have influenced Aethelweard senior, Aethelmaer's father, when he was translating the Anglo-Saxon Chronicle into Latin (see *The Chronicle of Aethelweard*, ed. A. Campbell, London, 1962). William of Malmesbury had little use for it:

> It is best to keep quiet about Aethelweard: he was a distinguished man, and indeed outstanding: and he attempted to set out those chronicles in Latin: I liked his intention, but his style was revolting

(from the Latin of *Wm. Malm. G.R.*, vol.1, Prologue).

Stenton thought it 'deplorable' (see *Stenton 1971*, p.461). A modern German scholar called it barbaric:

> The two great writers, Aldhelm and Bede, write, like all Anglo-Saxons, a stylistic-ally uncultivated (*verwildertes*), though grammatically correct Latin

(from the German of E. Norden, *Die antike Kunstprosa*, 1958, in M. Winterbottom, *Aldhelm's Prose Style and its Origins*, A.S.E., vol.6 (1977), pp.39-76).

It is perhaps better to see this Anglo-Latin as one among many legitimate growths from the great stock of ancient Latin.

A Latin, similarly obscure, but even more so, is found in a work called *Hisperica Famina* (ed. M.W. Herren, Toronto, 1974). It may have influenced Aldhelm, through the Irish monk Mailduibh, who was said to have played a part in founding Malmesbury abbey. But the connection, if any, between hisperic and hermeneutic Latin is by no means clear.

I have drawn attention to various examples of hermeneutic Latin, in considering charters E1 and E2 (see pp.10, 24, 28 & 66). Note also, in E1, the almost untranslatable description of the *witan, omnibus ecclesiastice pietatis ordinibus seu secularis potentie dignitatibus,* and the remarkable phrase *calce carens* (lit., lacking the chalk-mark for the end of a race) for 'eternal', and, in E2, *Apostolico nostro* (our apostolic man) for the Pope.

For further reading, see K. Sisam, *Anglo-Saxon Royal Genealogies, Procdgs. Brit. Acad.,* vol.39 (1953), pp.287-348, esp.p.320, n.4; L. Whitbread, *Aethelweard and the Anglo-Saxon Chronicle, E.H.R.,* vol.74 (1959), pp.577-89; M. Winterbottom, *The Style of Aethelweard, Medium Aevum,* vol.36 (1967), pp.109-118; M. Lapidge, *The Hermeneutic Style in 10th century Anglo-Latin Literature, A.S.E.,* vol.4 (1975), pp.67-111; C.P. Wormald, *The Uses of Literacy in Anglo-Saxon England and its Neighbours, Trans. Ryl. Hist. Soc.,* 5th ser., vol.27 (1977), pp.95-114; also the ongoing *Dictionary of Medieval Latin from British Sources,* ed. R.E. Latham, London, 1975-).

Appendix 5

Liturgical Drama at Eynsham Abbey

Jesus broke bread, and said, 'Do this . . .'; Jesus washed feet, and said, 'Do as I have done . . .'; Jesus was baptized, and said, 'Go, and baptize . . .': he knew the meaningfulness of dramatic symbolism, as also the grace which it could convey.

It is clear, from Aelfric's *Letter to the Monks of Eynsham* (see ch.8, above), that Anglo-Saxon monks found enrichment and enlivening in liturgical drama. And Holy Week had special excitements — the diminishing row of candles, the singing from four sides of the church, the coaxing of new fire from dead stone, the serpent uplifted, with a candle in its mouth. Such things would, of course, be anticipated and planned with simple, and even boyish, pleasure, and they would alleviate monotony and repetition; but they would also stir imagination and quicken the soul. They were drawn from the same deep wells as was so much Anglo-Saxon art.

The 10th-century monastic reformers, in their *Regularis Concordia*, had given special attention to liturgical drama for Easter morning. Here is Chambers' sensitive translation of directions for Mattins on that day:

> While the third lesson is being chanted, let four brethren vest themselves. Let one of these, vested in an alb, enter as though to take part in the service, and let him approach the sepulchre without attracting attention and sit there quietly with a palm in his hand. While the third respond is chanted, let the remaining three follow, and let them all, vested in copes, bearing in their hands thuribles with incense, and stepping delicately as those who seek something, approach the sepulchre. These things are done in imitation of the angel sitting in the monument, and the women with spices coming to anoint the body of Jesus. When therefore he who sits there beholds the three approach him like folk lost and seeking something, let him begin in a dulcet voice of medium pitch to sing *Quem quaeritis?* (Whom seek ye?) And when he has sung it to the end, let the three reply in unison *Ihesu Nazarenum* (Jesus of Nazareth). So he, *Non est hic, surrexit sicut praedixerat. Ite, nuntiate quia surrexit a mortuis* (He is not here: he has risen, just as he had foretold. Go, tell the news that he has risen from the dead). At the word of this bidding let those three turn to the choir and say *Alleluia! resurrexit Dominus!* (The Lord is risen!) This said, let the one still sitting there and as if recalling them, say the antiphon *Venite et videte locum* (Come and see the place). And saying this, let him rise, and lift the veil, and show them the place bare of the cross, but only the cloths laid there in which the cross was wrapped. And when they have seen this, let them set down the thuribles which they bare in that same sepulchre, and take the cloth, and hold it up in the face of the clergy, and as if to demonstrate that the Lord has risen and is no longer wrapped therein, let them sing the antiphon *Surrexit Dominus de sepulchro* (The Lord is risen from the sepulchre), and lay the cloth upon the altar. When the antiphon is done, let the prior, sharing in their gladness at the triumph of our King, in that, having vanquished death, he rose again, begin the hymn *Te Deum laudamus*. And this begun, all the bells chime out together
> (from E.K. Chambers, *The Medieval Stage*, vol.2, Oxford, 1903, pp.14f.& 309; for

the accompanying music, see G. Reese, *Music in the Middle Ages*, London, 1941, pp.193ff.).[1]

Aelfric's *Letter* (which, here as elsewhere, shows a certain independence from the *Regularis Concordia*) makes no mention of that particular drama. Yet, two centuries later, Eynsham abbey had its own form of it. For, on Easter morning, in 1196, the monk Edmund came back from his trance in time for it:

And there he persisted in constant weeping, whilst Mattins were sung right through, and as, in that same church, they followed their customs for Easter Day. The resurrection of the Lord was enacted before their eyes: and the angel was shown, speaking with the women at the tomb, and telling them the finished triumphs of their King, and bidding them tell the disciples: and then Christ himself was seen, as, in the guise of the gardener, he spoke with that Mary who loved him so much. And still the monk wept, until, when masses had been celebrated, he was deemed worthy to share in and feast upon the holy sacrament

(from the Latin of the Vision, ch.7; see *E.C.*, vol. 2, p.294).

And here is the same passage, in the anonymous and very delightful translation, printed by Wm. de Machlinia (Malines), in London, in *c.*1482-6:

And there in gret deuocyon and terys bode and contynewid til matens was doon and tyl the resurreccion of our lorde the whiche yerely in the same chirche is wont to be shewid vysybly and howe the angel apperid and spake to the women at the sepulture of the victoriose resurreccion of ther king and also that they shulde tel to his disciplys his glorious resurreccion and at the laste til our lord apperyd to his welbelouyd mary mawdelen and named her maria in the figure of a gardner and til the messys ware doone and had resceyuid the holy comyning of cristen men

(from *English Reprint* of the Vision, ed. E. Arber, 1869, p.27).

Notes

1. Following Reese, the word 'antiphon' (Latin, *antiphona*) has been substituted for Chambers' 'anthem'.

Appendix 6

Remigius: allegations of simony

Remigius had been with Duke William at Hastings, and had received his bishopric in the following year. The evidence for a charge of simony was circumstantial, but it was strong. The story that he had had to make the tiresome journey to Rome and back, in order to regularize his position, seemed authentic:

a) William of Malmesbury's account is brilliant and incisive. A monk and a scholar, half English, half Norman, he wrote prolifically from his Wiltshire cloister. Sometimes, in later editions, he modified acid judgements. In *c*.1125 he told of Remigius. In this case he never altered his verdict:

> Remigius had been a monk at Fécamp. When William, duke of Normandy, was coming to England, Remigius gave him considerable help. It had been agreed between them that, if William won, Remigius would receive a bishopric. And William was as quick in giving him one as Remigius was in taking it (*nec fuit Willelmus segnior in dando quam Remigius in accipiendo*)

> (from the Latin of *Wm. Malm. G.P.*, p.312).

b) A small Bodleian MS., written in *c*.1150 (see *Hardy 1862-5*, vol.2, p.l), may not be accurate, but confirms the rumour. It lists those who contributed to William's invading force. Participation and reward appear to be linked:

> William, duke of Normandy, coming to England, to take possession of the kingdom, which was his by right, had from his steward William Fitz Osbern 60 ships: from Hugh, later earl of Chester, the same number: from Hugh de Montfort, 50 ships, and 60 'knights': from Remigius, almoner of Fécamp, later bishop of Lincoln, one ship, with 20 'knights' . . . (*a romo*[1] *elemosinario fescanni postea episcopo Lincoliensi unam navem cum xx militibus*)

> (from the Latin of *Bodl. MS.* e. Mus. 93, p.16).

c) Eadmer of Canterbury was another monk, somewhat earlier in date than William of Malmesbury. He was of English blood, but a keen supporter of the new order, and particularly of archbishops Lanfranc and Anselm. He wrote:

> (Lanfranc) set off for Rome, to receive the *pallium*[2] which was due to him as archbishop. He took with him two bishops, companions on his way: one was Thomas, archbishop of York, who had been consecrated by him at Canterbury, after professing canonical subjection to him: the other was Remigius, bishop of Lincoln. They arrived in Rome at the same time, and were all received with courtesy and dignity, each according to his place.

> Afterwards there was an appointed day, when Father Lanfranc was presented to Alexander, pontiff of the apostolic see. To the astonishment of those who were familiar with Roman custom, the pope himself stood up, as Lanfranc came in to him, and sweetly bade him halt his steps. And he continued, 'We have shown this special respect, not because of your archbishopric, but because you are the teacher

to whose earnest care we owe all that we know. This done, it is meet and right for you, on your part, to offer appropriate reverence to Blessed Peter.' That said, he resumed his seat, and Lanfranc came forward, and prostrated himself at his feet. Swiftly, however, the pope uplifted him, and kissed him. And then they sat down together, and passed that day in happiness, the one with the other.

On the next morning, sundry affairs were brought to their attention. And then a charge, concerning Thomas and Remigius, was laid before the pope. By canon law, it was declared, neither of them should have been raised to the episcopate: Thomas, because he was the son of a priest, and not a monk, and such should not go forward in holy orders: Remigius, because he had made a bargain with William, and bought his bishopric: for, when William was hasting to conquer England, Remigius had come forward with all kinds of help and met sundry expenses: and when William had become king, he had rewarded him. Hearing this, both of them were aware that they had no plausible excuses to offer. So they handed back their staffs and their rings, together with their episcopal responsibilities, and they begged for mercy.

When Lanfranc heard their pleas, he threw himself between, mighty man that he was, both in faith and wisdom, and with ready speech he made plain that both these men were of wide and strong experience, both of them utterly essential to the new king in the re-ordering of his kingdom, both of them outstanding in many ways.

Hearing this, the Supreme Pontiff turned himself to Lanfranc and said, 'Lo, you are a veritable father to that fatherland: and thus you are at pains to see what is best for it. The pastoral staffs, which they returned, behold, here they are. Take them, and confer them, just exactly as you see is most profitable for the Christian faith in that place.' So Lanfranc took them, and there and then, in the very presence of the pope, invested those men again, each one with his own insignia.

And then, having received the stole of his own primacy from the pope, he retraced his steps to England, and came there quickly, together with his companions. He was given due reverence by the men of Canterbury, and was confirmed as primate of the whole of Britain (*primas totius Britanniae*)[3]

(from the Latin of *Eadmer*, pp.10-12).

d) Gerald of Wales was a secular priest, archdeacon of Brecon, twice elected bishop of St. David's, twice rejected by England. He was no lover of monks: but, in *c*.1198, he wrote a *Life of Remigius*, and made a vigorous case for his canonization. The alleged simony was an obvious problem. Gerald's answer was that Remigius had certainly helped out at Hastings, but that the whole thing had been utterly disagreeable to him, and a matter of grim duty, in no way sullying his impeccable priesthood:

Remigius, you should know, was a man of discretion, a man of foresight, a man of wide education and culture, Norman in origin, a monk of the house of Fécamp. And since

Giving pleasure to princes is by no means the least of human virtues,[4]
he had come to the notice of the king, and indeed to no small intimacy and favour. So it was that he accompanied the king into his new kingdom: and, like a high-born officer, responsible for essential service, he was set over 10 'knights': they had been sent by his abbot, to help him and serve him. It was an unpleasant task, undertaken unwillingly: for it carried him far from the quiet of the cloister. Nevertheless, mindful of his vow of obedience, he carried out what his superiors had bidden: and he did so with diligence and with a humble spirit: so much so that, becoming as it were all things to all men,[5] even in the midst of the din and confusion of battle, he did not affront the warriors of this world by overmuch

stiffness of bearing or peculiarity of religion, nor yet did he permit the contagions of the world to soil the dignity of his order or his habit with any spot or blemish whatsoever

(from the Latin of *Ger. Wales*, pp.14f.).

e) John of Schalby wrote about a century later. As a canon of Lincoln, and registrar to its bishop, Oliver Sutton, he had been schooled in diplomacy. His reference to Remigius was veiled and cautious. The monk of Fécamp had come to England 'for a certain reason (*ob certam causam*)' (from the Latin of *Ger. Wales*, p.193). What could be more tactful?

Notes

1. MS., *romo*, with interlinear *rumi*.
2. The *pallium* is a circular band, white in colour, woven of lamb's wool, with hanging strips before and behind, embroidered with six purple crosses. By this time it was worn on the shoulders by popes, and conferred by them upon archbishops, as a sign of delegated authority. In heraldic form it still appears on the Arms of the archbishop of Canterbury.
3. In point of fact even the archbishops of York, let alone archbishops in Scotland and Ireland, were not at all enthusiastic about Canterbury's special primacy.
4. From Horace, Epistles, 1, 17, 35 (*principibus placuisse viris non ultima laus est*).
5. See 1 Cor. 9, 22.

Appendix 7

The sad story of Yarnton

Land in Yarnton, Oxon. (see illustration 12) was given to Eynsham abbey in 1005 (see E1). In 1091 Bishop Remigius included it in his list of Eynsham abbey properties (see E5). By 1086, however, the abbey had already begun to lose ground there; although the Yarnton land still belonged to it, it was held by Roger d'Ivry (see ch.12, n.2, and *D.B., Oxon.*). Henry I's charter of 1109 seems to reflect that change, for Yarnton land is listed as Eynsham abbey's, but tacked on to the list in a somewhat uncertain manner (see E7).

The abbey evidently tried hard to regain possession, but felt that a curious chapter of accidents had come between them and what was theirs. In *c.*1270 they put their own summary version of the matter into an odd space in their cartulary. It reveals a somewhat erroneous grasp of the earlier portion of the saga, for it makes Bishop Remigius, who died in 1092, contemporary with King Henry II, who only began to reign in 1154. There is a lugubrious pathos about their litigation. Here is a translation; I have added relevant data in the margin:

The manor of Yarnton remained in the possession of the church of Eynsham for a long time. And a certain Remigius, then bishop of Lincoln, made request that that manor be lent to him, so that he could sojourn there for a while: and it was granted him. And shortly afterwards the said Remigius departed this life (*in fata decessit*), being at the time seised of the said manor, as a loan.

Remigius, bishop
of Lincoln,
1067-92

And Lord Henry II, king of England, took seisin of the barony of the said bishop, and also of the said manor of Yarnton: our Lord the said King then handed this manor over to a certain Bernard de St. Valéry. Abbot Godfrey of Eynsham frequently took this Bernard to the King's court, in pursuit of his rights (*sepius convenit coram rege de jure suo*), but to no avail. Bernard offered him homage, but Abbot Godfrey refused it: then, however, Robert II, bishop of Lincoln, accepted it, saving only the rights of the abbot and convent of Eynsham.

King, 1154-89

Abbot, 1150/51-95

Robert de Chesney,
1148-66
Abbot, 1197-1208

When Abbot Godfrey died, he was succeeded by an abbot named Robert, who sued the said Bernard, by a writ concerning his rights (*implacitavit per breve de recto*), in the court of the same (*sic*), William, then bishop of Lincoln. When, however, the bishop died before the end of the case, Abbot Robert pursued it in the court of King John. Twelve law-worthy men had been chosen from the neighbourhood (*duodecim homines legales de vineto*), and taken to the court at Southwick, all ready to

William de Blois,
1203-6

King, 1199-1216

King there,
May 9, 1206

165

make a sworn statement concerning the said manor; but just then all cases were held over, pending the return of the King from across the water. Soon afterwards Abbot Robert went to his Lord (*migravit ad Dominum*).

His successor was Abbot Adam, who took Thomas de St. Valéry to law, by a writ concerning his rights in the court of the lord bishop of Lincoln. But just when he was due to appear in court the affairs of the kingdom were thrown into confusion by the arrival of Louis in England: and laws fell silent before the clash of arms (*siluerunt leges in arma*).

Not long afterwards Thomas also died, and his inheritance went through his daughter to Robert, count of Dreux: this Robert was by royal letters summoned before the King's court: just when the justices had come down to Oxford, and jurors had been selected, and were in court, and when the day had come when the matter ought to have been brought to judgement, royal letters were produced, saying that Robert had lost seisin of all that he had in England, and that custody of his lands had been handed over to Lord Richard, brother to our Lord the King

(from the Latin of E44B).

King to Normandy,
June 1, 1206

Abbot, 1213/14-28

Thomas succeeded
brother Bernard,
*c.*1191

Louis (Dauphin)
landed, 1216

Hugh of Wells, bishop,
1209-35

Henry III,
1216-72

Richard of Cornwall,
brother to Henry III

Appendix 8

More about the Customary

1. *The prayers for use by travellers*

A short prayer in Middle English, and another in Middle French, are of special interest. Probably meant. to be memorized and said quickly at moments of emergency, they almost have the character of charms. They envisage Jesus himself, with three of his most relevant saints, invisibly present and very potent, behind and with the four lay-figures, upon whose integrity and efficiency a successful journey depended — the guide and leader who took the party, day by day, through England's wild and wooded tracks; the innkeeper, who sheltered the party night by night; the steward, who supervised the general practicalities of the expedition; and the marshal, who had particular responsibility for the horses, the mainstay of medieval transport. We must, I think, envisage a substantial party, joined up with similar parties, and reminiscent of the famous Canterbury pilgrims of Chaucer. Here are the texts of the prayers:

> Crist us helpe ant rede
> Crist us witte and lede
> Crist us fede and schrude
> Crist us leve spede
> Crist us wyssi lif to then ende
> an ware hure hedi mel
> and ure rith reste hup schal arise

> Jesu seyt nostre conduur
> sant Julien nostre herbergur
> saynt Phelippe nostre seneschal
> saynt Ypolyte nostre mareschal
> et deu nus duiut tel hoste de ki
> nus euns plus kil del nostre. Amen deus

> (from *E.Cust.*, ff.126R (see illustrations 31-32) and 126V).

The ends of each text are difficult to interpret, and may contain scribal errors. The Middle English may be translated as follows:

> Christ help and guard us
> Christ keep safe and lead us
> Christ feed and clothe us
> Christ grant us good fortune
> Christ guide us *lif* to the end
> and guard (us) against our *hedi mel*
> and our true rest will rise up.

(Notes: *schrude*, south-west Midland spelling; *schrede*, south-eastern spelling, would rhyme better. *Lif*, either noun or verb, 'life' or 'live'. *Hedi mel* may be a scribal mistake for *hedi iuel* (headstrong evil-doing); perhaps it means 'heady mell', that is 'heady or impetuous association, possibly with undesirable women', but that involves the use of 'mell' as a noun.)

The poem is not listed in C. Brown & R.H. Robbins, *The Index of Middle English Verse* (New York, 1943), or in R.H. Robbins & J.L. Cutler, *Supplement to the Index of Middle English Verse* (Lexington, 1965). There is a different travellers' prayer in R.H. Robbins, *Secular Lyrics of the XIVth and XVth centuries*, no.64 (2nd edn., Oxford, 1955).

The Middle French prayer may perhaps be translated as follows:

> Jesu be our guide
> Saint Julian our innkeeper
> Saint Philip our steward
> Saint Hippolytus our marshal
> and may God bring us unto such a host
> that we may have more from him than he from us. Amen God.

The name Philip means 'horse-lover', the name Hippolytus 'horse-looser'; 'hippos' is the Greek word for horse. That fact alone may have brought them into the list. The Ethiopian eunuch of Acts 8, 26-40, however, was travelling, and in a horse-drawn carriage, when St. Philip the Evangelist brought the gospel to him. The village of St. Ippolyts near Hitchin, Hertfordshire, took its name from its church of St. Hippolytus, a church to which people used to bring sick horses, in hope of healing.

The following jingle perhaps catches the 'feel' of the prayer:

> Jesu lead us on our way
> Saint Julian guard us where we stay
> Saint Philip husband our resources
> Saint Hippolytus give us healthy horses
> and God bestow us such a host
> that we (not he) may profit most
> O Father, Son, and Holy Ghost.

2. *Prayers for founders and benefactors*
Here are the French texts of the alternative prayers

> Deu pur sa grace assoile nostre seignour Eilmer ki cest liu funda, sa cumpaine, le cunte Leufriz, la cuntesse Godive, et tuz nos aultres fundius et benefaiturs, tuz les abbez et lez moines de ceste maisun, nos peres, nos meres, nos freres, nos sorurs, tuz nos benefaiturs et tuz iceus pur ki nus devuns prier e ki en nus unt lur esperance et tuz les almes ki cors en cest cimiterie reposent . . .

(from *Id.*, f.38V).

> Deu pur sa grace assoile nostre seignur Eilmer ki cest liu funda, sa compaine, labbe uel, labbe Columbel, labbe Walt', lautre Walt', labbe Will', labbe Godef', labbe Rob' et cetera, le cunte Leufriz, la cuntesse God', le rei Henri, Henri de Oxenford, Hug' de Mortemer, Rad' de Chaine, Rad' Murdac, Walkelin Hareng, Dam Ide, Dam Mald de Chaine, maistre Nich', Geffr' le Chamberleyn et cetera. Tuiz nos freres ki departirent puis ke la maisun fu funde

(from *Id.*, ff.38V/39R; for MS. of second prayer, see illustrations 31-32).

labbe uel (in the second, and older, prayer) presents problems:

i. Salter suggests that it might refer to the pre-Conquest Anglo-Saxon abbots, but the French words are in the singular, 'the old abbot' (see *E.C.*, vol.1, pp.xii ff.).

ii. It has been suggested to me that possibly *uel ‹ yvel* = equal, meaning 'the abbot likewise'; or perhaps *uel* = Latin *vel*, used rather like *scillicet*; or perhaps *Uel'* or *Vel'* is an abbreviated name.

iii. The last of those suggestions led me back to *H.R.H., 1972*, p.49, and its list of Eynsham abbots. It includes a little-known abbot Nigel of Eynsham, dying on 9 May

1128, and succeeded by abbot Walter. He may have been active, for some ten years before then, in connection with the foundation of a daughter house, Luffield Priory, on the Buckinghamshire/Northamptonshire border. His record appears in one MS. of John of Worcester's *Continuation* of Florence of Worcester's *Chronicon ex Chronicis* (see *Id.*, ed. J.R.H. Weaver, Oxford, 1908, p.29, n.1, *Decessit hoc anno (sc. 1128) reverendus Egeneshamensis aecclesiae abbas Nigellus vii°.* id. Maii, successit ei Walterius; see also *Luffield 1975*).

Abbot Nigel is not mentioned in the Eynsham Cartulary, a fact which presumably led to Salter ignoring him, as also to the omission of his name from the older prayer, in the Customary, for deceased abbots. Yet there is no reason to question his name or his date. It is just a small item amongst other notes at the end of the 1128 record. Abbeys regularly sent notes around to other abbeys, announcing abbatial deaths and appointments, and requesting prayers.

Nigellus was, in fact, a latinized form of a common Norman and English name, *Nel* or *Nele*, a name which had Irish and Scandinavian roots (see *O.D.E.C.N.* 1950). Can it be that abbot Nigel had once appeared in Eynsham's prayers, abbreviated as *Nel* or *Nele*, but that his reign had been forgotten? If so, it had also been misplaced and put before Columban's.

iv. Another possibility is worth consideration. The list in that old prayer ends with abbot Robert (1197-1208). His successor, abbot Adam, was deposed in 1228 but was evidently still alive, probably in retired abbots' quarters in the precincts, or at times perhaps on his portion of land at Little Rollright, Oxon. (see *E.R.*, no.3, 1986). Though discredited, he was a distinguished figure, famed both as a writer and for his contacts with St. Hugh. It might almost be said that he still haunted the abbey, some of the past living on into the present, appearing in church perhaps, but not, I imagine, in the chapter house where these prayers were used. Could it be that the phrase 'the old abbot', *labbe uel*, had almost slipped into the prayers during that period, and before he actually qualified, by death, to have his name included?

3. The prayers for founders and benefactors lead into detailed directions about what comes next:

Then, if they are to return from the chapter-house to the cloister, let them rise and say the *Verba mea*.

And, if they are to have a period for conversation, let the clapper be sounded by the prior (even if the abbot is present), and let the *Benedicite* be said by the abbot.

And thus, after a solemn bow (*facto ante et retro*),[1] let them have converse in the cloister, no *Benedicite* being said there.

If, however, some or other request for prayer (*aliquod breve*) has been received from another house and been read out in chapter, they must go to the church, and the bells will be sounded for that:

likewise, if the anniversary of one of our benefactors has been announced, or the death of some important person: and the bells must be sounded for that also:

or if perhaps there is some other occasion for going to church, as is the case, when, because of something that has happened, the seven penitential psalms have to be said after chapter . . .

And so on, and so on. It sounds tedious and irritating; but, in point of fact, a monk would soon get used to it, and the giving of signals by clapper, or by bells, or by the use of this or that prayer, made for order and quietness in their shared life.

It should be remembered that these monks had already been engaged, for several hours, in prayers and in devotional reading, followed by general business. By this time they were looking forward to a brief period of relaxed, though quiet, conversation in the cloister. In chapter, however, they may have heard of a special request or need for prayer, and prayer was their chief task. It would ill become them to delay. Conversation or not, therefore, they must return to church, and pray forthwith.

Notes

1. See *E.Cust.*, p.36, n.14; a solemn bow from the centre to those on the left and right; prescribed for numerous occasions in various places within the monastery.

Appendix 9

Vision of the Monk of Eynsham: Bibliography

1. Printed texts:
a. Salter, *E.C.*, vol.2 (1908), pp.255-371 (Latin text, with Introduction, notes, and summaries of each chapter, in English).

b. H. Thurston, in *Analecta Bollandiana*, vol.22 (1903), pp.225-319 (Latin text, with Introduction in Latin).

c. P.M. Huber, in *Romanische Forschungen*, vol.16 (1903), pp.641-733 (Latin text, with Introduction in German).

2. Translations into English:
a. *The Revelation of Saint Nicholas to a Monk of Evesham* (*sic*), printed by Wm. de Machlinia, London, *c*.1483 (reprinted, in *English Reprints*, ed. E. Arber, London, 1869).

b. *The Revelation of the Monk of Evesham* (*sic*), ed. J. Thomson, Glasgow, 1904 (in 'present-day English'; I have not seen it).

c. *The Revelation to the Monk of Evesham* (*sic*) *abbey*, ed. V. Paget, London, 1909 (a modernized version of Wm. de Machlinia).

3. There is a separate account of the same *Vision* in *Brit. Libr. Cotton MS. Calig. A. viii*, ff.192-209; like the other, it is in Latin, but it has been derived from a metrical version (now apparently lost) in French (see Salter, *E.C.*, vol.2, pp.278f. and H.L.D. Ward, *Catalogue of Romances in the Department of MSS. in the British Museum*, vol.2 (1893), pp.493-506).

4. References in Vita Hugonis:
1864 edn. (RS 37), pp.xxxiv-xlviii & 235-42.

5. Other medieval references:
a. *Ralph of Coggeshall* (RS 66), pp.71f.

b. *Roger of Wendover* (RS 84), vol.1, pp.246-66.

c. *Matthew Paris* (RS 57), vol.2, pp.423-37.

Appendix 10

Manipulation of monastic records

'Holy deceit' is, of course, a contradiction in terms; but godly people can, in fact, argue themselves into some very odd positions, and then claim that it is all for God's glory. Monks often found it convenient to falsify their records, to misapply their seals, and even to forge seals (see *Regesta*, vol.4, pp.1-23, and *Jocelin*, pp.2ff.). We have seen the tip of this iceberg in the manner in which Eynsham abbey's foundation-charter was virtually merged with a Stow charter. It is a factor to which attention must be paid at every point. To what (if any) extent were the Eynsham monks who, in *c*.1196, chose and ordered the earlier entries in their new cartulary manipulating their material in favour of their own institution?

It is distasteful to make such an assertion; so let the case of *Ingulf's Chronicle* demonstrate it. In the year 1076 Ingulf became abbot of Crowland, Lincolnshire. Later on, in the 14th century, the monks of that house were involved in fierce dispute with the citizens of Spalding and Moulton. However, they were short of evidence in support of their claims, so they proceeded to make it up. They concocted a detailed account of the earlier days of their abbey. They fabricated complete charters. And they attributed the whole story to Ingulf, and wrote it as if he were himself speaking. The whole work was fictional, and done with considerable imagination and romantic skill. It was trusted and quoted until last century. Then its falsity was exposed.

The following extract (including a once-valued reference to Stow) illustrates the quality and character of the writing. It refers to the year 1076. There is no evidence that Stow had any abbey at that time.

> In that monastery, to the service of which, under God, I am devoted, I found sixty-two monks, of whom four were lay brothers, besides monks from other monasteries who had become members of our chapter, and each of whom had a stall in the choir, a seat in the refectory, and a bed in the dormitory. These returned, according as they desired, some after half a year, some after a year, to their own monasteries; and they, especially in times of war, and when the least howling of the tempest threatened the disturbance of peace, took refuge at Crowland. Of this number there were ten from Thorney, six from Peterborough, eight from Ramsey, three from Hely, nine from St. Edmund's, twelve from St. Alban's, ten from Westminster, two from St. Andrew's at Northampton, fourteen from Christ's church at Norwich, fifteen from Thetford, seven from Coventry, six from St. Mary's without York, ten from St. Mary's at Stow, six from Michelneye, and five from Malmesbury, besides daily visitors, and some who seeing the security of the place, and the mutual affection of the brethren of Crowland, devoutly, besought us to allow them to become members of our college, and were permanently settled among us. The kindness which from a remote period had been engendered in our monastery rarely or never repelled any one who knocked at its gate

> (from the Latin of *The History of Ingulf*, in *The Church Historians of England*, as translated by J. Stevenson, 1854, vol.2, pt.2, p.675; see also *Ingulf's Chronicle*, transl. H.T. Riley, 1854, p.153).

Eynsham Cartulary: indications of structure

Related groups etc.	Charter numbers and dates (Salter)	Notes
Eynsham & Stow beginnings	1-7 (1005-1109)	
'Processions' to Eynsham	8-12 (*c*.1138-64)	
Insertion Grant from Thomas de St. Valéry	13 (1191-1205)	Early hand over erasure
Henry II grants royal protection	14 (1180-9)	
Bishops of Lincoln: Alexander Robert de Chesney	15-19 (1123-66)	No. 19 may be from Robert Bloet
Apparent diversion Hugh of Avalon	20-23A (1186-1200)	
Land at Fawler	24-25 (1213-1225)	Another hand
William I or II	26-28 (11th century)	
Stephen & Henry II (also Empress Matilda & Count de Meulan)	29-39 (1135-66)	No. 37 may be from Henry I (?1109)
Insertion Bishops Hugh of Avalon & William de Blois	40-40A (1186-1206)	Different hands, followed by fol.20 (recto) blank
Four archbishops of Canterbury	41-44 (1155-1200)	
Insertion New Land & Yarnton	44A-44B (1215-70)	Later hands
Six bishops, other than Lincoln	45-51 (1148-86)	
Archdeacons	52-58 (1151-92)	
Basset family	59-63 (1144-88)	
d'Oilly family	64-77 (*c*.1115-97)	

'Newark etc.': varying lists
(dates as suggested in sources)

1.	E1A	1053-5	Leofric & Godiva: 'lands' (O.E. *tha land*).

2.   E2   1054-7   Godiva: 'Newark and Fledborough, with what pertains to them, as also Brampton, and Marton in the wapentake of Well, with what pertains to them' (*Newercha . . . atque Flatburch cum appenditiis suis & Branthon & Martinewelle cum appenditiis*).

3.   E3   *c*.1080-87   Leofric & Godiva: 'Newark and Fledborough and Well wapentake, together with what pertains to them' (*Nuwercham & Flaburcam ac Welle wapentac cum appenditiis suis*):

4.   L3/3   1090   Leofric & Godiva: 'Newark, Fledborough, Well wapentake, excepting the third penny of the shire' (*Newercham, Flatburch, Wellewapentacum, excepto denario tercio comitatus*).

5.   E5   1091   Leofric & Godiva: 'Brampton and two-thirds of Well wapentake, together with all that' appertains to them, Newark also and Fledborough, similarly' (*Brantonam . . . & duas portiones Guelleguapentac cum omnibus sibi pertinentiis Newercham quoque ac Flatburch cum universis sibi adjacentibus*).

6.   E27   1075-92   Godiva: 'Newark and Fledborough and Brampton and Well wapentake, with sac and soke, and toll and team' (O.E. *Niweweorce & Fladburh & Brantune & Wylle Wepentaec mid sace & mid socne & tolle & teame*).

7.   E7   1109   Robert Bloet: 'in exchange for Newark and Stow' (*pro commutatione Niwerche & Stowe*).

Appendix 13

Salter and Chambers

Salter's *Eynsham Cartulary* (1907-8) dominates Eynsham abbey studies. Chambers' *Eynsham under the Monks* (1936) went on from Salter. So did Gransden's *Eynsham Customary* (1963).

Herbert Edward Salter (1863-1951) was at New College, Oxford, and gained a Second in Mods., a First in Greats, and a First in Theology. He was ordained in the Church of England, but abandoned parochial work, after being Vicar of Shirburn, Oxon. (1899-1909). He had already evinced a consuming interest in the local history of Oxford — the city, the university, the colleges, the neighbouring abbeys and churches etc. His *Eynsham Cartulary* was the first in an astonishing output of major publications. He remained near Oxford until 1942, and then moved to Dorset. Until well on in years he kept up an interest in vigorous country pursuits — bees, ferrets, fruit, vegetables, walking, cycling, even beagling! He had been a Research Fellow of Magdalen College, Oxford (1918-39). He had been made an Honorary Freeman of the City of Oxford (1930). He had been awarded an Oxford D.Litt. (1933). His work had been quiet, unassuming, unspectacular, but wide-ranging and very thorough, and of immense value to all who follow.

His working-papers are in the Bodleian library, Oxford. They indicate the firm boundaries which he had set for his research. He was familiar, for example, with Eynsham abbey's Harleian Rolls, and its Customary, and its Vision, but in each case left much further study to be done.

Oxford Essays in Medieval History: presented to Herbert Edward Salter was published in his honour in 1934. It contained a photograph of him. Each writer acknowledged Salter's encouragement and help, and F.M. Powicke, then Regius Professor of Modern History, at Oxford, added a perceptive Foreword:

> Dr. Salter has been a pioneer in exploring the far-reaching implications of minute investigation into local history, local topography, and local records. He is an expert guide in palaeographical matters and in diplomatic. His writings have illuminated the study of monastic and municipal history.

One of the essayists is of special interest to Eynsham. Evelyn Emma Stefanos Procter spent her last years at Little Newland, Eynsham. Shy, devout, austere, independent, determined, wise, she had been a pillar of St. Hugh's College, Oxford, first as Fellow (1926-46), and then as Principal (1946-62). She was an authority on the royal courts of medieval Spain, particularly those of Leon and Castile.

Edmund Kerchever Chambers (1866-1954) was at Corpus Christi College, Oxford, and gained a First in Mods. and a First in Greats. He went into the Civil Service (1892-1926), and rose to be Second Secretary in the Board of Education. He was made C.B. in 1912 and K.B.E. in 1925. He was, however, 'a notable example of a man who followed two careers, both with distinction' (from *D.N.B. 1951-60*). Right from his Oxford days he had shown a profound interest in English poetry, especially dramatic verse, and particularly Shakespeare. He applied himself to its social and political context. Whilst still in the Civil Service, he published two valuable works, *The Medieval Stage* (2 vols., 1903) and *The Elizabethan Stage* (4 vols., 1923). Numerous other writings followed. He received a Durham D.Litt. in 1922 and an Oxford D.Litt. in 1939. In 1934 he became an Honorary Fellow of his old college.

After 1926, and until 1938, when he moved to Devon, he lived at Hythe Croft, Eynsham, and pursued his literary work. His *Eynsham under the Monks* was a by-product of those days.

In July 1960 his voluminous papers went from his family to the Bodleian library, Oxford. They contain many gems like the following. Edith Sitwell was asking for permission to use some of his *Early English Lyrics*. It seems that at times he was somewhat unapproachable. Like Agag before Samuel, the writer felt it wise to come 'delicately' (see 1 Sam. 15, 32)!

> May I take this opportunity of expressing some of the great gratitude all poets and poetry-lovers and all students of the art of poetry must feel towards you, and of sending you my homage

(from *Bodley Chambers MS.* Autogr. d.24).

She got what she wanted!

Amongst all the papers that went to the Bodleian library in 1960 there was a packet of Chambers' notes for his book on Eynsham. It seems that they were simply jottings, worthless to others, and very slight. They appear to have been discarded and destroyed. (Information in a letter, dated 8 July 1983, from the Keeper of Western Manuscripts at the Bodleian library to the present writer.)[1]

Notes

1. These notes owe much to *Who was Who 1951-60*, as well as to *D.N.B. 1951-60*.

Abbreviated references

Aelfric: Homilies
I (fac.)
    Aelfric's First Series of Catholic Homilies, facsimile, ed. N. Eliason & P. Clemoes (Early English MSS. in facsimile, vol.13), Copenhagen, 1966

Aelfric c.1567
    A Testimonie of Antiquitie: Aelfric's Sermon of the Paschall Lambe, ed. anon., London, *c.*1567

Aelfric, Saints
    Aelfric's Lives of Saints, ed. W.W. Skeat (EETS 76, 82, 94, 114: 4 pts. in 2 vols.), Oxford, 1881-1900; vol.1, revised & reprinted, 1966

A.S.E.
    Anglo-Saxon England, ed. P. Clemoes & others, vols. 1- , Cambridge, 1972-

Bailey 1989
    K. Bailey, *The Boundaries of Hanborough*, OLHA *Jnl.*, vol.3, pp.109ff.

Barlow 1
    F. Barlow, *The English Church 1000-1066*, 2nd edn., London, 1979

Barlow 2
    F. Barlow, *The English Church 1066-1154*, London, 1979

Bateson 1892
    Aelfric's Abridgement of St. Aethelwold's Concordia Regularis, ed. M. Bateson (Hants. Rec. Soc., 1892, pp.171-98, with *Obedientiary Rolls of St. Swithun's Priory, Winchester* (= *Letter to the Monks of Eynsham*)

Bateson 1894
    M. Bateson, *Rules for Monks and Secular Canons after the Revival under King Edgar*, E.H.R., 1894, pp.690-708

Benham 1916
    A.R. Benham, *English Literature from Widsith to Chaucer: a Source Book*, Yale & Oxford, 1916

Bennett 1947
    H.S. Bennett, *Life on the English Manor, A Study of Peasant Conditions, 1150-1400*, 3rd imprssn., Cambridge, 1947

Blair & Steane 1982
    J. Blair & J.M. Steane, *Investigations at Cogges, Oxfordshire, 1978-81*, Oxoniensia, vol.47 (1982), pp.37-125

Brooke 1957
    C.N.L. Brooke, *The Earliest Times to 1485*, in *A History of St. Paul's Cathedral*, ed. W.R. Matthews & W.M. Atkins, London, 1957, pp.1-99

Brooks 1974
    N. Brooks, *Anglo-Saxon Charters: the work of the last 20 years*, A.S.E., vol.3 (1974), pp.211-31

Brooks 1984
    N. Brooks, *The Early History of the Church of Canterbury*, Leicester, 1984

Butler 1924
    C. Butler, *Benedictine Monachism*, 2nd edn., 1924

Campbell 1949
    Encomium Emmae Reginae, ed. A. Campbell, Camden 3rd ser., vol.72, Ryl. Hist. Soc., 1949

Campbell 1982
    The Anglo-Saxons, ed. J. Campbell, Phaidon, 1982

Clemoes 1959
    P. Clemoes, *The Chronology of Aelfric's Works*, in *The Anglo-Saxons. Studies in some Aspects of their History & Culture. Presented to Bruce Dickins*, ed. P. Clemoes, London, 1959, pp.212-47 (reprinted, O.E. Newsletter, *Subsidia*, no.5, 1980)

Clemoes 1966
    P. Clemoes, *Aelfric*, in *Continuations and Beginnings. Studies in O.E. Literature*, ed. E.G. Stanley, Nelson, 1966, pp.176-209

Close Rolls
    Rotuli Litterarum Clausarum. In Turri Londinensi, ed. T.D. Hardy, vol.1 (1204-24), London, 1833

Cooper 1961/70
    H.C.D. Cooper, *The Saxon Bound of Eynsham*, Top. Oxon., vol.7 (1961) & vol.16 (1970), Oxford

Crawford 1922
    O.E. Version of the Heptateuch: Aelfric's Treatise on the O. & N.T., and his Preface to Genesis, ed. S.J. Crawford (EETS 160), 1922

C.S.
    Cartularium Saxonicum, ed. W. de Birch, 3 vols., London, 1885-93

Darby 1973
    A New Historical Geography of England, ed. H.C. Darby, Cambridge, 1973

Davis 1973
    R.H.C. Davis, *The Ford, the River and the City*, in *Oxoniensia*, vol.38 (1973), pp.258-67

D.B.
    Domesday Book, shire vols., ed. J. Morris, London & Chichester

Dickinson 1950	J.C. Dickinson, *The Origins of the Austin Canons and their Introduction into England*, London, 1950
Dietrich 1855-6	E. Dietrich, *Abt Aelfrik*, in *Zeitschrift für die Historische Theologie*, ed. C.W. Niedner, new ser., vol.19, pp.487-594 & vol.20, pp.163-256, Gotha, 1855-6
D.N.B.	*Dictionary of National Biography*
Douglas 1964	D.C. Douglas, *William the Conqueror. The Norman Impact upon England*, London, 1964
Dugdale 1817-30	W. Dugdale, *Monasticon Anglicanum*, ed. J. Caley, H. Ellis & B. Bandinel, 6 vols. in 8, London, 1817-30
E	Eynsham abbey charters, as numbered in *E.C.*
Eadmer	Eadmer, *Historia Novorum in Anglia, et opuscula duo, De Vita Sancti Anselmi et quibusdam miraculis eius*, ed. M. Rule (RS 81), London, 1884
E.C.	*Eynsham Cartulary*, ed. H.E. Salter (Oxf. Hist. Soc., vols.49, 51), 1907-8
E.Cust.	*The Customary of the Benedictine Abbey of Eynsham in Oxon.*, ed. A. Gransden (Corpus Consuetudinum Monasticarum, vol.2), Siegburg, 1963
EETS	Early English Text Society
E.H.D.	*English Historical Documents*, vol.1, *c*.500-1042, ed. D. Whitelock, 2nd edn., London, 1979
E.H.R.	*English Historical Review*
Ekwall 1960	*Concise Oxford Dictionary of English Place-Names*, ed. E. Ekwall, 4th edn., Oxford, 1960
E.M.	E.K. Chambers, *Eynsham under the Monks* (Oxon. Rec. Soc., vol.18), 1936
EPNS	English Place-Name Society
E.R.	*The Eynsham Record*, ed. F.B. Atkins, nos.1- , Eynsham Hist. Grp., 1984-
Exeter Book 1933	*The Exeter Book of O.E. Poetry*, facsimile, ed. R.W. Chambers, M. Förster, & R. Flower, London, 1933
Farmer 1985	D.H. Farmer, *Saint Hugh of Lincoln*, London, 1985
Fehr 1914	*Die Hirtenbriefe Aelfrics*, ed. B. Fehr, in *Bibl. der ags. Prosa*, vol.9, Hamburg, 1914 (reprinted 1966, with supplmt. by P. Clemoes)
Fernie 1983	E. Fernie, *The Architecture of the Anglo-Saxons*, London, 1983
Finn 1973	R.W. Finn, *Domesday Book: A Guide*, London and Chichester, 1973
Galbraith 1974	V.H. Galbraith, *Domesday Book. Its Place in Administrative History*, Oxford, 1974
Garmonsway 1978	*Aelfric's Colloquy*, ed. G.N. Garmonsway, rev. edn., Exeter, 1978
G.A.S. Alb.	T. Walsingham, *Gesta Abbatum Monasterii S. Albani*, ed. H.T. Riley (RS 28), 3 vols., London, 1867
Gatch 1977	M. McC. Gatch, *Preaching and Theology in Anglo-Saxon England: Aelfric and Wulfstan*, Toronto, 1977
Gelling 1953-4	*The Place-Names of Oxon.*, ed. M. Gelling (EPNS vols. 23-4), Cambridge, 1953-4
Gelling 1979	*The Early Charters of the Thames Valley*, ed. M. Gelling, Leicester, 1979
Gem 1912	S.H. Gem, *An Anglo-Saxon Abbot: Aelfric of Eynsham*, Edinburgh, 1912
Ger. Wales	Gerald of Wales (Giraldus Cambrensis), *Vita S. Remigii et Vita S. Hugonis*, ed. J.F. Dimock (RS 21g), London, 1877
Gibson 1978	M. Gibson, *Lanfranc of Bec*, Oxford, 1978
Godden 1979	*Aelfric's Catholic Homilies: Second Series*, ed. M. Godden (EETS 2nd ser., 5), 1979
Gordon 1978-9	E. Gordon, *The Site of Eynsham Abbey: a Historical Note*, in *Gray & Clayton 1978*, pp.105-8, & *1979*, p.104
Gray & Clayton 1978-9	M. Gray & N. Clayton, *Excavations on the Site of Eynsham Abbey, 1971*, in *Oxoniensia*, vol.43 (1978), pp.100-22, & Plate 4; and vol.44 (1979), p.104

Grundy 1933	G.B. Grundy, *Saxon Oxfordshire* (Oxon. Rec. Soc., vol.15), Oxford 1933
Hardy 1862-5	*Descriptive Catalogue of Materials relating to the Hist. of Gt. Brit. & Ireld: to the end of the Reign of Henry VII*, ed. T.D. Hardy (RS 26), 2 vols. in 3, London, 1862-5
Harmer 1950	F.E. Harmer, *Chipping and Market. A Lexicographical Investigation*, in *The Early Cultures of North-West Europe*, ed. C. Fox & B. Dickins, Cambridge, 1950
Hart 1966	*The Early Charters of Eastern England*, ed. C.R. Hart, Leicester, 1966
Haskins 1918	C.H. Haskins, *A Charter of Canute for Fécamp*, E.H.R., vol.33 (1918), pp.312-4
H.B.C.	*Handbook of British Chronology*, ed. F.M. Powicke & E.B. Fryde, 2nd edn., London, 1961
Hill 1948	J.W.F. Hill, *Medieval Lincoln*, Cambridge, 1948
Hill 1981	D.H. Hill, *An Atlas of Anglo-Saxon England*, Oxford, 1981
Howden: Chron.	Roger de Howden, *Chronica Magistri Rogeri de Hovedene*, ed. W. Stubbs (RS 51), 4 vols., London, 1868
H.R.H.	*The Heads of Religious Houses: England & Wales 940-1216*, ed. D. Knowles, C.N.L. Brooke & V.C.M. London, Cambridge, 1972
Hy. Hunt.	Henry of Huntingdon, *Historia Anglorum and De Contemptu Mundi etc.*, ed. T. Arnold (RS 74), London, 1879
Jocelin	*The Chronicle of Jocelin of Brakelond*, ed. H.E. Butler, London, 1949
John 1983	E. John, *The World of Abbot Aelfric*, in *Ideal & Reality in Frankish and Anglo-Saxon Society*, ed. P. Wormald, 1983, pp.300-16
Kemble	*Codex Diplomaticus Aevi Saxonici*, ed. J.M. Kemble, 6 vols., London, 1839-48
Kennett 1695	W. Kennett, *Parochial Antiquities*, Oxford, 1695
Ker 1964	*Medieval Libraries of Gt. Britn: a List of Surviving Books*, ed. N.R. Ker, 2nd edn., London, 1964
Keynes 1980	S. Keynes, *The Diplomas of King Aethelred 'The Unready' 978-1016*, Cambridge, 1980
Knowles 1963	D. Knowles, *The Monastic Order in England 940-1216*, 2nd edn., Cambridge, 1963
L	Lincoln cathedral charters, as numbered in *Linc. Reg. Ant.*
Lennard 1959	R. Lennard, *Rural England 1086-1135. A Study of Social & Agrarian Conditions*, Oxford, 1959
Liebermann 1913	F. Liebermann, *The National Assembly in the Anglo-Saxon Period*, Halle, 1913
Linc. Reg. Ant.	*The Registrum Antiquissimum of the Cathedral Church of Lincoln*, eds. C.W. Foster (vols.1-3, & some of 4) & K. Major (the remainder), 10 vols.& 2 vols. facsimiles (Linc. Rec. Soc., vols.27 etc.-68), Lincoln, 1931-73
Luffield 1975	*Luffield Priory Charters*, ed. G.R. Elvey (Northants. Rec. Soc., vols. 22, 25), 1968, 1975
Matthew 1962	D. Matthew, *The Norman Monasteries and their English Possessions*, Oxford, 1962
Matthew Paris	Matthew Paris, *Chronica Maiora*, ed. H.R. Luard (RS 57), 7 vols., London, 1872-84
M.R.H.	*Medieval Religious Houses: England & Wales*, ed. D. Knowles & R.N. Hadcock, London, 1971
O.D.E.C.N. 1950	*Oxford Dictionary of English Christian Names*, ed. E.G. Withycombe, 2nd edn., 1950
O.E.	Old English (variously called Early English or Anglo-Saxon)
Oleson 1955	T.J. Oleson, *The Witenagemot in the Reign of Edward the Confessor*, Oxford, 1955
OLHA	Oxfordshire Local History Association

Owen 1984   D. Owen, *The Norman Cathedral at Lincoln*, in *Anglo-Norman Studies*, ed. R.A. Brown, vol.6, pp.188-99, Boydell, 1984

Pope 1967-8   *Homilies of Aelfric. Supplementary Collection*, ed. J.C. Pope (EETS 259-60), 1967-8

Postan 1972   M.M. Postan, *The Medieval Economy and Society*, Pelican, 1975

RB 1980   *The Rule of St. Benedict. In Latin and English with Notes*, ed. T. Fry, Minnesota, 1981

Rees 1978   *Consider your Call*, ed. D. Rees & others, London, 1978

Regesta   *Regesta Regum Anglo-Normannorum 1066-1154*, ed. H.W.C. Davis, C. Johnson, H.A. Cronne & R.H.C. Davis, 3 vols. & 1 vol. facsimiles, Oxford, 1913-69

Regularis Concordia *Regularis Concordia*, ed. T. Symons, Nelson, 1953

Robertson 1925   *The Laws of the Kings of England: from Edmund to Henry I*, ed. A.J. Robertson, Cambridge, 1925

Robertson 1956   *Anglo-Saxon Charters*, ed. A.J. Robertson, 2nd edn., Cambridge, 1956

RS   Rolls Series

Salter: Archives   *Medieval Archives of the University of Oxford*, ed. H.E. Salter (Oxf. Hist. Soc., vols.70, 73), 1920-1

Salter 1936   H.E. Salter, *Medieval Oxford* (Oxf. Hist. Soc., vol.100), 1936

Salway 1981   P. Salway, *Roman Britain*, Oxford, 1981

Sawyer 1968   *Anglo-Saxon Charters. An Annotated List and Bibliography*, ed. P.H. Sawyer, 1968

Sherwood/Pevsner   *Oxfordshire* (The Buildings of England), ed. J. Sherwood & N. Pevsner, *1974*   Penguin, 1974

Spurrell 1984   *Stow Church Restored 1846-66*, ed. M. Spurrell (Linc. Rec. Soc., vol.75), 1984

Steed 1961/2   V. Steed, *The Bounds of Wychwood Forest, Top. Oxon.*, 7-8 (1961/2)

Steed 1963   V. Steed, *Hermitages and Chapels in Wychwood Forest, Top.Oxon.*, 10 (1963)

Stenton 1955   F.M. Stenton, *The Latin Charters of the Anglo-Saxon Period*, Oxford, 1955

Stenton 1971   F.M. Stenton, *Anglo-Saxon England*, 3rd edn., Oxford, 1971

Stevenson 1858   *Life of St. Aethelwold*, with *Chronicon Monasterii de Abingdon*, vol.2, ed. J. Stevenson (RS 2b), London, 1858, pp.255-66

Swanton 1975   *Anglo-Saxon Prose*, ed. M. Swanton, London, 1975

Sympson 1905-6   E.M. Sympson, *Where was Sidnacester?* (Assoctd. Architectural Socs. Rpts. & Pprs., vol.28), 1905-6, pp.87-94

Tanner 1744   T. Tanner, *Notitia Monastica*, ed. J. Tanner, 1744

Taylor 1965   H.M. & J. Taylor, *Anglo-Saxon Architecture*, 2 vols., Cambridge, 1965

Thorpe 1840   *Ancient Laws & Institutes of England*, ed. B. Thorpe, 2 vols., 1840

Thorpe 1844-6   *Sermones Catholici: Homilies of Aelfric*, ed. B. Thorpe (Aelfric Society), 2 vols., London, 1844-6

V.C.H.   *Victoria County History*

Vita Hugonis 1864   *Magna Vita Sancti Hugonis*, ed. J.F. Dimock (RS 37), London, 1864

Vita Hugonis 1985   *The Life of St. Hugh of Lincoln*, ed. D.L. Douie & H. Farmer, 2 vols., new edn., Oxford, 1985

Walter Cov.   *Memoriale Walteri de Coventria*, ed. W. Stubbs (RS 58), 2 vols., London, 1872

Westlake 1907   J.S. Westlake, *From Alfred to the Conquest*, in *Cambridge History of English Literature*, vol.1, pp.108ff. (Aelfric), Cambridge, 1907

White 1898   C.L. White, *Aelfric. A new Study of his Life and Writings* (Yale Studies in English, 2), Boston, New York & London, 1898; reprinted, with addtns. by M.R. Godden (pp.199-237), Hamden, Connecticut (see *A.S.E.*, vol.4, 1975)

Whitelock 1930   *Anglo-Saxon Wills*, ed. D. Whitelock, Cambridge, 1930

Whitelock 1943   D. Whitelock, *Two Notes on Aelfric & Wulfstan: the Date of Aelfric's Death*, *Mod. Langu. Rvw.*, vol.38 (1943), pp.122-4

Whitelock 1952   D. Whitelock, *The Beginnings of English Society*, Pelican, 1952

Willis 1718-19   B. Willis, *Mitred Abbies*, 2 vols., London, 1718-19

Wm. Malm. G.P.   William of Malmesbury, *Gesta Pontificum*, ed. N.E.S.A. Hamilton (RS 52), London, 1870

Wm. Malm. G.R.   William of Malmesbury, *Gesta Regum*, ed. W. Stubbs (RS 90), London, 1887

Wood: Life   *The Life and Times of Anthony Wood*, ed. A. Clark (Oxf. Hist. Soc., vol.19 etc.-40), 5 vols., 1891-1900 (see also abbreviated version, ed. L. Powys, 319pp. & 2 Plates, Wishart, London, 1932)

Zupitza 1880   *Grammatik und Glossar* (Aelfric), ed. J. Zupitza, Berlin, 1880; 2nd edn., with addtn. by H. Gneuss, Berlin, 1966

Index

1. Translations of Eynsham Charters

2. General

Adam, abbot of Eynsham, 112, 116, 128ff., 131ff., 169

Aelfric, abbot of Eynsham, 7f., 14f., 34ff., 40, 42

Aethelmaer, ealdorman, 14ff., 26ff., 42

Aethelred II, king, 6ff.

Aethelweard sen., ealdorman, 14, 158

Aethelwold, bp. of Winchester, 13f., 34f.

Anglo-Saxon Chronicle, 21

Baldwin, abp. of Canterbury, 115

Bampton, Oxon., 31f.

Banbury, Oxon., 88

Benedictines: general, 11ff., 17ff., 92; cells, 57ff., 65f., 92ff.; oblates, 25; revivals 10th/11th centuries, 7f., 13ff., 31, 34ff., 47f.

Boethius, influence of, 10

Cassington, Oxon., 88f.

Chambers, Sir Edmund, 3, 175f.

Charlbury, Oxon., 132

Cnut, king, 8, 42f.

Cogges, Oxon., 32, 79

Columban, abbot, 56ff., 70ff., 168f.

Combe, Oxon., 89f.

Domesday: general, 53; Eynsham, 55ff.; Stow, 67ff.

Eadmer of Canterbury, 162f.

Eadric Streona, 26

Emma/Aelfgifu, queen, see Aethelred II and Cnut

Eynsham and its abbey: abbatial appointments (including *Eigenkloster* issue), 15f., 57f., 70ff., 81f., 121ff., 131; abbots, see Adam, Aelfric, Columban, Godfrey and Nigel; architecture, 95ff.; before 1005?, 29ff.; cartulary, 1ff., 137ff., 173; customary, 104ff., 167ff.; destruction (1066), 49f.; dissolution (1538), 147f.; diversion of road, 132; excavation, 32f.; foundation-charter (1005), 5ff., 155f.; founders and benefactors, see Aethelweard sen., Aethelmaer, Leofric and Godiva; library, 28, 70, 157; market, 1f., 89, 91; New Land, 128ff.; Pentecostal processions, 87; place-name, 29f.; return from Stow (1109), 75f., 81ff.; seals, use of, 133f.; situation, 21f., 31f.; vision of monk Edmund, 116ff., 171

Fécamp, abbey, 42f., 47, 51, 59, 79

Gerald of Wales (Giraldus Cembrensis), 77, 163f.

Godfrey, abbot of Eynsham, 118ff.

Hanborough, Oxon., 132

Howden, Roger de, 65

Hugh of Avalon, bp. of Lincoln, 111ff., 121ff.

Huntingdon, Henry of, 82ff.

Ingulf (pseudo), 172

Lanfranc, abp. of Canterbury, 47, 52f., 68

Leofric and Godiva, 61ff., 106, 137ff., 168, 174

Lincoln, see moved to, 52f.

Luffield priory, 132, 169

Malmesbury, William of, 74ff., 162

Matilda, abbess of Essen, 14, 33

Mercia, supremacy of, 29ff., 155f.

Merton, Oxon., 87f.

Nigel, abbot of Eynsham, 168f.

Oxford: Eynsham abbey property, 48, 56, 73, 81, 84; St. Frideswide's, 8, 31f.; hanging of clerks, 125ff.

Pheleleie, Oxon., 92f.

Rameslie, Sussex, 24, 42f.

Remigius, bp. of Dorchester/Lincoln, 51ff., 55ff., 68, 70ff., 162ff.

Robert Bloet, bp. of Lincoln, 75ff.

List of Subscribers

Abingdon Area Archaeological and
   Historical Society
Dr. & Mrs. G.F. Adams
Dr. David Adshead
Harry & Marjorie Adshead
Mr. & Mrs. H.G. Adshead
Sir Robert & Lady Aitken
Mr. & Mrs. Al-Jeboury
Richard A. Andrews
Chief & Mrs. G.K. Animashawun
Mrs. J.M. Annetts
Prof. & Mrs. T. Arie
Dr. F.B. & Mrs P.M. Atkins
Jennifer Atkins
J.F. Atkins
Susy Atkins
Bishop Arthur Attwell
Mr. & Mrs. N.W. Ayles
The Rev. F.J. Bacon
Mrs. F.J. Bacon
Mr. William Bainbridge
Dr. Arnold H.J. Baines
Balliol College Library
John & Sara Bannister
Bartholomew School Library
Mr. & Mrs. Geoffrey Batts
The Revd. Dr. E. & Mrs. H. Baty
Mr. P.G. Beak, M.B.E.
William J. Beauchamp
Arthur Beckett
Mr. T.J. Beesley
Dr. Nicholas Bennett
Mr. Francis Bennion
Molly Benson
Mrs. C. Berry
Mr. & Mrs. L.F. Berry
Mr. B.H.J. Bevan
C.A. Bishop
Mrs. Marguerite Blackwell
John Blair
Mrs. Judy Bleay
Y. Bolsover
Mr. C.J. Bond
Mrs. Rita Botcherby

The Reverend Tony Bowering
David Bradley
G.A. Bradley
John Bradley
Dr. & Mrs. M.D. Brasier
Mr. D. Britton
Mr. & Mrs. D.J. Brooks
Mr. & Mrs. W. Brooks
Diana Brown
Mrs. Patricia E. Brown
Mrs. Shelley Bruce
Mr. & Mrs. D. Bryce
Constance & Norman Buchanan
Lilian Buchanan
Mrs. B.R. Buckingham
Dr. & Mrs. C.A. Caine
Mr. Jonathan C. Calcutt
Campion Hall
Andrew Carden, R.I.B.A.
Mr. & Mrs. E.S. Carlton
Alec. H.R. Chalmers
Dr. Joyce Chalmers
Anna Chapman
Don & Sue Chapman
Katie Chapman
Mr. R. Charlton
Clifford Charman
Chelmsford Cathedral Library
Rev. T.J. & Mrs. B.M. Childs
Dennis Chiles
Mrs. J.M. Clements
Prof. Peter Clemoes
Mr. S.B. Clennett
Mr. & Mrs. John C. Clucas
Hilary & Charles Collins
H.M. Cooke
Dr. A.J. Cox
Dickon & Enid Cuthbertson
Flora McDonald Daniel
Miss Margaret A. Dankworth
Jane Darnell
Mr. G.H. Davies, C.Eng.
Mr. J.B. Davies
Mrs. Elizabeth Day

Edward De Gabriele
Lee J. Denney
Roy & Val Denney
Mr. Robert P. Dobbyn
Mrs. Christina Dorward
Downside Abbey Library
Mr. B.W. Duffield
Cecil du Heaume
Miss Rebecca Duke
Mr. & Mrs R. Duval
Dr. Joan Ebeid
Mr. R.G. Edwards
Mr. & Mrs. R. Elliot
Mrs. D.E. Elliott
Mr. F. Evans
Mrs. P. Evans
Raymond J. Evans
S.J. Evans
Revd T.G. Evans-Pughe
Eynsham History Group
Eynsham Primary School
Susan Eysackers
Mr. & Mrs. A. Fallon
Mr. & Mrs. D.O. Faulkner
Dr. J.F. Ferrier
Mr. Colin J. Fisk
Mr. & Mrs. J.L.M. Fletcher
Elsie M. Floyd
Brian & Carol Foster
Air Marshal The Rev Sir Paterson Fraser
Charles Freeman
Malcolm & Ruth Fry
Mr. & Mrs. B.C. Gall
Mrs. Inez E.B. Galletly
R.A. Gardner
Peggy Garland
Mrs. G. Garner
Mrs. Mona F. Gascoigne
Prof. Milton McC. Gatch
Dr. Margaret Gelling
Mr. P.G.W. Glare
Mrs. Iris Godwin
Jean Goodman
Gwynneth Gordon
Leslie & Ursula Goulding
Mrs. Margaret Graber
Mr. John L. Green
Mr. Stanley G. Green
Mr. & Mrs. Bernard Gregor-Smith
Mrs. Dorothy Griffiths
Dr. Lynne Grundy
Dr. C.J.M.R. & Mrs. Gullick
Mr. Denis Gunstone
Mr. R.W. Haden-Jones
The Venerable John C. & Mrs. Hadfield

Mr. & Mrs. W.J. Hall
Mrs. Delia Hammond
Mr. C.R. Hanks
Mr. W. John Hanson
Dr. Anthony Harris
Miss Julia Harris
Miss June Harris
Mollie Harris
Pamella Harvey
John Harwood
Mrs. Beryl Hastings
Mrs. Sonia Hawkes, M.A., F.S.A.
Elizabeth Hayes
Mrs. Eileen Hedges
Kathleen Heijink-Stanley
Edward & Vera Hibbert
Dr. J.W. & Mrs. T.A. Higgins
Mrs. Anne P. Hills
William & Ruth Hodges
Janet & Martin Holland
Mr. & Mrs. C.A. Hollinshead
Mrs. H.E. Hollis
Dr. M. Holmes-Siedle
Constance Holt
Mr. & Mrs. Frank Hopkinson
Mr. & Mrs. J.T.A. Howard-Drake
Mrs. L.M. Huggett
The Very Revd. John C. Hughes
Dr. B.J. & Mrs J.M. Hyde
Mr. & Mrs. J.G.O. Jackson
Mrs. Jasmine James
The Revd. John M. James
Jennifer F. Johnson
David J. Jones
Donna Nadine Jones
Marjorie Keed
Mrs. Rhona Kelly
Mr. F.H. Kempton
The Revd. Robert Key
Dr. S.D. Keynes
Mr. & Mrs. A.J. King
Mrs. Antonia Lacey
The Rev. Edgar Landen
Dr. Philip Ledger
Rev. A.J. & Mrs. K.M. Lee
Mr. Ronald G. Lee
Lincoln Cathedral Library
Mr. & Mrs. R.E.D. Lister
Dom Ian Wilfrid Mackenzie, O.S.B.
Mr. Neil Mackie
Mrs. Rhona Mackintosh
Celia & Michael Magnus
V. Rev. Mgr. J.P. Mahony
Mr. G.P. Mansfield
Edward Martin

Revd. & Mrs. William H. Martin
The Rev. D.W. & Mrs. Mason
Jane Mason
Mr. & Mrs. John Mason
Mrs. Eileen McAlister
Denis & Margaret McCall
Mr. & Mrs. Ian McGhee
Monica McKnight
Miss Margot Mears
Mrs. Monica Meeneghan
Robin & Jean Mitchell
Jean Mittell
Jacqueline S. Money
Mrs. J.N. Montague Jones
Eileen Morley
The Revd & Mrs. John Morley
Mr. & Mrs. M.F. Morley
Dr. A.A. Morris
Mrs. S. Moss
Liz & Andy Mosson
Sally Moyes
Sasha Moyes
Simon Moyes
Canon R.M. & Mrs. B.E. Nichols
Miss M. Oakeley
Mr. & Mrs. A.J. Oakley
Bernard & Ruth O'Leary
Mrs. J.A. Ormrod
Oxfordshire County Libraries
Oxfordshire County Museum, Woodstock
Mrs. J.E. Parker
Reverend Canon John W. Parker
Mr. R.D. Parsons
Barbara Payne
James C. Penny
Mr. & Mrs. R. Perrett
Miss M.A. Philcox
Miss E. Phillipps-Treby
Coral Pill (née Woodhouse)
Mr. & Mrs. A.G. Pimm
Alan Pimm
Mr. G.S. Pimm
Mr. H.D. Pimm
Miss Lottie Pimm
Mrs. H. Plumb
H.P. Powell
Mr. John B. Pukaniuk
Pusey House Library
Mrs. Marjorie Quine
Mr. Darsie Rawlins
Mr. Andrew Jeremy Redhead
Mrs. E. Redman
Mrs. Mairhi J.P. Regent
Mr. A.H. Richards
Mr. & Mrs. D.S. Richards

Mr. & Mrs. Tom Richards
Mrs. E.M. Riddoch
The Rev. & Mrs. Peter Ridley
Mrs. Margaret J. Rimmer
Mr. William A. Robbins
Lynne Marie Roberts
Mr. & Mrs. R.R. Robertson
Mr. R.G. Room
Deborah Rose
Mrs. A. Rowland
David Russell
Mrs. Marian Russell
Mrs. Phyllis Russell
Dr. A. Salter
Prof. Peter Salway
Kaye Sawtell
Mr. William Sawyer
Mrs. Ruth Scott
Mrs. D.L.M. Sharp
Mr. K.J.W. Sheffield
Mr. G. Simmons
Mr. & Mrs. J. Slatter
Judy Slinn
Mrs. Claudine M. Smith
Mrs. Josie Smith
E. & J.M. Snowden
Dom Alberic Stacpoole
Sir Peter Stallard
P.N. Stenhouse Martin (Mr.)
V. Stenhouse Martin (Mrs.)
Mr. & Mrs. E.C. Stevenson
Mr. Basil Streat
Mary Streat
Dr. D.A. Sutherland
Mrs. Irene Sutton
Dr. Richard Swann, Senior
Ruth E. Taylor
Mr. & Mrs. M.A. Thompson
Mrs. Mary Thomson
Miss J.C.C. Thornton-Duesbery
Dr. & Mrs. G.R. Tibbetts
Miss K.J. Tibbetts
Dr. P.B.H. Tinker
The Right Revd John Tinsley
Dr. T.W. Tinsley
Ms. Angie Titchen
Rev. John Tolkien, M.A.
Mrs. Elizabeth Tow
Yvonne Townsend
Mrs. K.M. Turnbull
Dr. Stanley Vann
Mrs. V. Vaughan
Dr. K.M. Vernon
Ronald W.T. Vint
Mrs. Daphne Irene Walker

Kathleen E. Walker (Lincoln)
Mr. & Mrs. D.J. Walsh
Mrs. G.D. Walton
Frank & Margaret Ware
Dr. Tamie Watters
Peter & Elizabeth Way
Barbara Weare
Mr. Kenneth Webb
Mrs. Joan Weedon
Bishop Neville Welch
Mr. J.F. Wells
Dr. Marian Wenzel
Mr. E.F. Whelan
Mr. & Mrs. E. White
Mrs. Jane Eleanor White
Mr. Michael White
Mr. C.F. Whitlock
Mrs. Gwen Whitlock
Mr. R. Whitlock

Joseph & Vivian Whitt
Dorothy Whittaker
Peter G. Wickson
Mr. C.B.N. Willis
The Revd Dr. & Mrs. Alan Wilson
Mr. John A. Wilson
Mrs. Marjorie M. Wilson
Mr. A. & Mrs. D.J. Wooldridge
Miss Iris Woolford
Worcester College, Oxford
Anne Wrapson
Dr. & Mrs. F.W. Wright
Mrs. Patricia H.M. Wymer
Mr. Rowland Wymer
The Rev. John & Mrs. Wynne
Dr. Philip & Mrs. Margaret Youle
Mrs. Brenda Young
Dr. Christopher Young